I0800458

IMAGES
of America

EAST COOPER
A MARITIME HERITAGE

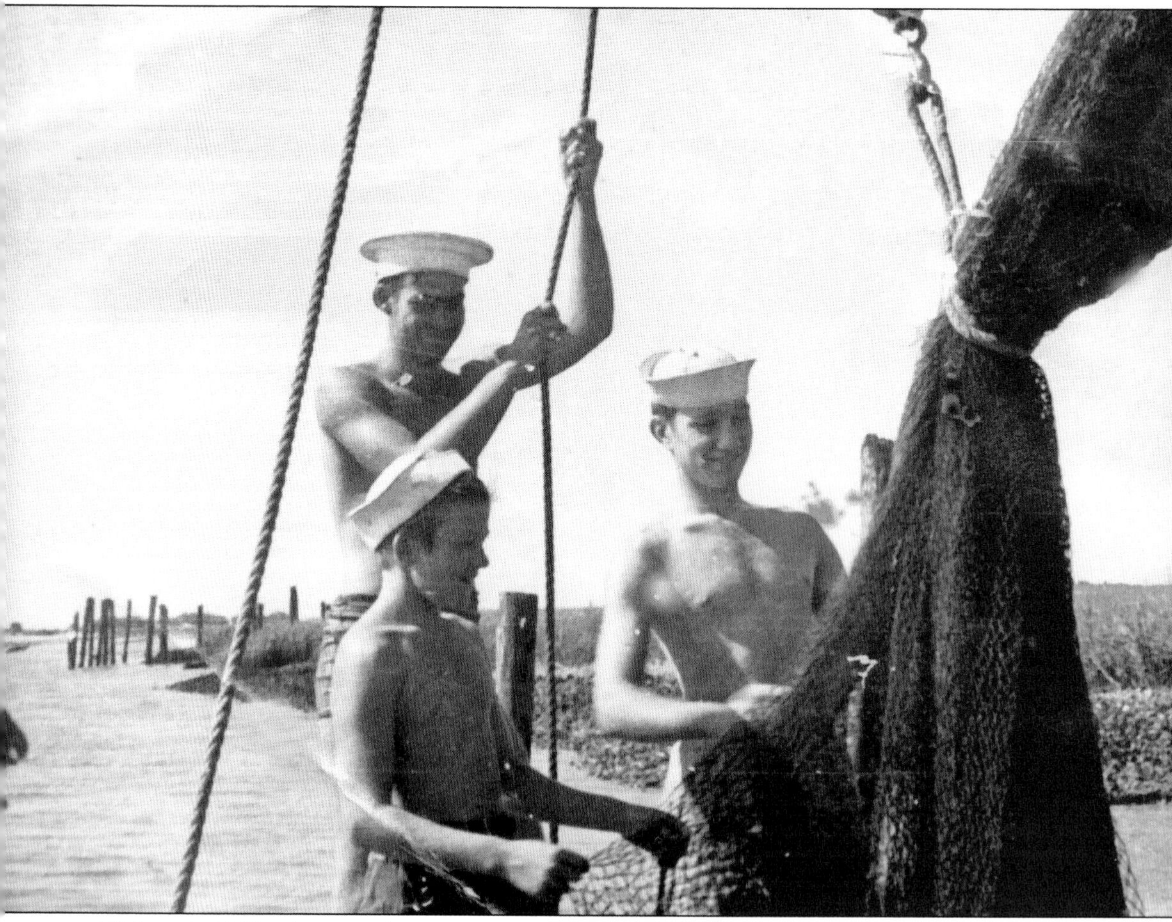

This early-1940s photograph captures the spirits of three young apprentices sewing shrimp nets. Brothers Clarence "Captain Junior" A Magwood Jr. (right) and "Captain Dan" L Magwood Sr. (below), and cousin "Captain Rob" E. Magwood Jr. (above) handle the net while Rob's brother, "Captain John" M. Magwood, looks on. (Courtesy of the authors.)

On the Cover: Here the Magwood Fleet of Shem Creek is moored six boats deep at C. A. Magwood Jr. and Sons fish house in the late 1970s. Boats were painted the Magwood signature colors of white trimmed in dark green with bright orange rigging. In line are the *Miss Alva*, the *Ethel and Clarence*, the *Scotty and Sherryl*, the *Skipper and Wayne*, the *Playboy*, and the *Hope*, all owned and operated by different captains in the family. (Photograph by Martin Puckhaber, courtesy of Wayne Magwood.)

IMAGES
of America

EAST COOPER
A MARITIME HERITAGE

Tressy Magwood Mellichamp
and Lily Herndon Weaks

ARCADIA
PUBLISHING

ISBN 978-0-7385-5382-5

Published by Arcadia Publishing
Charleston SC, Chicago IL, Portsmouth NH, San Francisco CA

Printed in the United States of America

Library of Congress Catalog Card Number: 2007941430

For all general information contact Arcadia Publishing at:
Telephone 843-853-2070
Fax 843-853-0044
E-mail sales@arcadiapublishing.com
For customer service and orders:
Toll-Free 1-888-313-2665

Visit us on the Internet at www.arcadiapublishing.com

This book is dedicated to the men and women who have made their livings working the coastal waters east of the Cooper River and offshore; to the locals who have lost their lives to the sea throughout the centuries; to the boatbuilders and craftspeople who have provided work and pleasure craft to East Cooper residents, past and present; to the many fishermen who have harvested our waters to provide fresh, quality seafood to this community and beyond; and to all who love these local waterways. This book is lovingly presented to all East Cooper residents so that we do not forget.

Contents

ACKNOWLEDGMENTS

For space considerations and editorial reasons, it was impossible to include every picture, topic, and story we were so graciously given. However, we thank everyone who participated for his or her generous contribution in oral histories, research, and donation of images, and we gratefully acknowledge the following people: Frank Blum, Donnie Brown, Ronald Burbage, Tommy Cannon, Michael Cobb, Mike Coker, Mike Cox, Jimmy and Andy Crane, Tommy Edwards, Rial Fitch, Rusty Fleetwood, Tony Geisman, Earl Glines, Rick Hatcher, Mary Anne Hay and her sister, Waring and Bunny Hills, Jan Hiester, David Jones, Sue McManus-Frost, Ann Magwood, John Magwood, John Henry Middleton, Hugh Missroon and his daughter Carrie, Kimberly Morales, Harold Olsen, Mrs. Porcher, Marian Puckhaber, Stuart Reeves, Drew Ruddy, Richard Salmons Jr., John Santos, Robert Santos, Robert Schirmer Jr., Fred Scott, Phyllis Shaffer, MaeRe Chandler Skinner, Lisa Sigman, Billy Simmons, Alec W. Smalls, Walter D. Toler, Cindy Vaughn, Jim Vickers, Gary Weaks, Ralph Wilbanks, Rev. Len Williams, Louis Williams, Barry Wilson, the South Carolina Department of Natural Resources, and Eternal Reefs.

Several excellent books and other resources served as sources and guides for facts and for image searches. These include *Tidecraft* by W. Fleetwood Jr.; *Plantations of the Low Country* by William P. Baldwin Jr.; *The Papers of Henry Laurens, Vol. 8*, edited by George C. Rogers Jr., David R. Chesnutt, and Peggy J. Clark; *Charleston in the Age of the Pinkneys* by George C. Rogers Jr.; *A Day of Cooper River* by John B. Irving M.D., enlarged and edited by Louisa Cheves Stoney and reprinted with additional notes by Samuel Gaillard Stoney; *Colonial South Carolina: A History* by Robert M. Weir; *History of Mount Pleasant* by Petrona Royall McIver; *Cooper River Plantations Tour* by the Historic Charleston Foundation; *Plantations of the Carolina Low Country* by Samuel Gaillard Stoney; *Bull's Island Memories* by Robert Elliott Magwood; and *The Mepkin Abbey Shipwreck: Diving in Mepkin Plantation's Past*, a thesis by Susan Lynn Vezeau. A variety of news articles were also used, as well as the video *A History of the Shrimp Industry in the Southeast*, which was produced by the University of Georgia in association with the National Fisheries Institute.

All images without acknowledgements are the properties of the authors or are considered in the public domain and come from a variety of graphic sources.

A special thanks goes to captains Wayne Magwood, Warren Rector, and Andrew Magwood.

Finally, thanks to our families for living patiently with months of research, piles of notes and images on respective tables and other household surfaces, and the great distraction of and often negligence from the writers.

INTRODUCTION

The area known as "East of the Cooper" (reaching roughly from the Charleston Harbor and Cooper River and her branches eastward to the southern portion of Bull's Bay) can hardly help but have an intimate relationship with the surrounding waters; it officially lies barely 24 feet above sea level. East Cooper's maritime history and currently thriving maritime industry have evolved over time, making the area a major destination on the South Carolina coast. The charming town of Mount Pleasant is perhaps the epicenter of East Cooper, and the town's location on the Charleston Harbor and its deep-water access have ensured that this "friendly town" (a term coined by Mary-Julia C. Royall) has not been left in the shadow of her bustling sister city, Charleston. The once tiny village is now the fourth largest municipality in the state of South Carolina.

East Cooper is the site of some of the most important events in South Carolina's history and is home to many of the most significant plantations in the Lowcountry. In fact, the Cooper River is so historically significant, a 25-mile area—30,020 acres to be exact—is listed as a National Register Historic District and is considered by the National Park Service to be "a remarkably intact historic and cultural landscape." The plantation culture, which shaped the destiny of South Carolina and, indeed, the whole South from the Colonial days onward, was developed along East Cooper rivers in the form of rice cultivation, in addition to utilizing numerous other natural and developed resources. East Cooper shipbuilding and small craft production ensured goods from the area could be transported to market, be it overseas commerce or local coastal trade, and needed supplies could be conveyed back to the planter families.

It was not just Carolinians who desired the fortunes associated with plantation goods and other local products; pirates, the French, the Spanish, and the English coveted the Charleston area's bounty, which of course included that of the East Cooper region. Additionally, this locale's strategic position along the lower eastern seaboard made it greatly desired in order to gain or maintain a foothold in the area. For these reasons, East Cooper's coast and the mouth of the harbor, which lies along her boundaries, boasts three out of four of what historians call the "ringing forts" Charleston Harbor is famous for.

In 1776, Fort Moultrie was considered by Gen. Charles Lee as a "slaughterhouse" not worth reinforcing, and yet it was the site of the first decisive victory in the Revolutionary War. And Fort Sumter stands as one of America's most famous landmarks, being associated with the birthplace of the Civil War. The waters off Sullivan's Island provided the backdrop for yet another famous event, the first successful submarine attack, tragically followed by the first submarine loss when she sank to the bottom of the sea, lying unrecovered until August 2000.

Beyond this region's many significant historical events is the sea's importance. South Carolina's coast is lined with more than 500,000 acres of salt marshes, which are living estuaries inhabited by countless saltwater species. The abundance of sea life found within these coastal marshes have supported a thriving industry throughout history, providing thousands of pounds of fresh, local seafood to its residents. For generations, fishing, shrimping, crabbing, oystering, and clamming have been major parts of the state's seafood industry. Of all of these, shrimping is the largest and has had the most impact on the East Cooper community. These industries produce money for the economy and have played a role in the growth and development of coastal communities in the state. In East Cooper, the focal point of these industries is famous Shem Creek, and the seafaring entrepreneurs plying their trade to and from the creek have reshaped the local community and become the impetus for many innovative seafood businesses.

There are other maritime legacies in East Cooper that have an important impact as well, such as sports fishing and recreational boating and diving. The lure of the area for fishermen, water buffs, and even historians increases yearly. Mount Pleasant hosts many fishing tournaments large and small, and sport fishers take full advantage of local creeks and rivers, as well as offshore sunken wrecks and artificial reefs. What lies beneath these teeming waters fascinates divers as well as anglers. East Cooper rivers and coastal waters hold a vast array of fascinating historical artifacts, making the area a top recreational and professional dive center. Long blessed by an abundance of wildlife, Mount Pleasant's shores also attract nature enthusiasts who take advantage of her coastal and river waterways to canoe, kayak, motor, and sail throughout the area, appropriately echoing the vignettes of the past, where every conceivable vessel could be seen on any given day along her peaceful waters. Today the area's legacy continues.

One

Nine of Thirteen
South Carolina Is Born

"Our sovereign lord the King having, out of his royal grace and bounty, granted unto us the province of Carolina . . ." So begins the Fundamental Constitutions of Carolina, a royal charter from King Charles II granting a vast amount of land in America to the eight Lords Proprietors, the first official rulers of Carolina. The year was 1669, and the following year saw the vessel *Carolina* lying just off the harbor. Arriving on the ship was the governor of the expedition and the other 92 original settlers, including a man whom Walter Fraser describes as a "brawling Irish soldier of fortune" and whom others on the voyage declared was an "ill-natured buggerer of children." This man, Florence O'Sullivan, was also probably East Cooper's first resident, having been granted jurisdiction of the island that now bears his name, and he likely maintained a residence in the vicinity of what is now the Old Village of Mount Pleasant.

These were hardly the first visitors or residents in the area. Attempts had been made by both the French and the Spanish to settle in proximity to what is now East Cooper several decades earlier. However, far preceding these intrepid explorers were the indigenous peoples whose oyster middens and rings have been officially dated as far back as 4120–4170 BC. It was ancestors of these ancient people, the Sewee tribe, who were likely among the first to note the appearance of the English ship sailing southward past Bull's Bay.

Tragically, according to English settlers, by 1700 the tribe was virtually decimated due to smallpox and drunkenness. An attempt by the remaining tribesmen to sail directly to England to trade proved their final undoing when a squall capsized the vessels, drowning most of the men. The survivors were "rescued" by a nearby British ship and sold into slavery. The few women remaining assimilated into neighboring tribes. All that remains of the tribe are names such as Wando, Copahee, Hobcaw, and Shem that were given to East Cooper waterways and are still in use today.

Native Americans, pirates, the French, and the British made their mark on East Cooper residents in the ensuing decades before the plantation culture was so thoroughly established, taming the wild frontier.

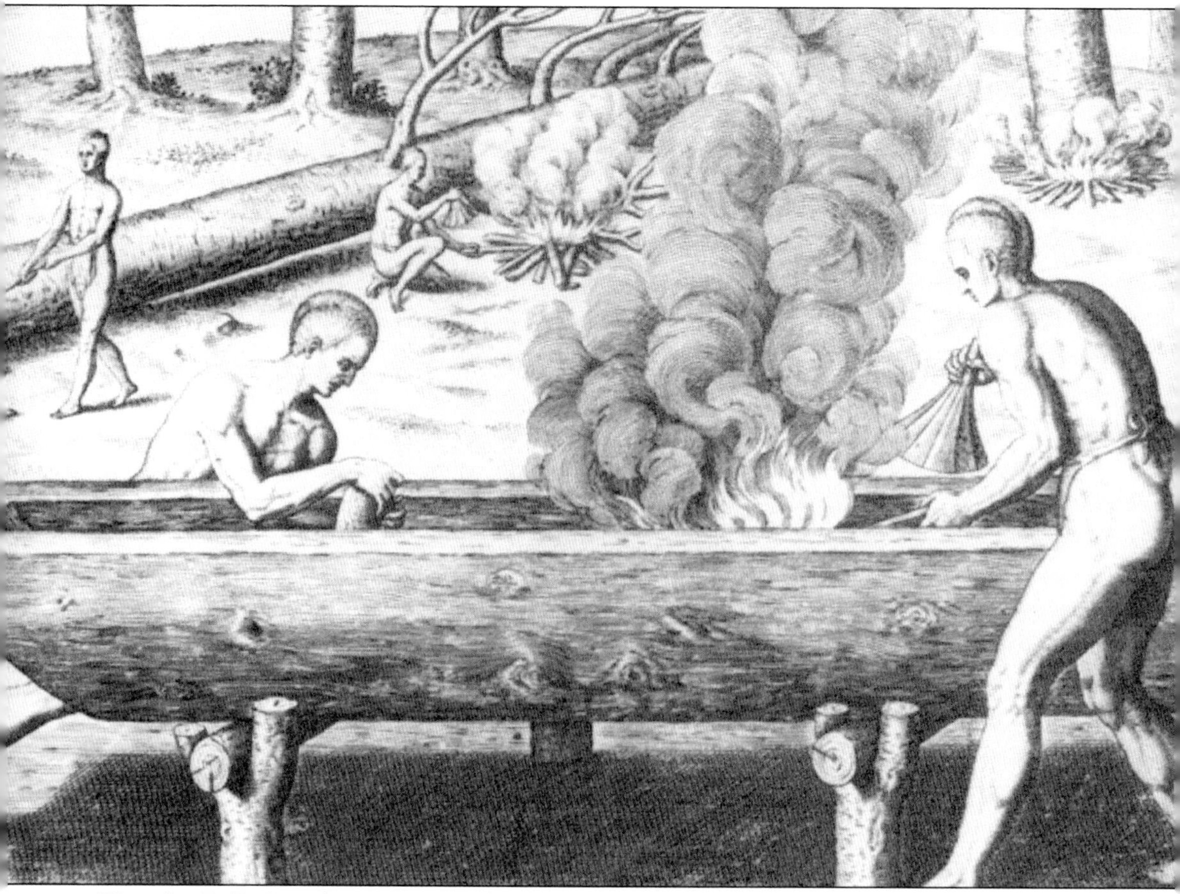

Theodor DeBry's early engravings of Native Americans captured typical daily activities. When white Europeans came to Carolina in the late 1600s, little had changed. Here the construction of a sea-going dugout canoe represents how the Sewees and other local tribes probably built their vessels. Before metal implements were widely used, a result of trade with settlers, natives would hollow out a large log using controlled fire and then shape the vessel with curved bows and sterns. Settlers utilized dugouts made from local trees as well, as evidenced by documents from the era describing their presence in the region's waterways. Derivations of the term "periagua" are used most often in these descriptions, the vessel in question being a large dugout canoe with European alterations such as additional planks or even a small mast and sail. These were so useful that in 1702 the South Carolina Commons House ordered "six Cyprus Periagers, forty foot Long and five foot wide . . . with Seventy-Eight pair of oars" to carry a military unit up the rivers and patrol the nearby waters.

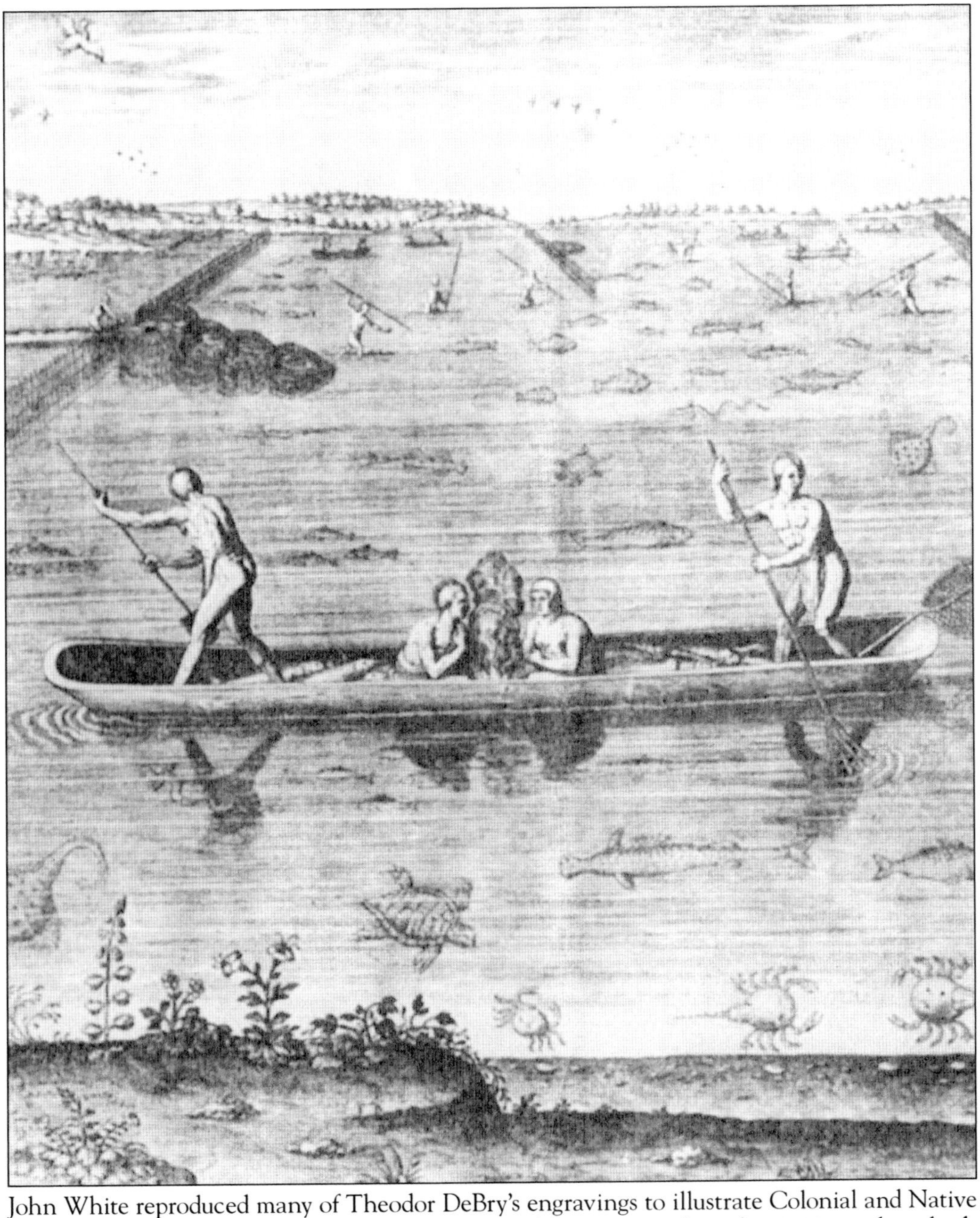

John White reproduced many of Theodor DeBry's engravings to illustrate Colonial and Native American events in America. In this famous reproduction, a number of activities and methods are represented. The natives in the bow and stern are maneuvering the canoe, while men in the center hover over a small fire. Large fish, possibly shad, are piled in the vessel. In the background, two other natives stand in the water, poised with spears. Also in the water are a hammerhead shark, a king crab, a hermit crab, and possibly a horseshoe crab, a catfish, and some other types of fish, including a skate or stingray, which can be seen in the fish weir. According to archeologist K. Kris Hirst, "a fish weir is constructed by placing a row of stakes in the middle of a stream, in an estuary, or near a coastline. Plant material is then wrapped around and between the stakes, and the fish are herded into the impoundment area where they can be retrieved with some facility."

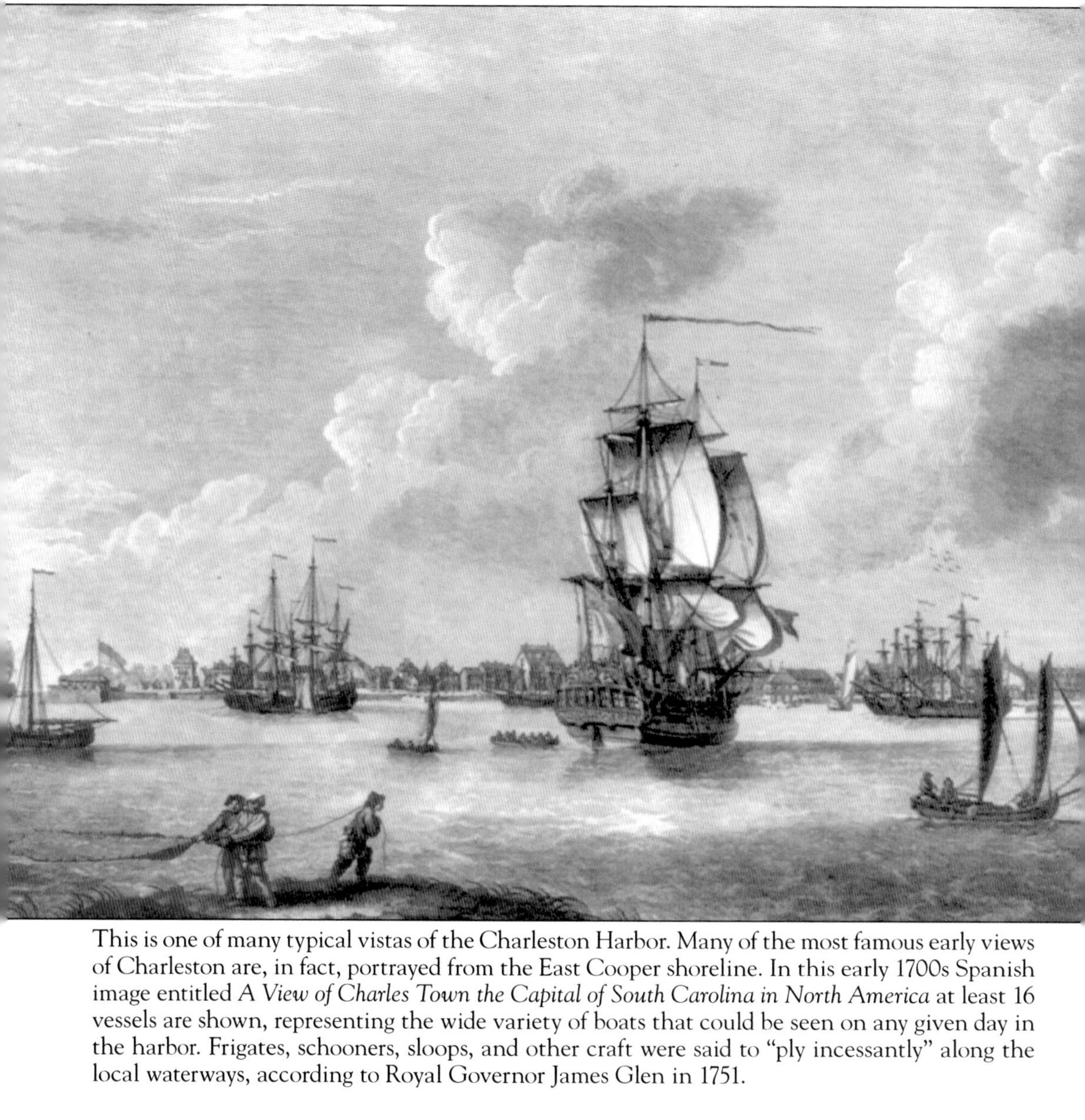

This is one of many typical vistas of the Charleston Harbor. Many of the most famous early views of Charleston are, in fact, portrayed from the East Cooper shoreline. In this early 1700s Spanish image entitled *A View of Charles Town the Capital of South Carolina in North America* at least 16 vessels are shown, representing the wide variety of boats that could be seen on any given day in the harbor. Frigates, schooners, sloops, and other craft were said to "ply incessantly" along the local waterways, according to Royal Governor James Glen in 1751.

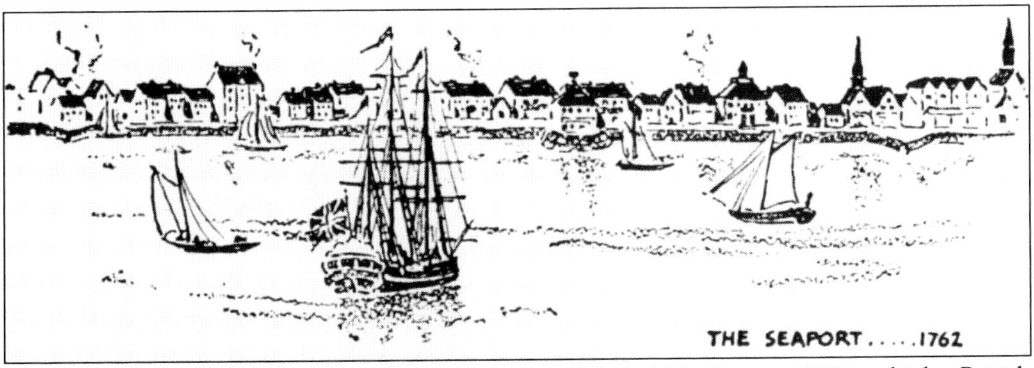

Here an unknown Colonial artist has sketched a view entitled *The Seaport 1762* in which a British frigate approaches the town from the busy harbor. Ships played a greater role in the area's history than many realize: it was a brigantine arriving in the harbor for repairs in 1685 that indirectly led to the creation of the most famous cash crop in the colony, rice. The ship was from Madagascar, and after coming into the port for an unscheduled visit after a violent storm, the captain reportedly gave a bag of rice to a local resident. It was that settler, named Henry Woodward, who is often credited with experimenting with the first successful rice crop in the colony. The drawing below by John Batchelu depicts a Colonial-era brig typical of those plying Charleston's waters.

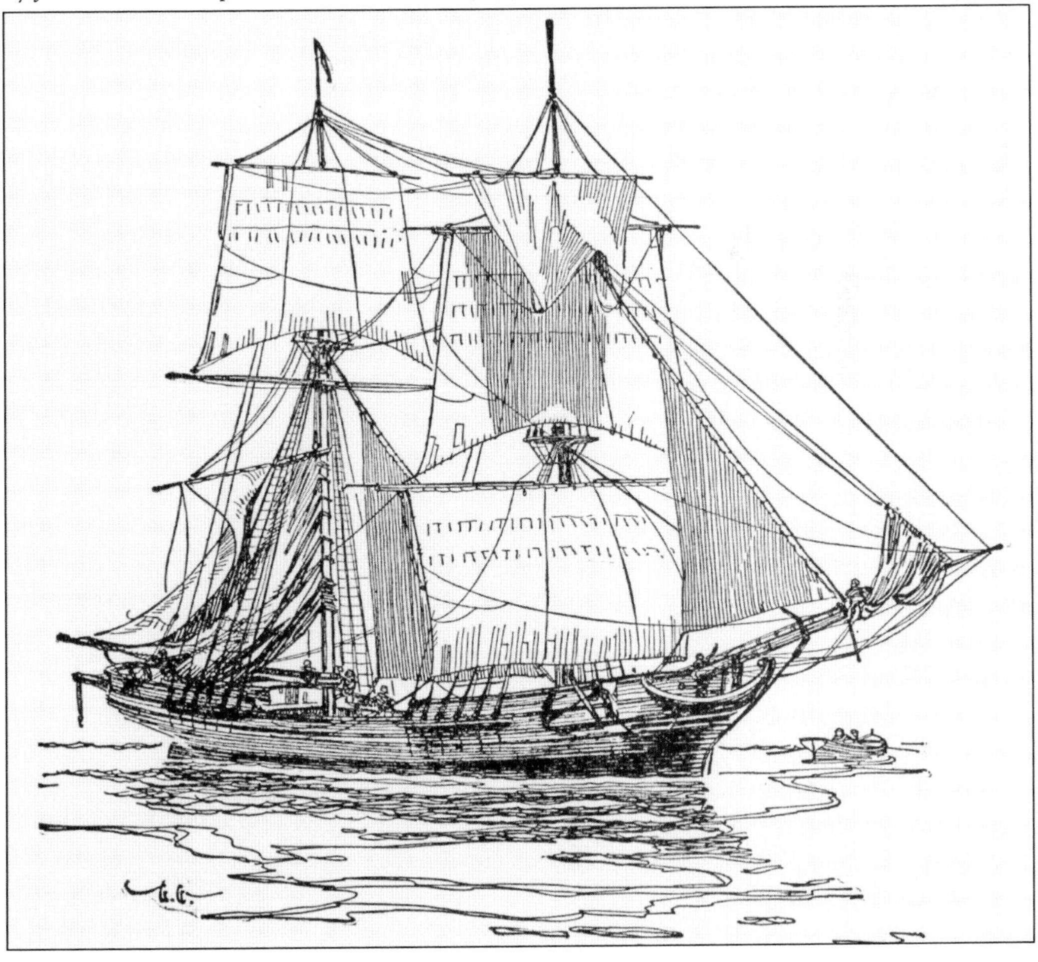

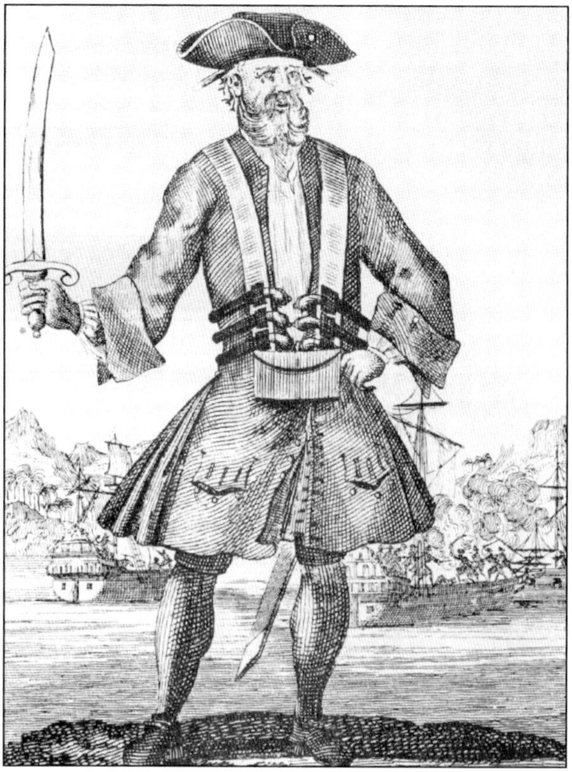

Perhaps the most famous pirate in history, Edward Teach, also known as "Blackbeard," was a frequent visitor to the shores and towns of the Carolinas. In 1718, he and his accompanying ships bottled up Charleston Harbor, capturing vessels and holding passengers hostage in return for medicines and threatening the town if his conditions were not met. Blackbeard convinced (and some say coerced) Stede Bonnet to sail with him while he plagued the Carolinas. (Original engraving by Daniel Defoe.)

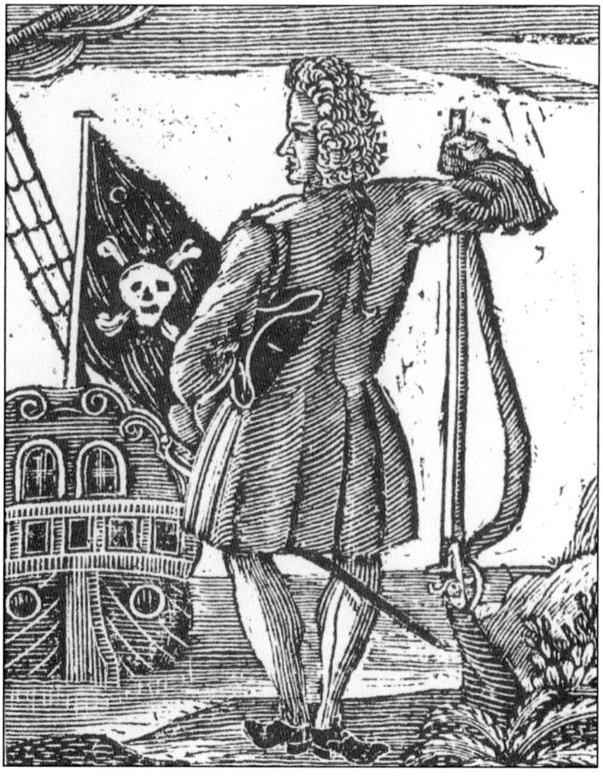

Stede Bonnet, known as the "Gentleman Pirate," figured prominently in this area. He was captured shortly after the Blackbeard incident and returned to Charleston to be tried. Bonnet's escape from imprisonment while aided by sympathetic locals is the stuff of legend, and he attempted to flee via rowboat into the storm-tossed harbor. Bonnet was washed ashore and recaptured on Sullivan's Island, imprisoned in the dungeon of the Exchange Building, and hung at the Battery. (Original engraving by Daniel Defoe.)

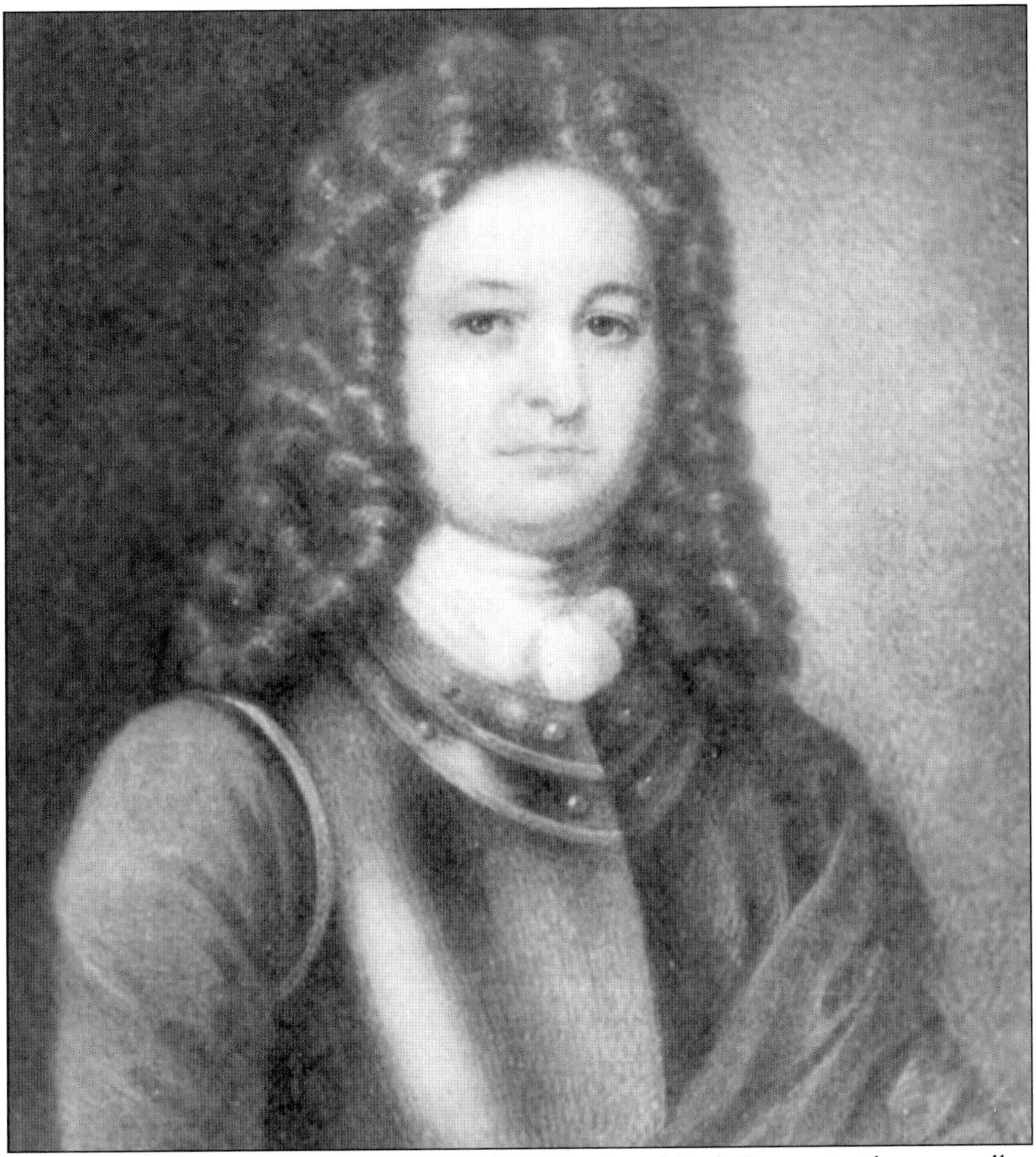

Col. William Rhett was a key player in the Edward Teach and Stede Bonnet incidents, as well as other important Colonial military events. He was incensed at Blackbeard's audacity in holding the city hostage and set about immediately to capture the notorious pirate. It was while seeking Teach and his crew that Rhett discovered Bonnet's ship in the Cape Fear River in North Carolina. After a violent and bloody battle, Rhett captured Bonnet's ship and brought him to trial in Charleston. Rhett returned with a hero's welcome, but it was not his first heroic feat. The East Cooper area owed Rhett a debt of gratitude for the repulsion of a French invasion that began in Sewee Bay. The enemy force worked its way toward Charleston Harbor, burning and looting the area as far west as Dearsley's (Shem) Creek. Forces led by Rhett repelled the French, and a skirmish was reported in the vicinity of "Abcaw" (Hobcaw). Some historians think this skirmish resulted in the construction of a fort named after Queen Anne that was built where King Street meets the harbor.

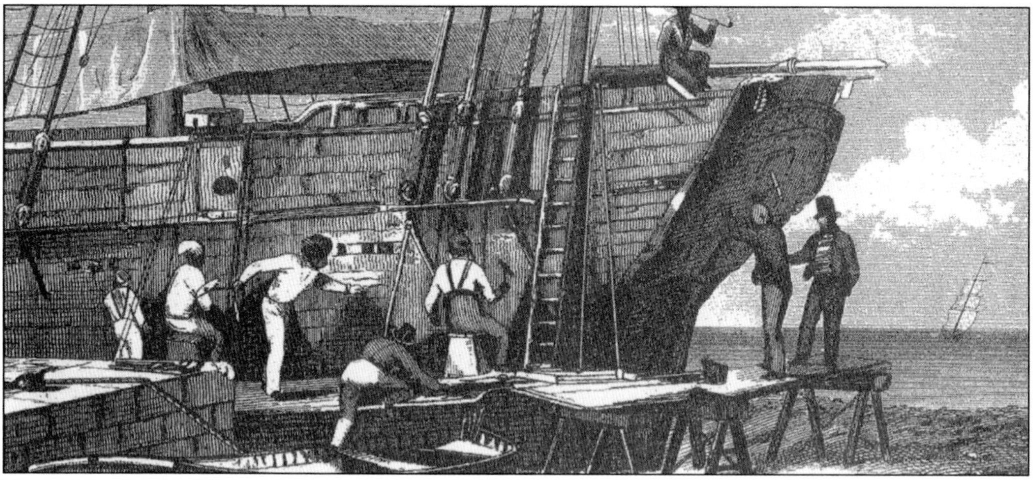

Regarding shipbuilding, surveyor and original settler Maurice Matthews writes of "several vessels built here" and of four vessels "on the stocks" being constructed in the year 1680. East Cooper was undoubtedly the site of several Colonial shipyards, where scenes like this were typical. (Courtesy Library of Congress.)

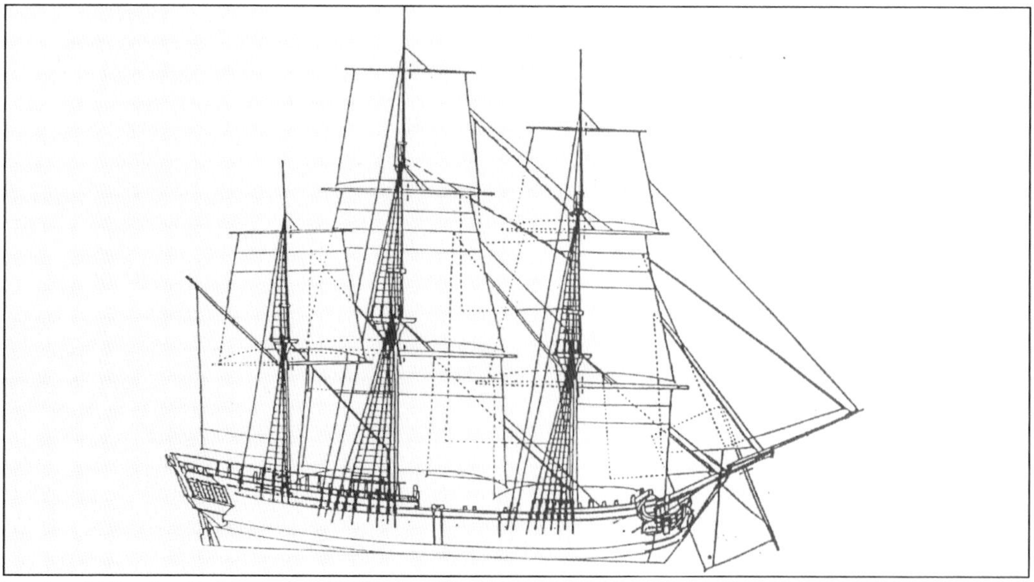

By the 1750s, the Hobcaw shipyard was sold to famous shipbuilders John Rose and James Steward, who were trained in England. In 1763, they constructed the most famous ship to come out of Carolina, the *Heart of Oak*, pictured. Considered the epitome of a fine ship, Rose sailed her to England on her maiden voyage to recruit shipwrights to Carolina. The ship was so valuable that within three years of being built, famous patriot and planter Henry Laurens estimated his quarter interest in her to be £4,000. His 3,000-acre plantation, Mepkin, located on the Cooper River, was comparatively valued at £7,000. (Courtesy Dianne Cobb.)

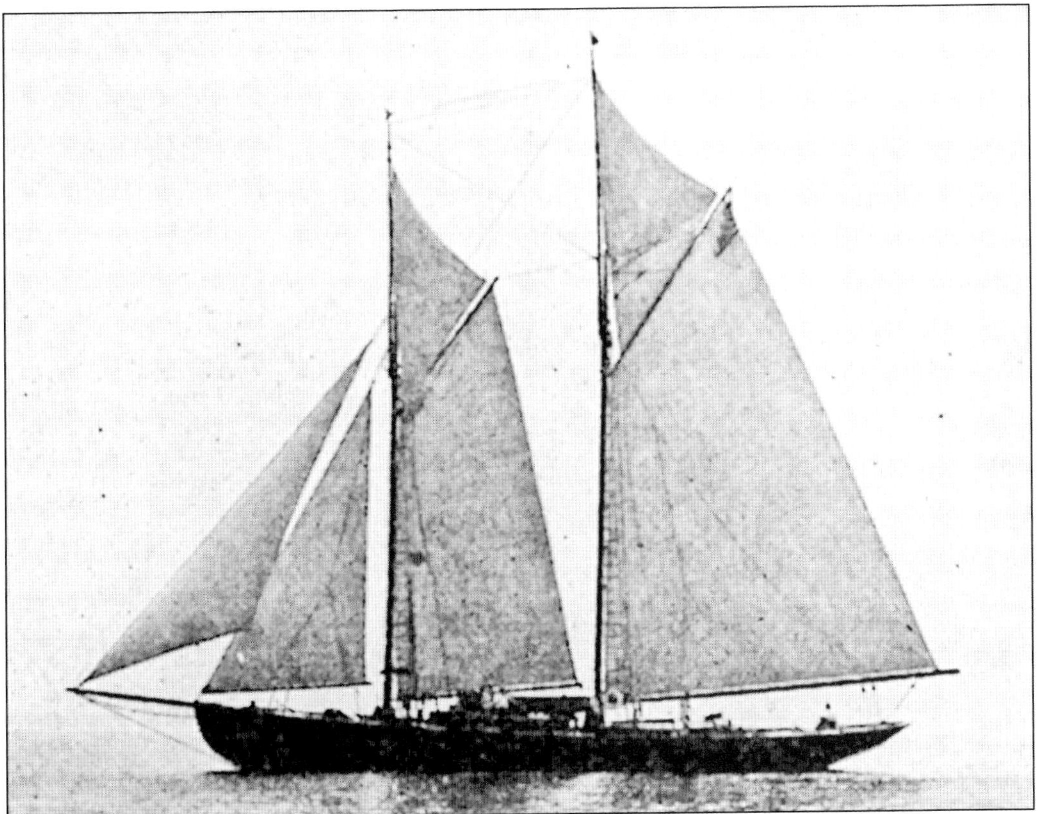

A schooner is a fore-and-aft rigged vessel with two or more masts, such as the one pictured. While all types of vessels were built in the East Cooper and other area shipyards, schooners were definitely the ship of choice; local shipwrights built more schooners than all other types of vessels. In fact, by the 1760s, about 80 percent of all registered local vessels were schooners.

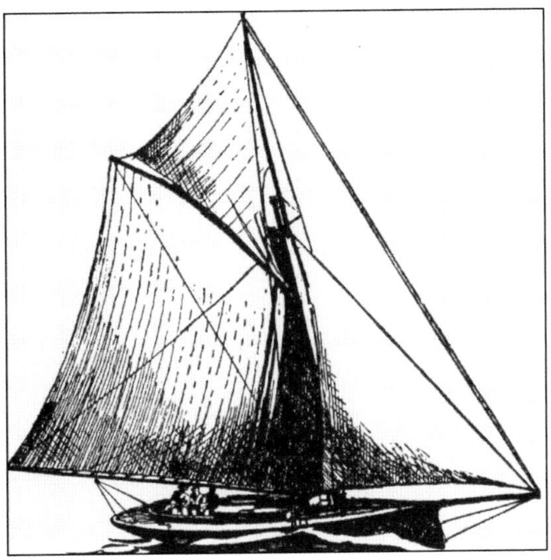

Another popular Carolina vessel was the sloop, built in the shipyards of the area and in "shade yards," a makeshift yard with one or two people building a small vessel along the banks of a creek or river. Sloops were handy vessels for planters and coastal traders because they were capable of traversing shallow waters such as tidal creeks and areas riddled with sand bars while still transporting a large quantity of good or people.

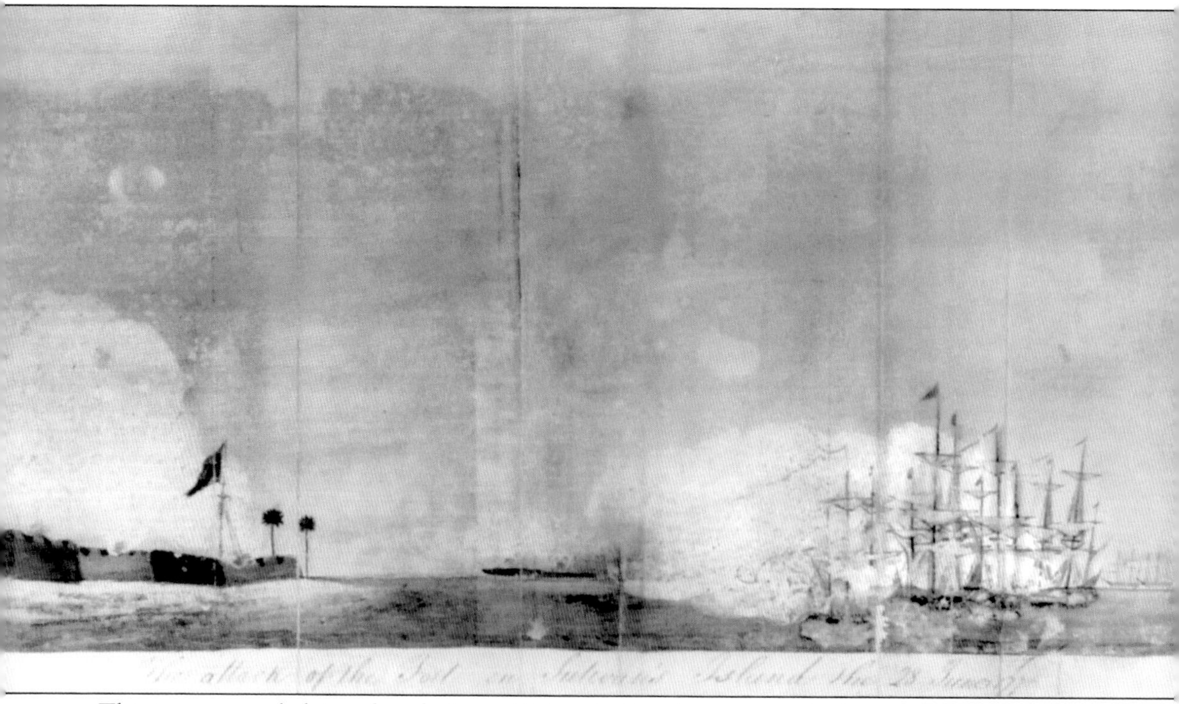

This image, entitled *Attack at the Fort of Sulivan's Island*, represents the beginning of what became America's first Revolutionary victory. What happened in this battle was unheard of: a superior British force was pummeled by soldiers manning a fort that was not only incomplete, but also inadequately supplied. The garrison at Fort Sullivan lacked gunpowder. Having only 28 rounds for the 26 guns, the commander of the fort, Colonel Moultrie, instructed his men to wait a full 10 minutes between firing each round. Fatefully, all British attempts regarding Sullivan's Island failed; the endeavor of attacking from Long Island (present-day Isle of Palms) via Breach's Inlet was a complete disaster, and the bombardment of Fort Sullivan ended in the British ships running aground. Every person aboard the quarterdeck of one ship, the flagship HMS *Bristol*, was killed or wounded. (Courtesy Library of Congress.)

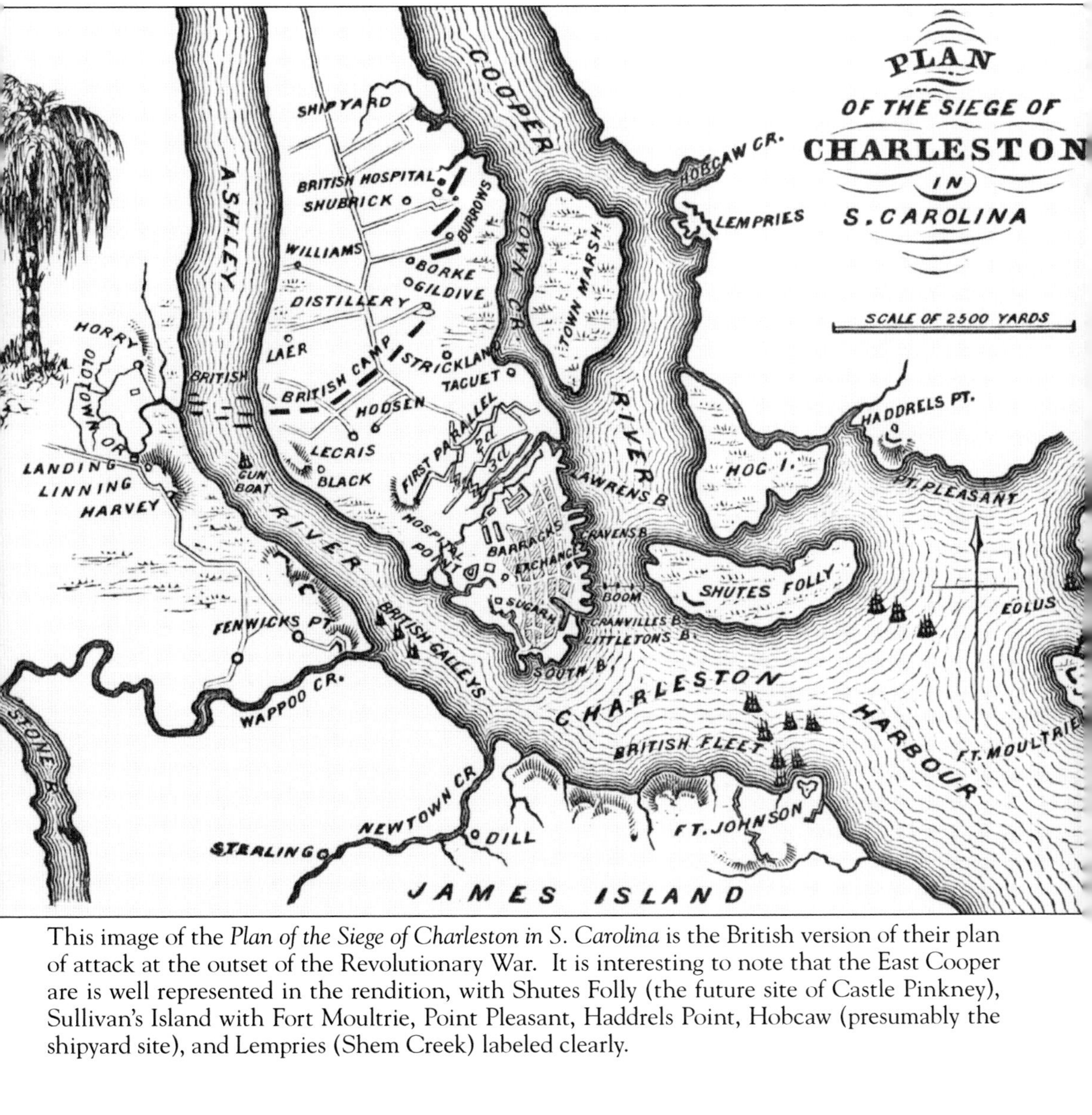

This image of the *Plan of the Siege of Charleston in S. Carolina* is the British version of their plan of attack at the outset of the Revolutionary War. It is interesting to note that the East Cooper are is well represented in the rendition, with Shutes Folly (the future site of Castle Pinkney), Sullivan's Island with Fort Moultrie, Point Pleasant, Haddrels Point, Hobcaw (presumably the shipyard site), and Lempries (Shem Creek) labeled clearly.

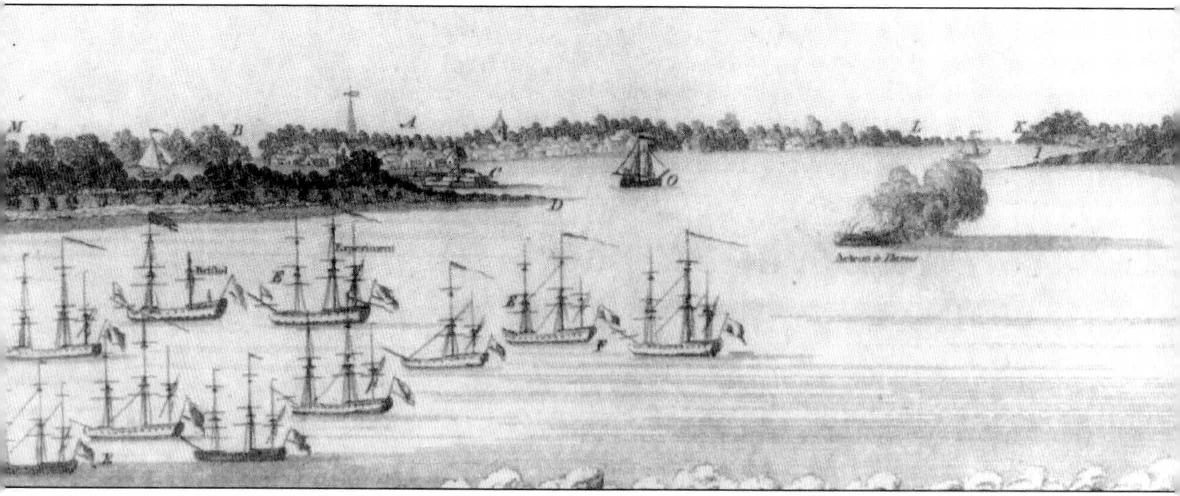

Here the British retreat from the debacle at Sullivan's Island. The caption reads "view . . . from on board the Bristol, Commodore Sir Peter Parker . . . taken in Five Fathom Hole the day after the Attack upon Fort Sulivan by the Commodore and his Squadron, which Action continued 9 hours and 40 minutes." Listed and lettered are the royal ships and various points of interest, including the Cooper and Wando Rivers, and Coming's Point in Mount Pleasant. (Courtesy Library of Congress.)

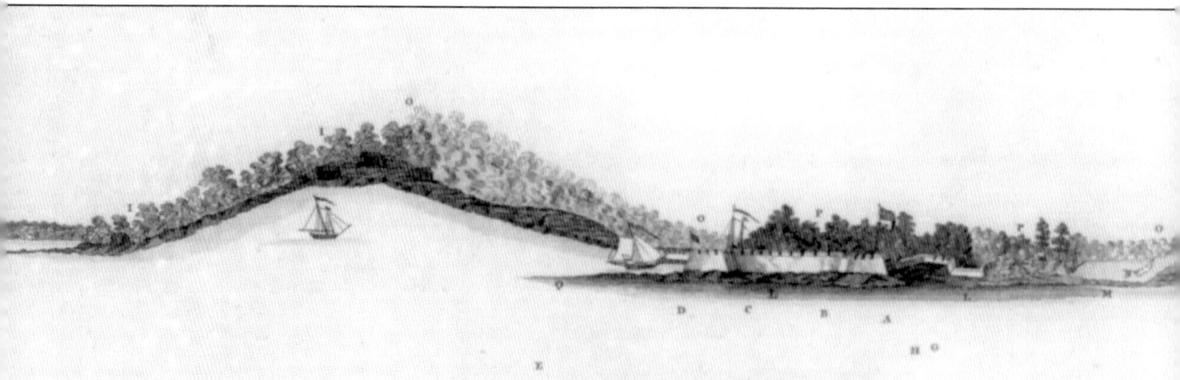

Another portrayal of the Sullivan's Island attack by the British shows the fort from the water. The caption describes the ships *Actaeon* and *Sphinx* stranded on a shoal and the burning of the *Actaeon* "by ourselves." The British did, indeed, set fire to the ship, which was considered one of the finest of their navy, having been commissioned only the year before. Americans salvaged a great deal before the ship finally exploded. (Courtesy Library of Congress.)

Two

Plantation Days on the Cooper River

"On quitting the wharf a fine view is obtained of the city . . . whilst the lofty masts of the vessels in the harbor, give the promise of active business, as the young day spreads more and more its widening glow, and advances to maturity. Innumerable little boats may also be seen dotting the river in all directions—some heavily laden bearing provisions to the city from the neighboring islands. . . . In proceeding up the river by the steamboat, moving steadily along as the current of a brook in summer, there is very soon presented to the eye of the visitor, luxuriant fields, bearing on their ample bosoms, the rich staples of our country. On the left, as we ascend, several well settled farms, under high cultivation, are studded along the margin of the river." In 1842, Dr. John B. Irving, a physician and East Cooper planter, wrote those phrases in a series of letters that were to become a book entitled *A Day on Cooper River*. The delightful book describes the journey and the landmarks and people encountered along the way while traveling upriver via steamship, then considered a marvel of maritime engineering.

After the Revolutionary War, East Cooper planters continued to endeavor to create a rich, opulent lifestyle by means of slave labor and rice cultivation, and with the exception of the steamship, little had changed with regard to planting methods and means of conveyance to and from plantations. River landings were simple, causeway-like affairs, and because the local wood used in construction of vessels was of superior quality, a plantation boat would often be in service for generations before sinking or being scuttled.

The ruins of plantation landings, the remnants of ingenious rice cultivation structures, sunken vessels, and plantation artifacts recovered from East Cooper rivers illustrate the surprising maritime savvy of these enterprising planters, who often began their careers as transatlantic traders. It was not unusual to see a variety of watercraft at any given plantation landing, including pleasure craft for racing, visiting, and picnicking.

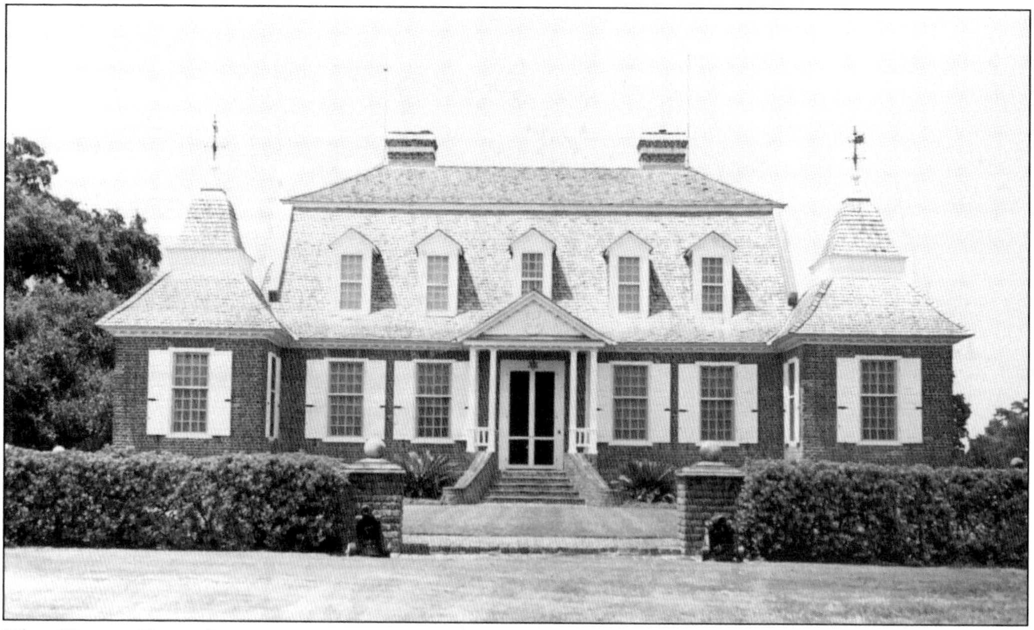

The Cooper River boasts many gorgeous plantations, including Mulberry, built in 1711. Hardly the standard in style, its uniquely Jacobean features and elegant facade belied the fact that the home was, necessarily, a fortress. Built on a high bluff, the site of a former Native American camp, it boasts four towers, which were said to have underground powder magazines beneath them. Cannons have been uncovered on the property as well.

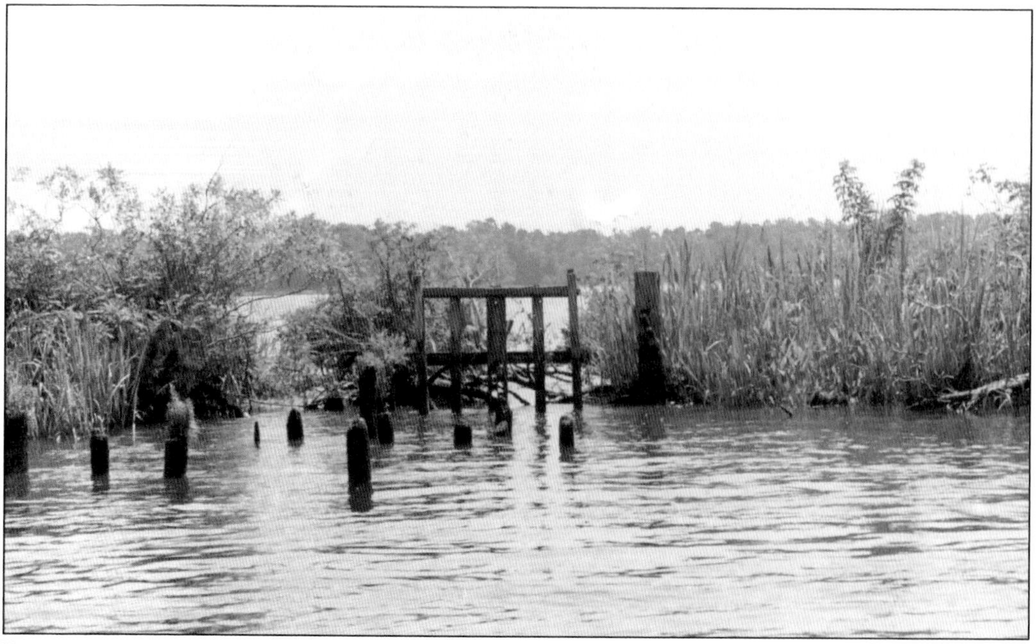

East Cooper rivers are riddled with old rice trunks and dikes. Here is the relic of a trunk, used in controlling fresh water levels in a rice field. Fresh water would drain out of this swinging gate at low tide, and the resulting pressure of an incoming tide would close it. To refill a field with fresh water from a rising tide, another trunk, swinging in an opposite direction, would be used.

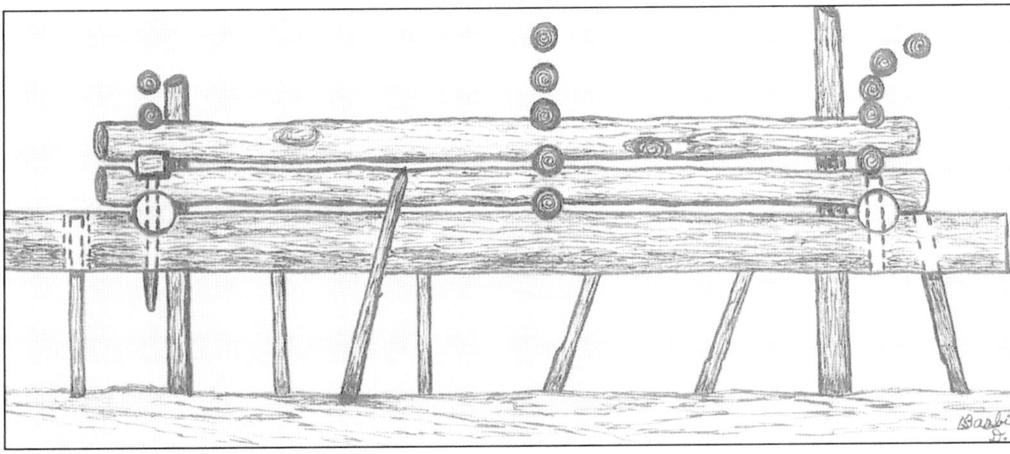

Structures called "crib docks" were the landing of choice at most local plantations. The South Carolina Institute of Archaeology and Anthropology (SCIAA) describes the docks as wooden structures resembling a log cabin without a roof. These docks were constructed using interlocking palmetto logs to construct a crib, which was weighted down and sunk into a river. The cribs were filled with old bricks (often made on-site or nearby at a plantation kiln) and other rubble, and were reinforced with earth or a wooden platform on top. The artist's rendition above shows the long wooden pegs, or guideposts, which attached the logs together, as well as the long posts that were driven deep into the river bottom. The image below is the sluice and landing at the old rice mill on Middleburg plantation, where the crib is plainly seen. Vessels would be loaded and unloaded at high tide. (Above, courtesy Drew Ruddy; below, courtesy South Carolina Historic Society.)

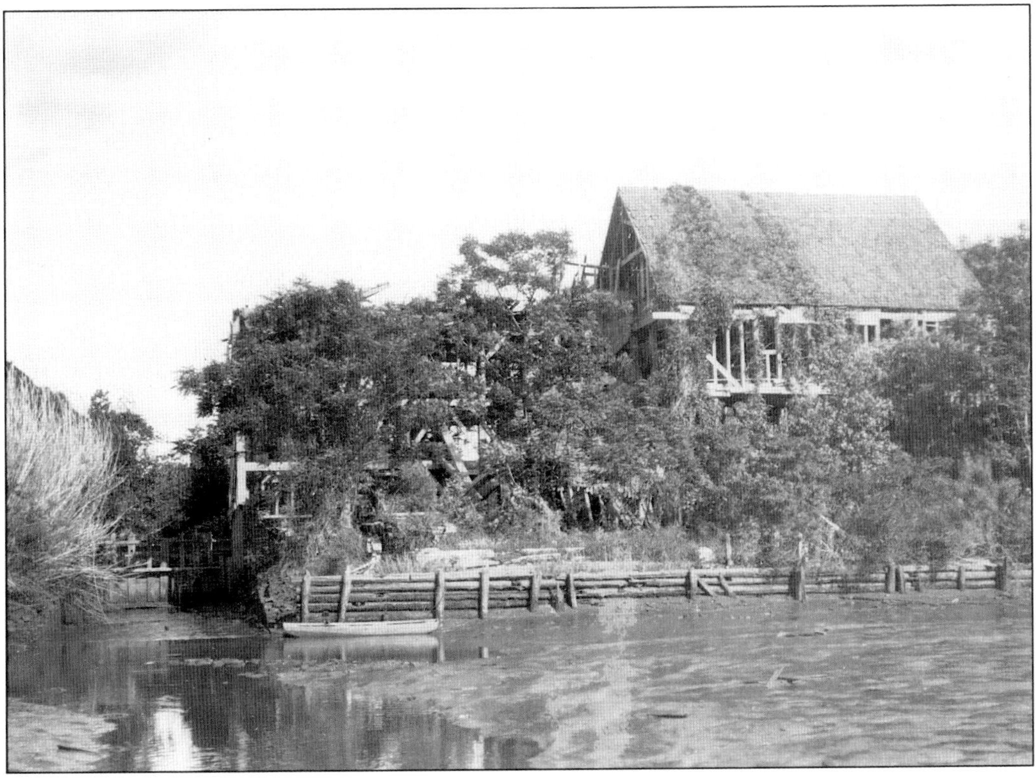

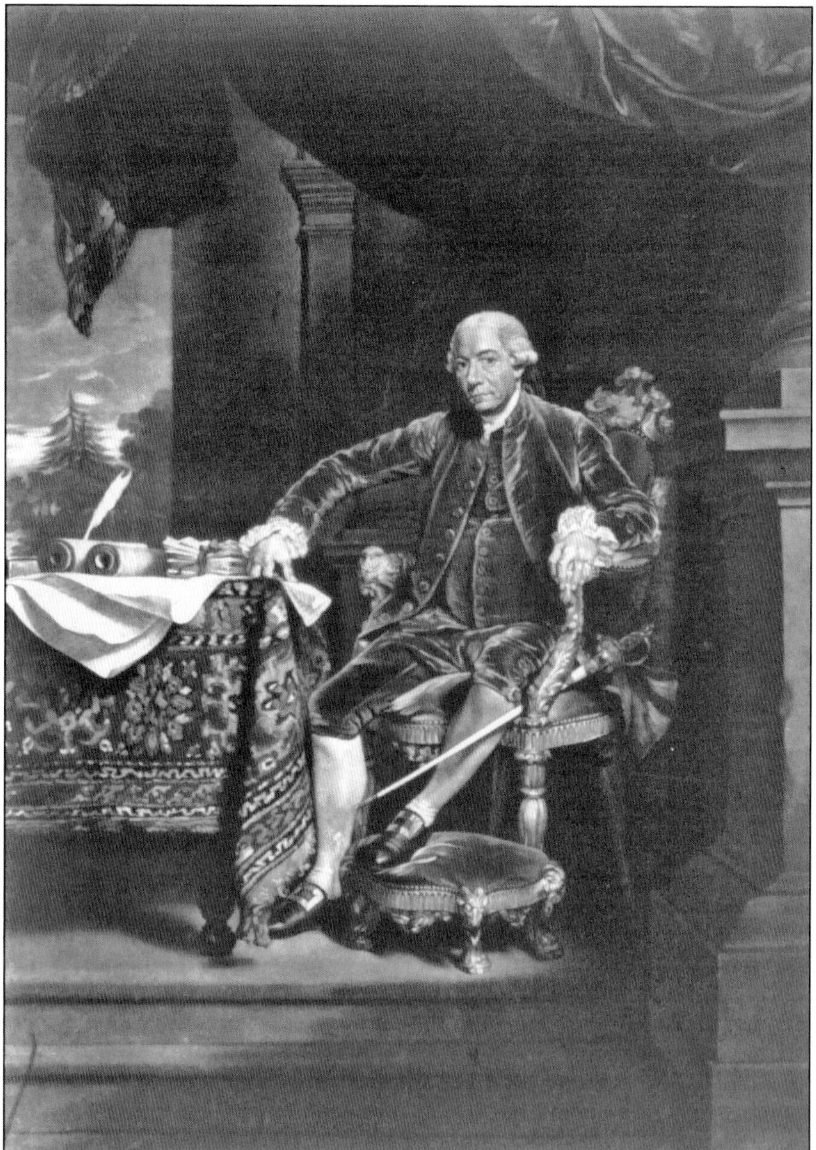

Henry Laurens was a famous Cooper River planter who began amassing his fortune as a merchant, transporting, buying, and selling many commodities, including slaves. One of the wealthiest men in America, Laurens demonstrated more than just business acumen when he described, in a series of letters, a thorough knowledge of boats and of various types of vessels and methods of construction. One of his more famous vessels was the *Baker*, a plantation boat he had converted from a schooner into a sloop because of observations he made while traveling north. Laurens's letters regarding this schooner are intriguing; when mentioning the "labor and expense of at least one man" being "saved by such rigging" and the "advantage gained in point of sailing," Laurens illustrates an understanding of sailing that perhaps harkened back to his days as a shipowner engaged in transatlantic voyages. He also mentions a Mr. Rose in regard to repairing the vessel, which might indicate the famous shipbuilder John Rose of the Hobcaw Shipyard. Laurens's correspondence regarding the *Baker* is an invaluable resource for understanding plantation vessels. (Courtesy Library of Congress.)

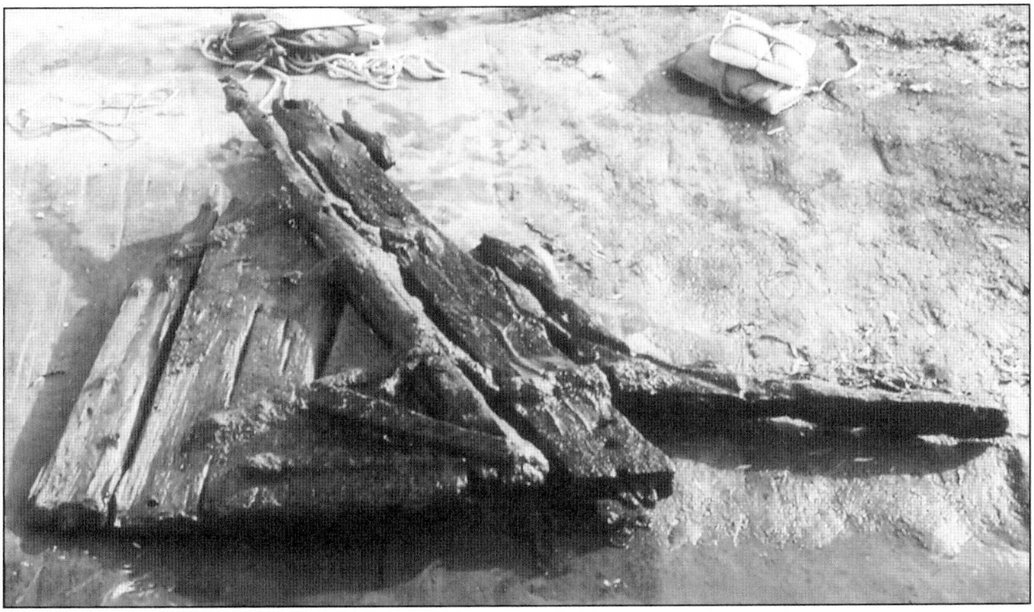

A rudder taken from a famous underwater wreck at Mepkin is shown here. It was originally thought to be from the *Baker*. While the vessel proved to be of a much later era, it is still extremely significant. Rumor has it this rudder had quite an adventure, being carefully excavated and recovered, preserved via submersion for a number of years, almost accidentally thrown away, and then submerged again at its original site in the Cooper River! (Photograph by Ralph Wilbanks; courtesy Drew Ruddy.)

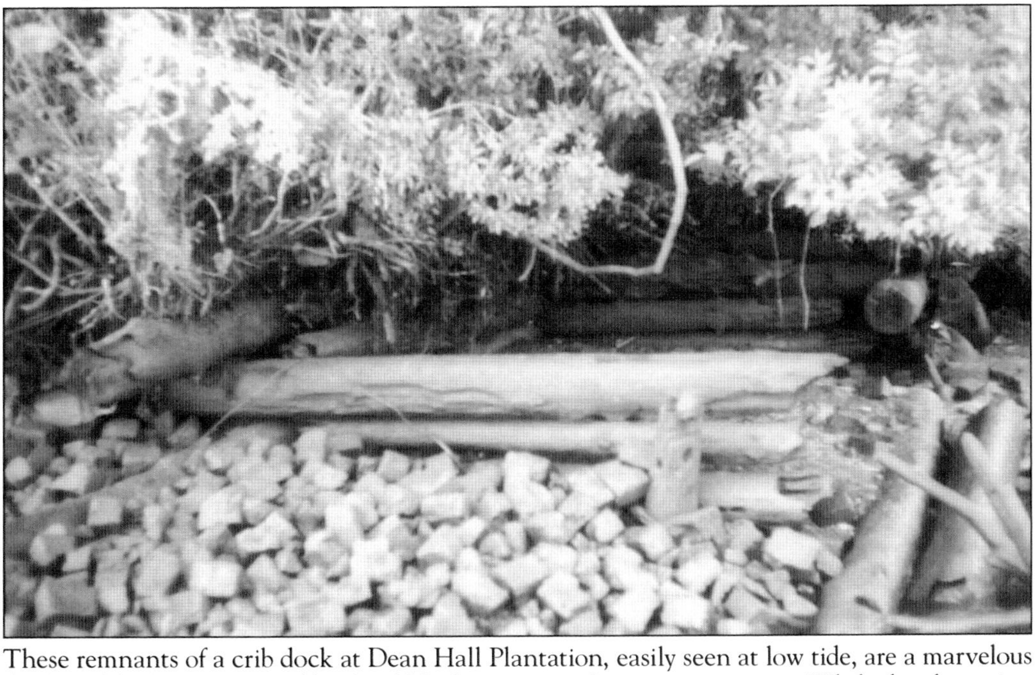

These remnants of a crib dock at Dean Hall Plantation, easily seen at low tide, are a marvelous display of the logs, posts, and brick rubble that were used in its construction. While the plantation home here was built at the *T* of the Cooper River in 1827, the plantation itself dates from 1725. It is impossible to date the dock, but it is definitely of the plantation era. (Courtesy Drew Ruddy.)

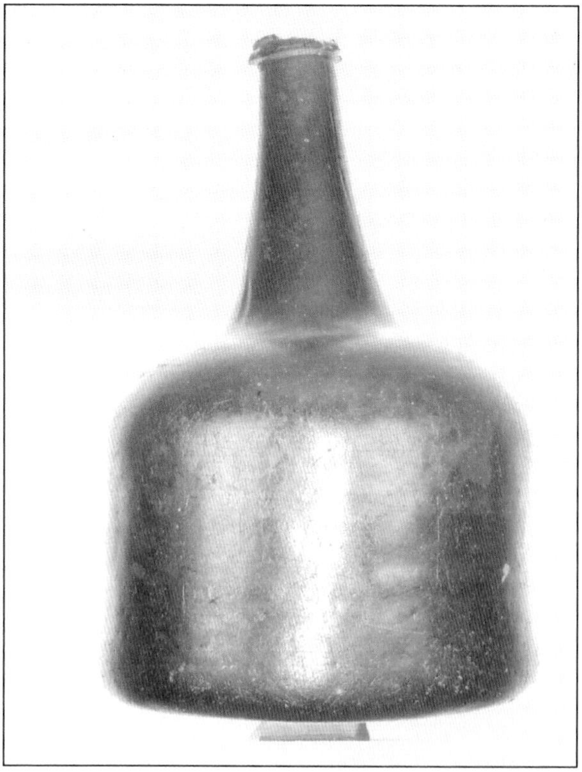

These are different types of vessels recovered from the Cooper River. Artifacts tell the story of the kinds of materials that were typically transported in plantation boats. Styles and shapes of bottles hint at their age, and clay artifacts often attest to the skill and artistry of local slaves who created these vessels and containers on the plantations. (Courtesy Drew Ruddy.)

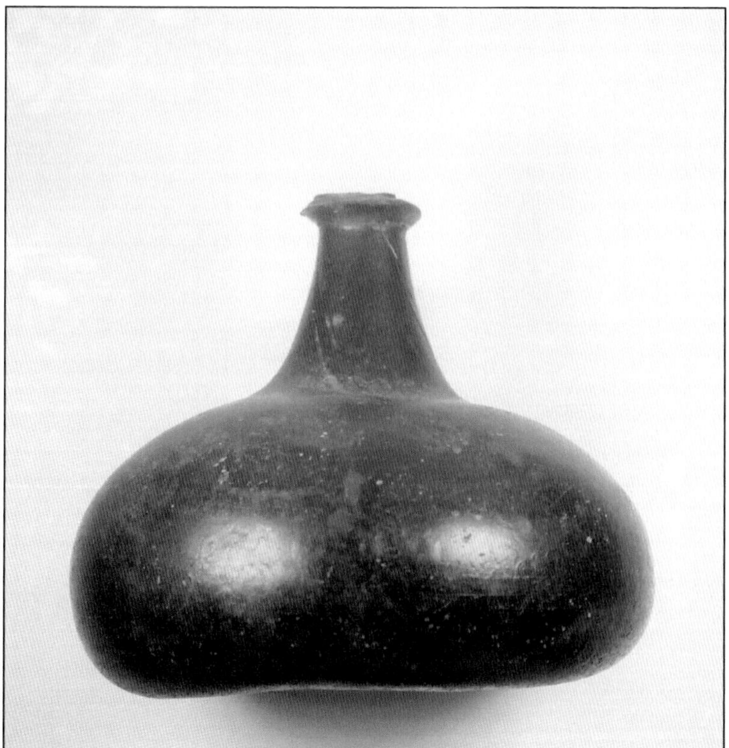

Three

Civil War off the East Cooper Shore

It is common knowledge that Charleston is the birthplace of the Civil War, with the first shots of the war being fired in the harbor in response to a federal ship, the *Star of the West*, attempting to bring reinforcements and supplies to Maj. Robert Anderson at Fort Sumter in January 1861. What many do not realize is that on September 24, 1860, a public meeting was held in Mount Pleasant that produced the first secession resolution in the state. It was three months later that the famous secession convention met in Charleston and the Confederacy was born. So, in a sense, perhaps the Civil War, itself, was birthed in the East Cooper area.

A floating battery, ironclads, blockade runners, and even a submarine were features of the coastal waters off the East Cooper area, and Mount Pleasant boasts yet another, significant Confederate contribution to history: it was the secret training ground for the final nine crewmembers of the famous Confederate submarine, the *H. L. Hunley*. The crewmen resided at Shell Hall on the Mount Pleasant side of the harbor, which was used during the war as an arsenal and had some sleeping facilities. It was from Breach Inlet, between Sullivan's Island and Long Island, in 1864 that this famous vessel was launched. The submarine attacked and sank the USS *Housatonic*, a federal sloop-of-war.

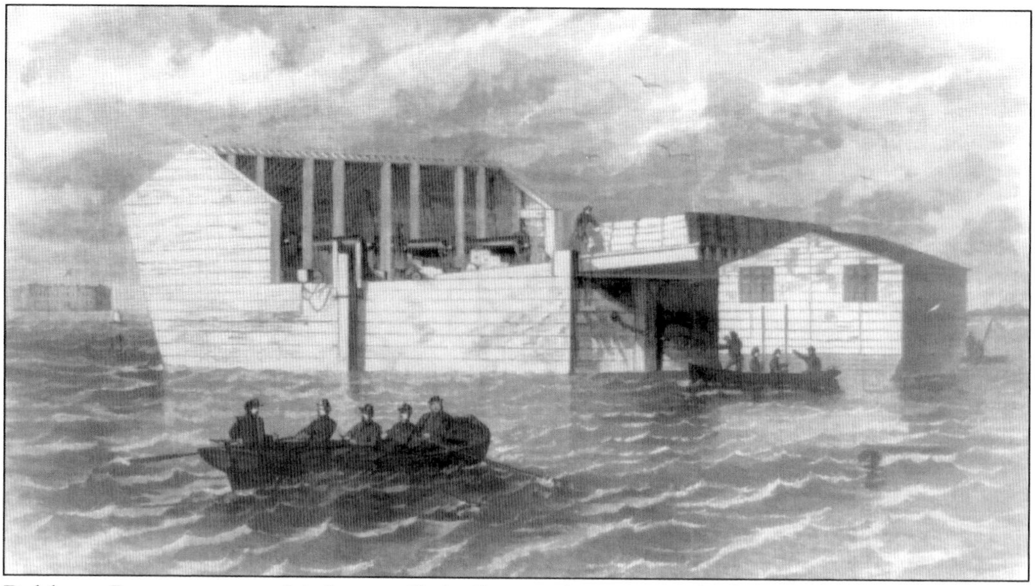

Dahlgren Battery, a type of defence called a floating battery, was built in Charleston in response to the threat of war and was towed to the western end of Sullivan's Island. Nicknamed "the slaughter pen" by critics, the structure was 100 feet long and 25 feet wide. Protected by two layers of iron, it participated in the bombardment of Fort Sumter. The unwieldy structure was later broken apart, and the metal was used in constructing a Confederate ironclad. (Courtesy *Frank Leslie's Illustrated Newspaper.*)

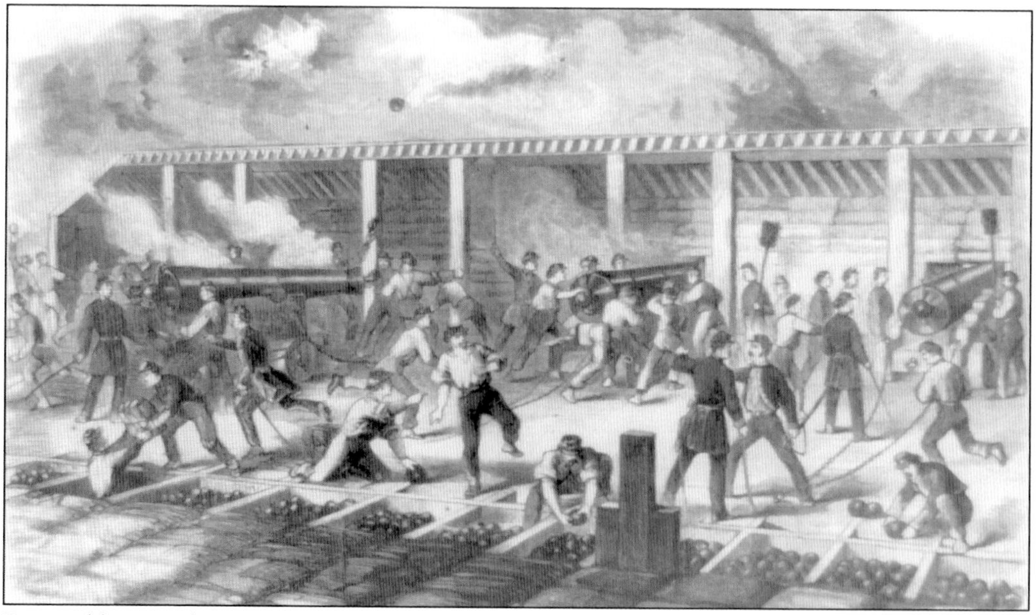

Pictured here is the interior of the floating battery from *Frank Leslie's Illustrated Newspaper.* In his battle report regarding the bombardment of Fort Sumter, Gen. P. G. T. Beauregard noted that "the enemy next opened on Fort Moultrie. . . . These three points—Fort Moultrie, Cummings Point, and the end of Sullivan's Island, where the floating battery, Dahlgren Battery, and the enfilade battery were placed—were the points to which the enemy seemed almost to confine his attention." (Courtesy *Frank Leslie's Illustrated Newspaper.*)

Another infamous event in the Charleston Harbor was the incredible running out of a Confederate gunboat, the *Planter*, by Robert Smalls. This slave was an experienced navigator who was, incredibly, left in charge of an African American crew of eight while the three white Confederate officers went ashore. Sneaking his family aboard, Smalls moved the steamer toward the Union blockade fleet while flying a white flag. Touted as a "gallant" hero by the North, he was given command of the *Planter* and made a second lieutenant in the 33rd Regiment of the U.S. Colored Troops. His former commanders, the Confederate officers, were not so lucky; they were court martialed for neglect of duty. (Both engravings by *Harper's Weekly*; courtesy Library of Congress.)

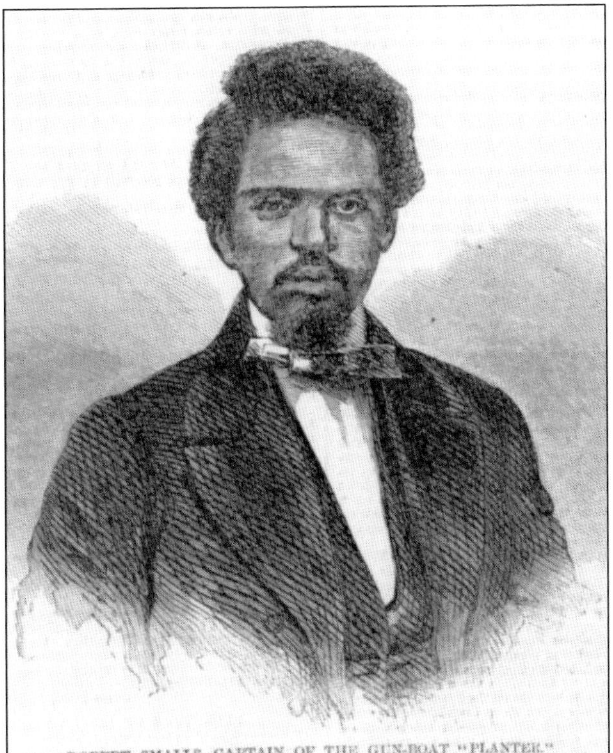

ROBERT SMALLS, CAPTAIN OF THE GUN-BOAT "PLANTER."

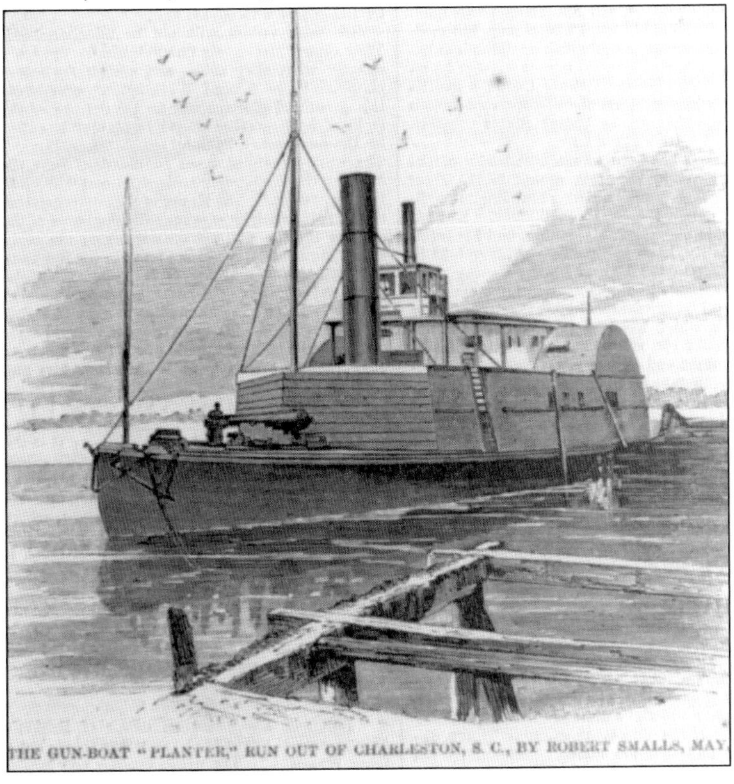

THE GUN-BOAT "PLANTER," RUN OUT OF CHARLESTON, S. C., BY ROBERT SMALLS, MAY,

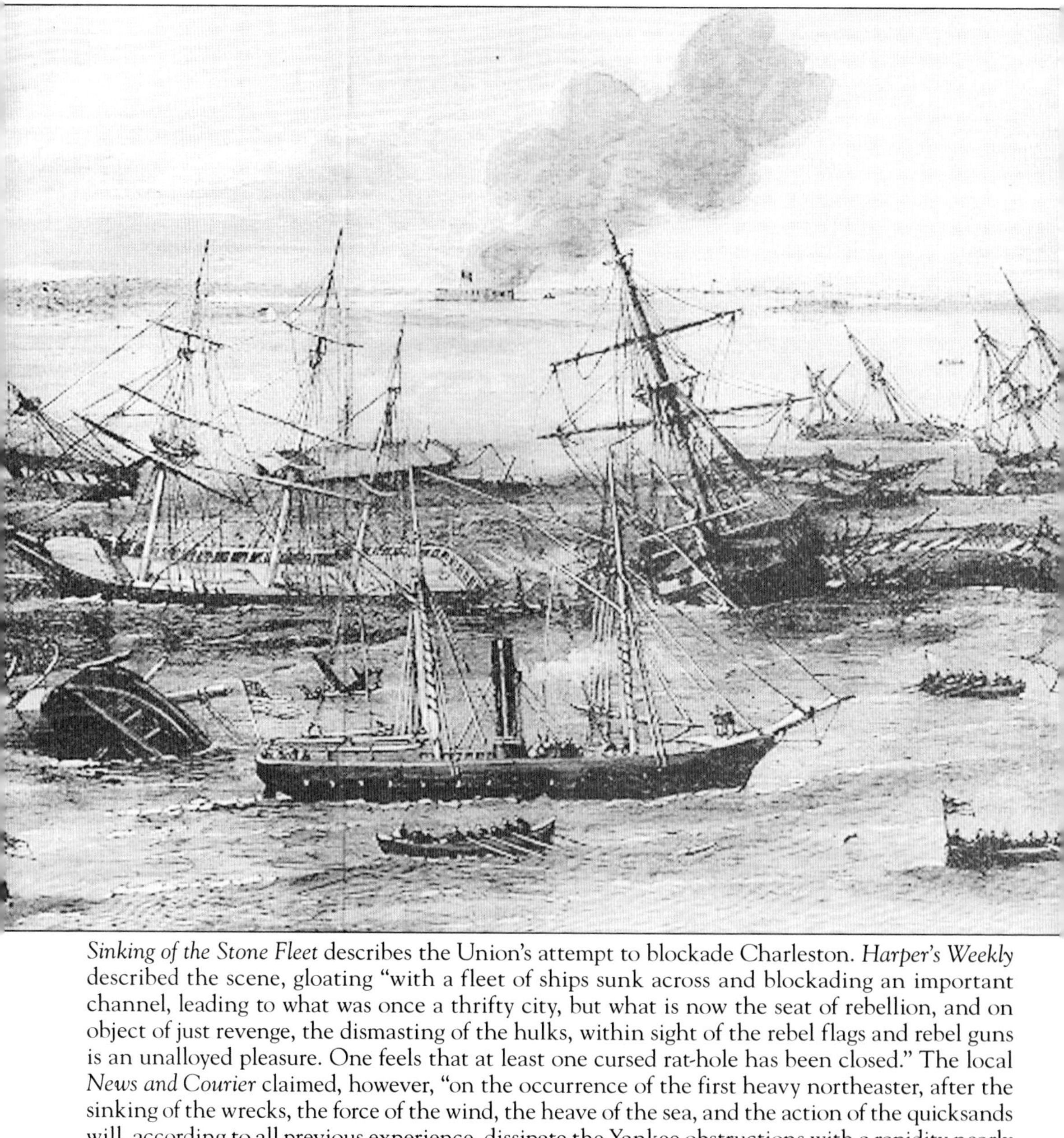

Sinking of the Stone Fleet describes the Union's attempt to blockade Charleston. *Harper's Weekly* described the scene, gloating "with a fleet of ships sunk across and blockading an important channel, leading to what was once a thrifty city, but what is now the seat of rebellion, and on object of just revenge, the dismasting of the hulks, within sight of the rebel flags and rebel guns is an unalloyed pleasure. One feels that at least one cursed rat-hole has been closed." The local *News and Courier* claimed, however, "on the occurrence of the first heavy northeaster, after the sinking of the wrecks, the force of the wind, the heave of the sea, and the action of the quicksands will, according to all previous experience, dissipate the Yankee obstructions with a rapidity nearly as great as that of the late conflagration." (Courtesy Library of Congress.)

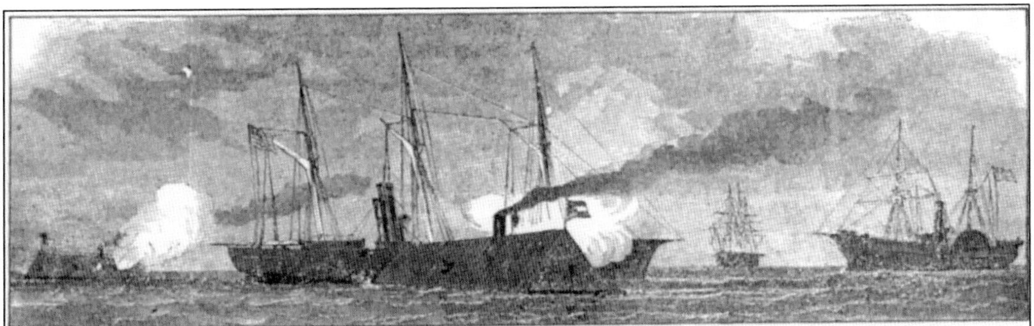

275 Confederate Rams engaging the Federal Blockading Fleet off Charleston, from a sketch in *Harper's Weekly*, Feb. 21, 1863

Pictured above is a sketch in *Harper's Weekly* entitled *Confederate Rams Engaging Federal Blockading Fleet in Charleston*. The Confederate navy was an effective force, despite the fact that at the outset of war it was comprised of 10 ships carrying 15 guns. Although the U.S. Navy in 1861 had 90 vessels, according to historian John W. Mauzey Jr., most of them were in foreign ports, or were either stranded in navy yards in various states of disrepair and in various states of unreadiness, or were unfit for sea at all. Pictured below is the dramatic sinking of the USS *Weehawken* during a moderate gale early on the morning of December 6, 1863, in Charleston Harbor. The vessel was famous for bombarding Sumter and withstanding concentrated gunfire from the Confederate forts while grounded in an earlier battle and tragically lost 4 officers and 27 enlisted men when she sank in 30 feet of water.

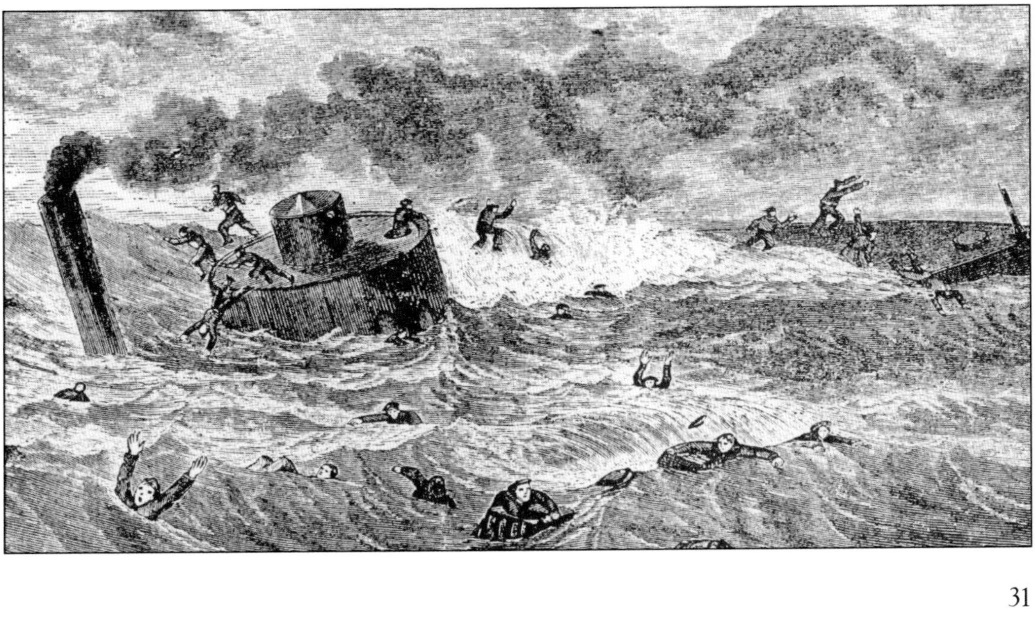

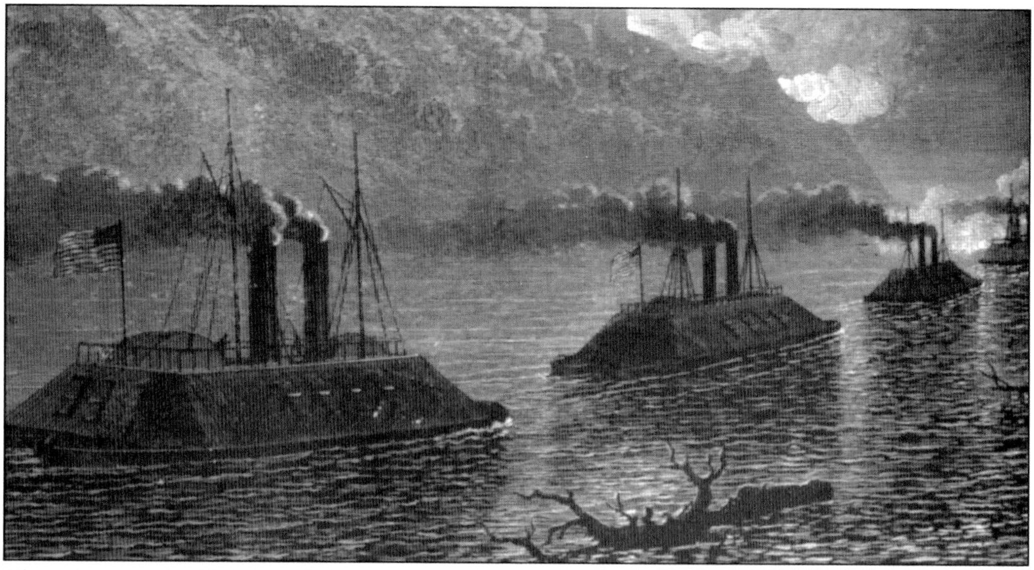

The advance of a U.S. ironclad convoy south toward Charleston is a famous scene showing the silhouette of the ironclads, vessels that were extremely cumbersome to maneuver and uncomfortable to occupy but very effective in maritime warfare during the Civil War. The two types of ironclads of the Civil War were called casemates and monitors, and Southern ironclads were largely casemates. A casemate had slanting sides, which served to protect the guns and crew from enemy fire, and Southern casemates were famous for having sharp bows with which to ram the enemy, which led to their nickname of "southern rams." A monitor was a steamship that traveled very low in the water with a small number of heavy guns in a turret that could rotate for firing. These vessels were swelteringly hot in the summer and freezing cold in the water. They were also famous for leaking and for requiring frequent, heavy repairs after engagements.

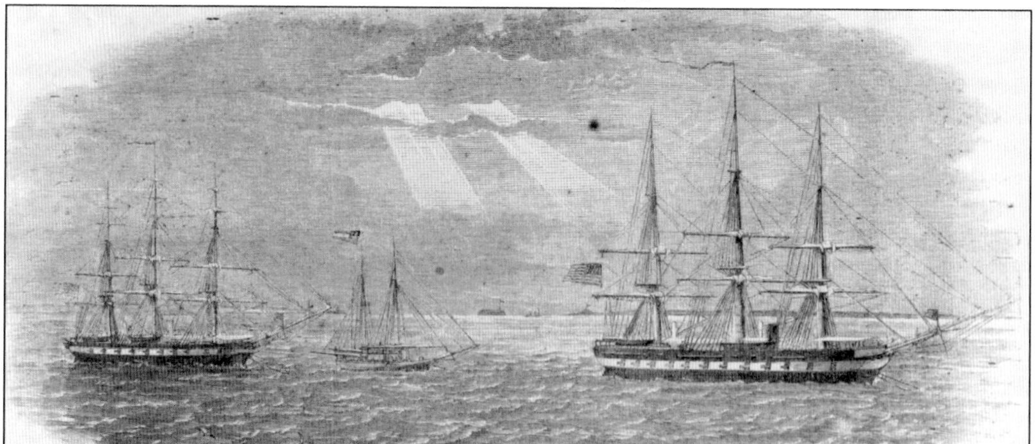

This image portrays an earlier Union triumph in the capture of a prize, the *Arthur Middleton*, which lies centered between the USS *Vandalia* and the USS *Roanoke*, still flying a Confederate flag. After the war, an article in the *London Times* claimed that "the number of blockade runners engaged . . . between British and Confederate ports between the years 1861 and 1865 . . . were no less than 250 vessels." (Courtesy Library of Congress.)

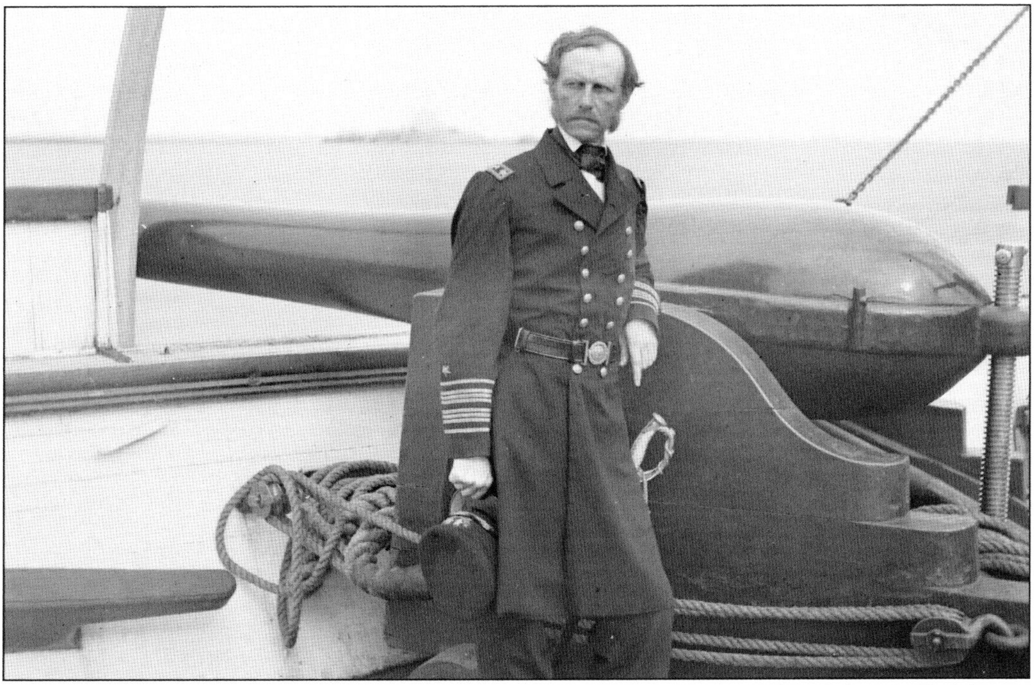

Commanding the South Atlantic Blockading Squadron was Rear Adm. John A. Dahlgren, shown here aboard the USS *Pawnee*, a familiar sight off the East Cooper's shores, as well as other Southern coastal waters. (Courtesy Library of Congress.)

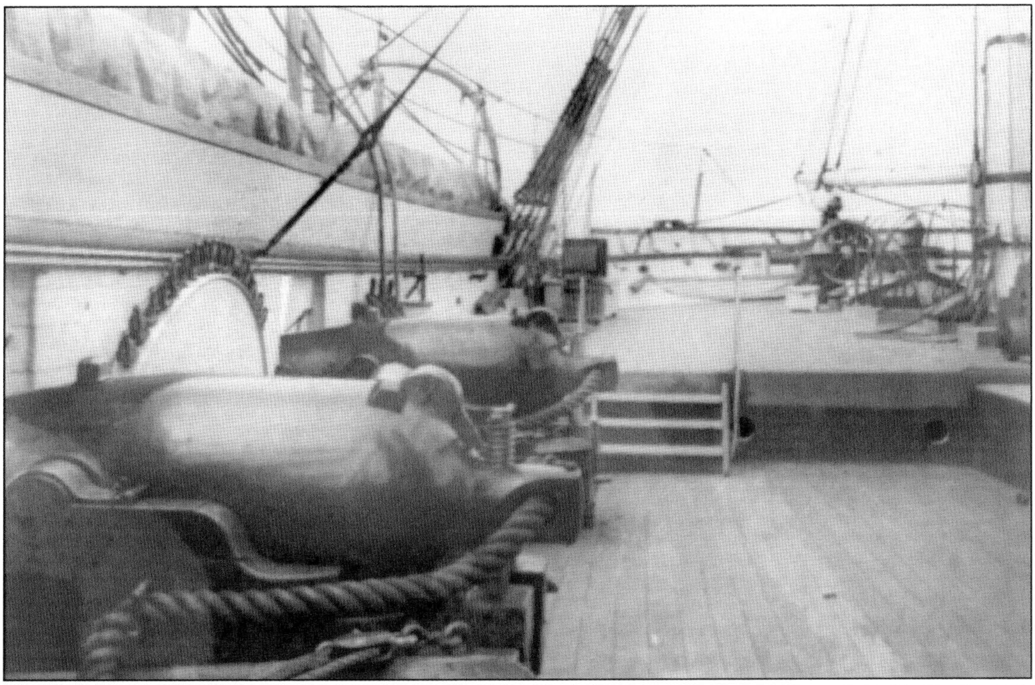

This is a view of the immaculate deck of the *Pawnee*, taken between 1863 and 1865. To the left is a "50 pounder" smooth-bore naval gun. The *Pawnee* was a 1,533-ton, light draft, steam sloop-of-war. (Courtesy Library of Congress.)

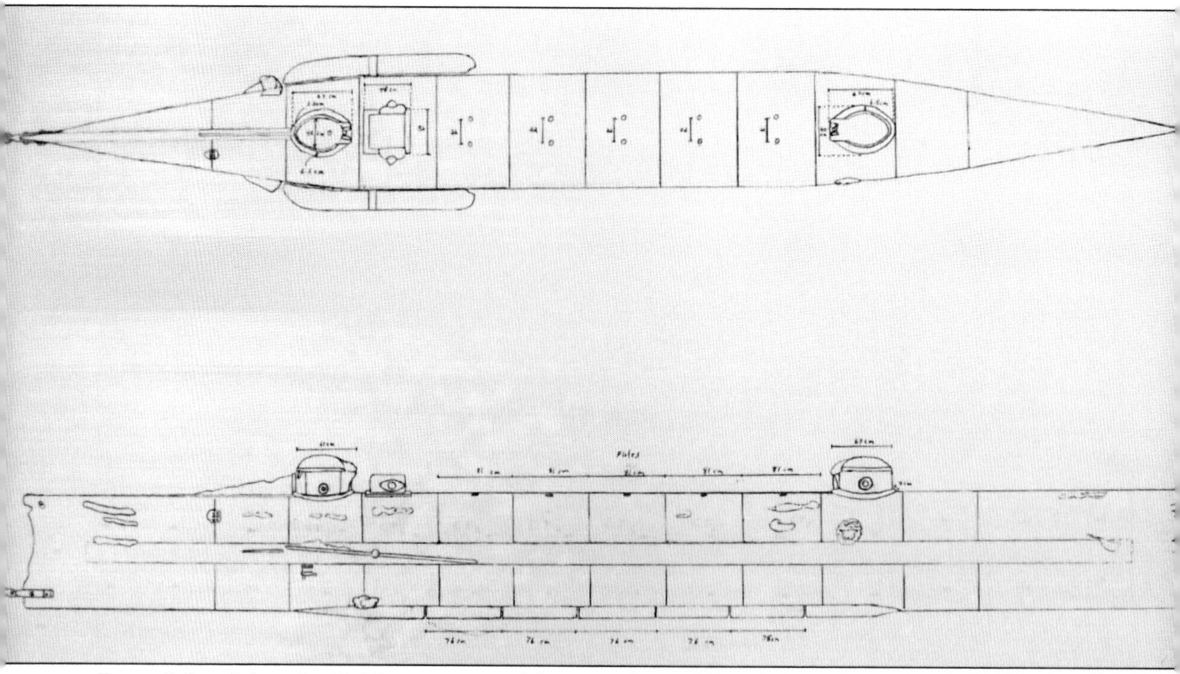

Rear Adm. John A. Dahlgren warned his superiors about a mysterious new weapon of the Confederacy, writing "I have reliable information that the rebels have two torpedo boats ready for service, which may be expected on the first night when the water is suitable for their movement. . . . There is also one of another kind [*H. L. Hunley*], which is nearly submerged and can be entirely so. It is intended to go under the bottoms of vessels and there operate. This is believed by my informant to be sure of well working, though from bad management it has hitherto met with accidents, and was lying off Mount Pleasant two nights since. There being every reason to expect a visit from some or all of these torpedoes, the greatest vigilance will be needed to guard against them." His warning was for naught, for the *H. L. Hunley* made history, ramming her long metal spar into the stern of the USS *Housatonic*, planting a torpedo into the warship, and sinking her. (Courtesy Library of Congress.)

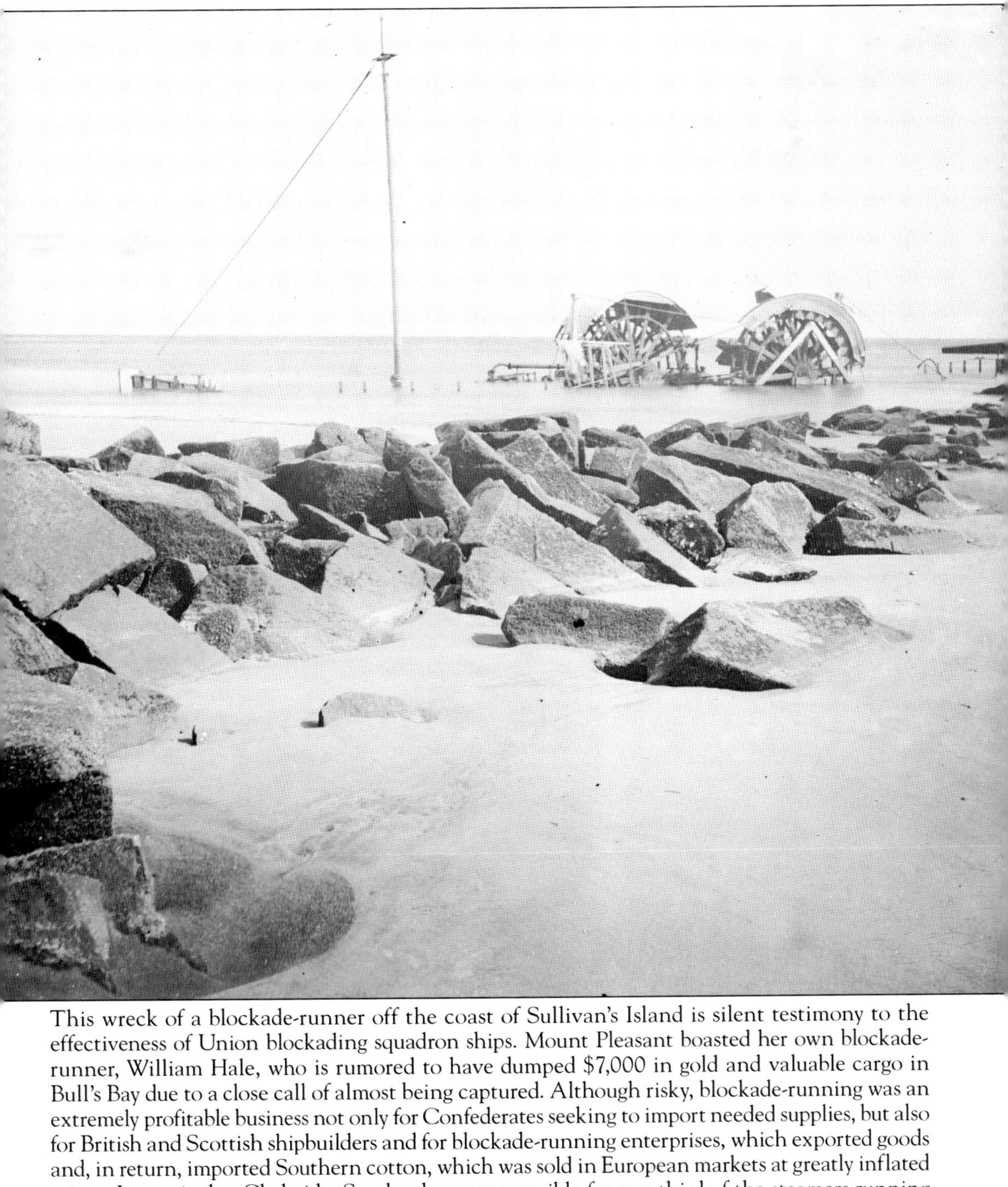

This wreck of a blockade-runner off the coast of Sullivan's Island is silent testimony to the effectiveness of Union blockading squadron ships. Mount Pleasant boasted her own blockade-runner, William Hale, who is rumored to have dumped $7,000 in gold and valuable cargo in Bull's Bay due to a close call of almost being captured. Although risky, blockade-running was an extremely profitable business not only for Confederates seeking to import needed supplies, but also for British and Scottish shipbuilders and for blockade-running enterprises, which exported goods and, in return, imported Southern cotton, which was sold in European markets at greatly inflated prices. In particular, Clydeside, Scotland, was responsible for one third of the steamers running the blockade and for four of the ships used in the Confederate navy. This covert relationship between the Confederacy and Clydside, Scotland, resulted in political headaches for Britain, which was supposed to be a neutral party. (Courtesy Library of Congress.)

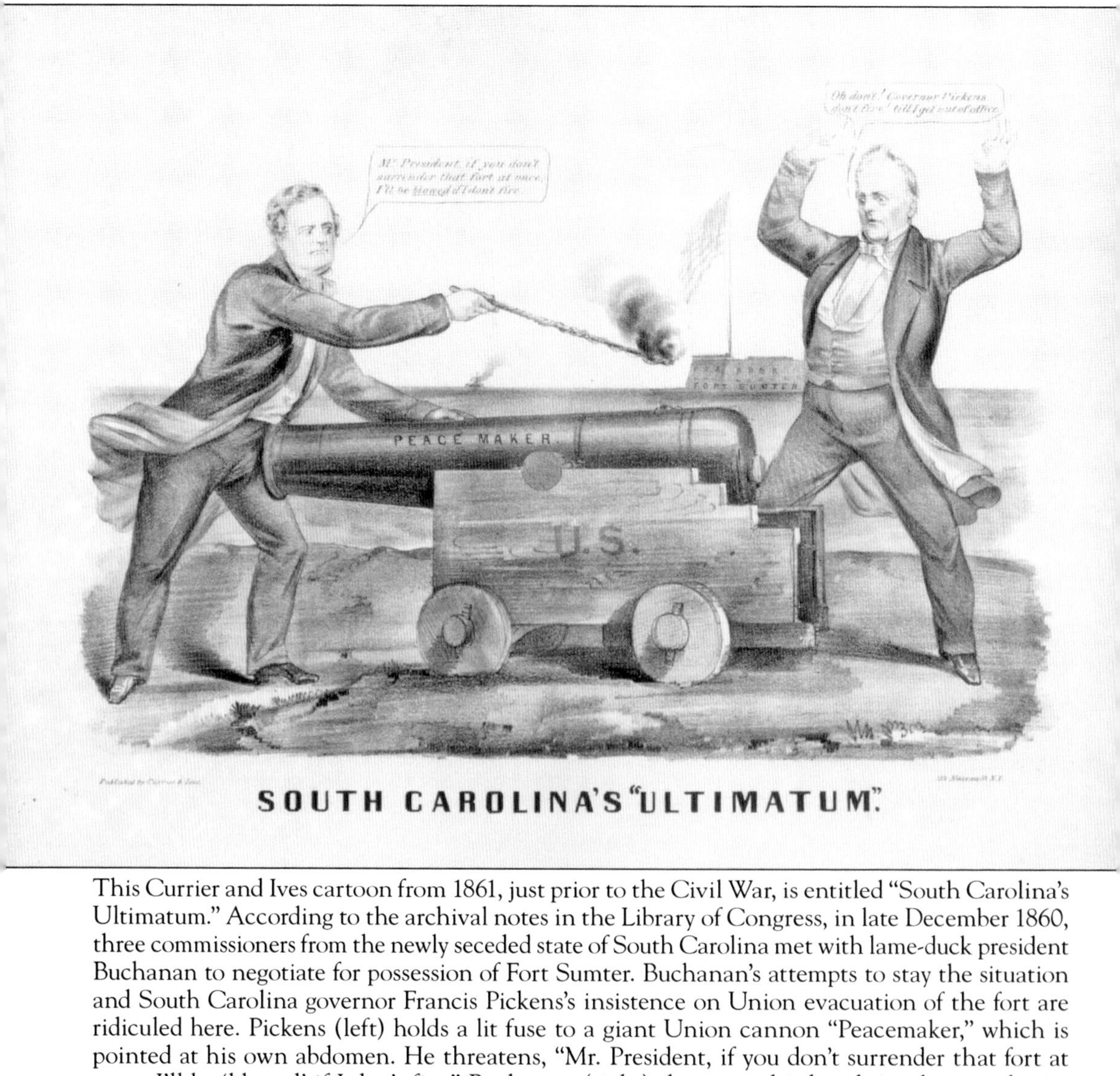

This Currier and Ives cartoon from 1861, just prior to the Civil War, is entitled "South Carolina's Ultimatum." According to the archival notes in the Library of Congress, in late December 1860, three commissioners from the newly seceded state of South Carolina met with lame-duck president Buchanan to negotiate for possession of Fort Sumter. Buchanan's attempts to stay the situation and South Carolina governor Francis Pickens's insistence on Union evacuation of the fort are ridiculed here. Pickens (left) holds a lit fuse to a giant Union cannon "Peacemaker," which is pointed at his own abdomen. He threatens, "Mr. President, if you don't surrender that fort at once, I'll be 'blowed' if I don't fire." Buchanan (right) throws up his hands in alarm and cries "Oh don't! Governor Pickens, don't fire! till I get out of office." In the background, a steamer makes its way across Charleston Harbor to Fort Sumter. The print probably appeared early in 1861, amid mounting tensions over the fate of the fort and uneasy relations between Washington and South Carolina.

This rather glorified rendition of Maj. Robert Anderson raising the Stars and Stripes over Fort Sumter in 1860 does not foreshadow the coming bombardment by the Confederates. The 56-year-old Southerner from Kentucky had only been at his post at Fort Moultrie for one month before his troubles began, and he made the decision to remove to Fort Sumter, which he considered far more strategic and important. (Courtesy Library of Congress.)

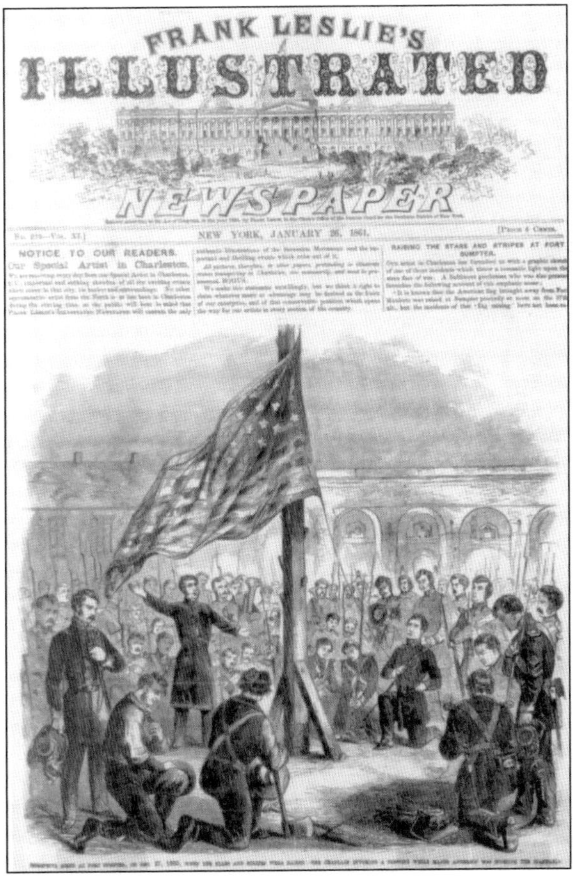
FRANK LESLIE'S ILLUSTRATED NEWSPAPER

NEW YORK, JANUARY 26, 1861.

NOTICE TO OUR READERS.

Our Special Artist in Charleston.

RAISING THE STARS AND STRIPES AT FORT SUMPTER.

By 1863, the interior of Fort Sumter had been all but demolished, as evidenced by this photograph. Although an initial triumph for the Confederates, the episode proved the warnings of Robert Toombs, Confederate secretary of state, to be prophetic. He warned the Confederate president that to take the fort would prove to be "suicide" and that "you will wantonly strike a hornets nest" and "lose every friend at the North." (Courtesy Library of Congress.)

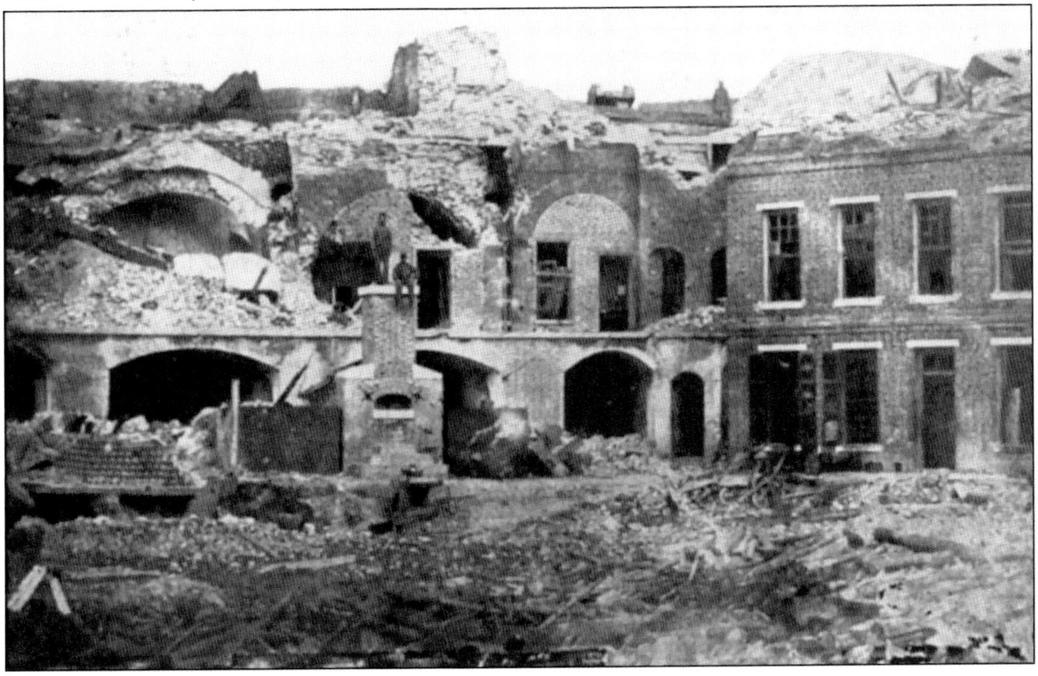

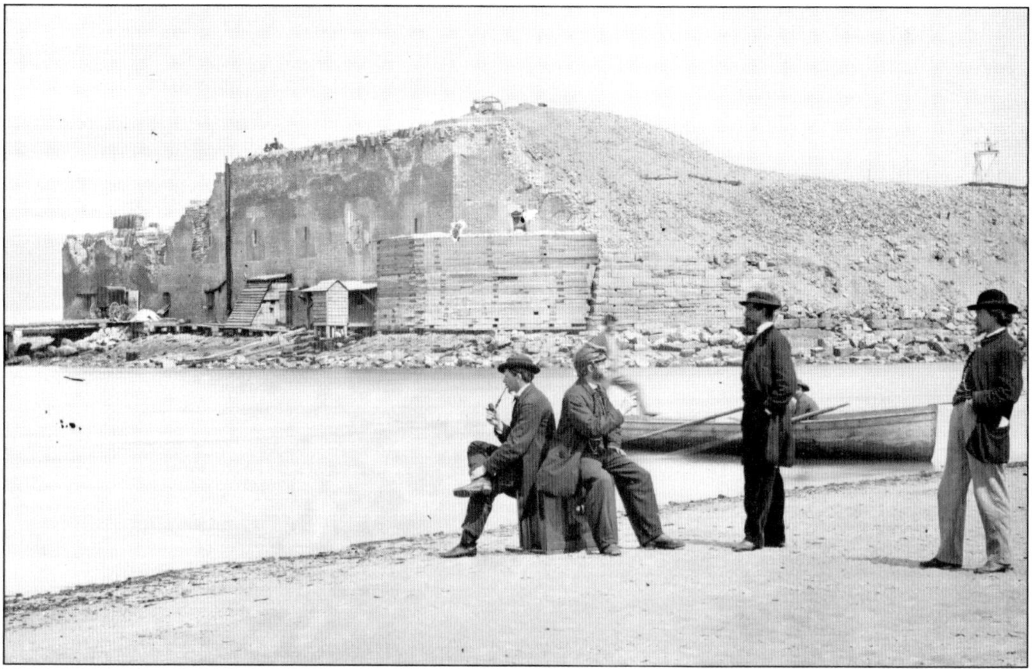

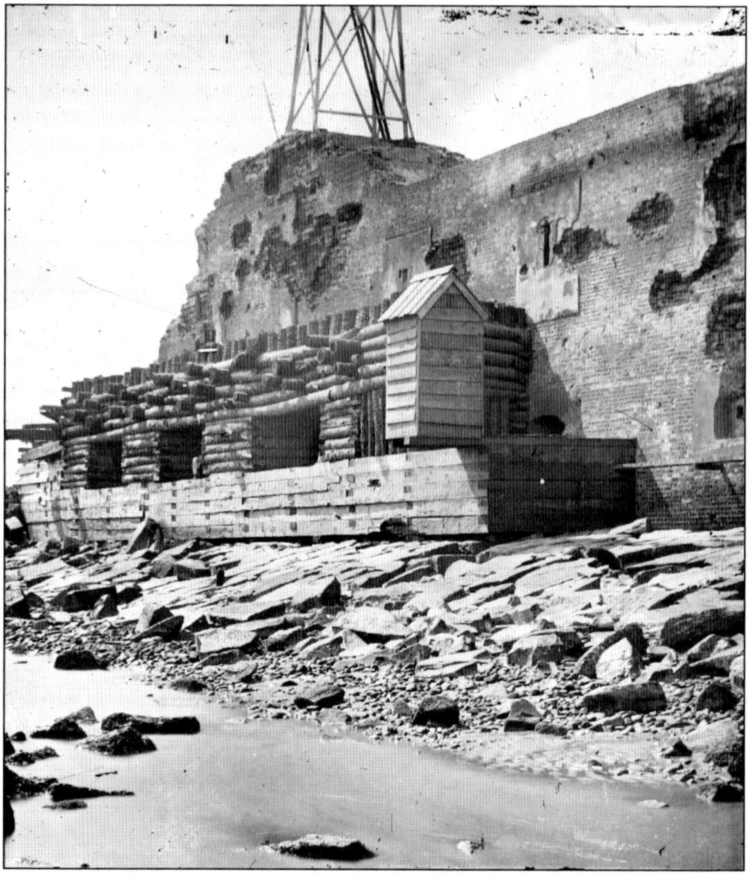

These images show interesting views of Fort Sumter. The image above was taken from a nearby sandbar, and the image at left is a close-up view of the eastern face of the fortification. Note the brick walls, which have been damaged by shelling, and the timber reinforcements. Despite the pummeling, Fort Sumter, like Fort Moultrie, remained standing, a testimony to design and determination. (Courtesy Library of Congress.)

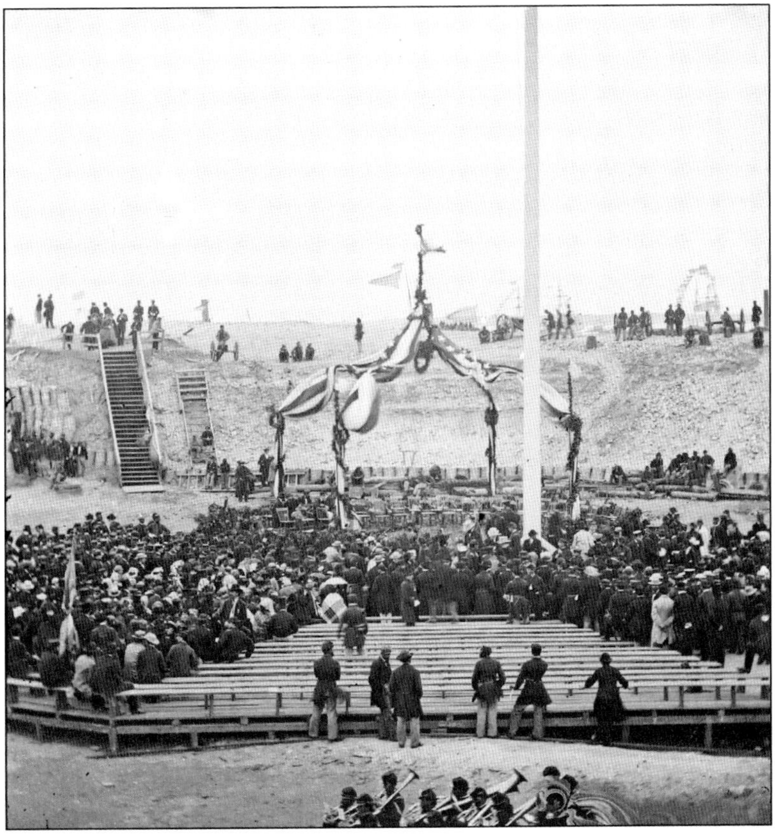

Exactly four years after the flag had been lost from Fort Sumter, an elaborate ceremony saw the raising of the Stars and Stripes again. Abner Doubleday, who had witnessed the initial bombardment by and subsequent loss of the fort to the Confederates, witnessed the festivities. Note the nearby ships with flags and pennants flying. (Courtesy U.S. Naval Archives.)

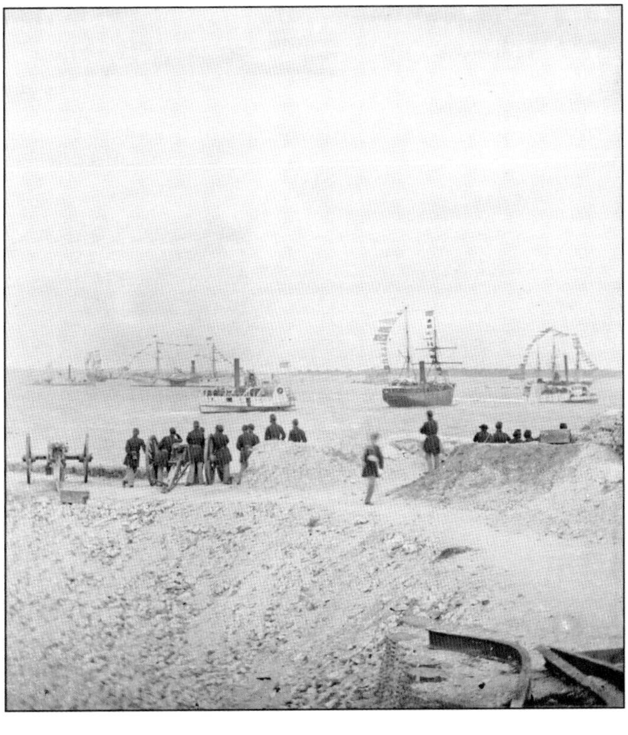

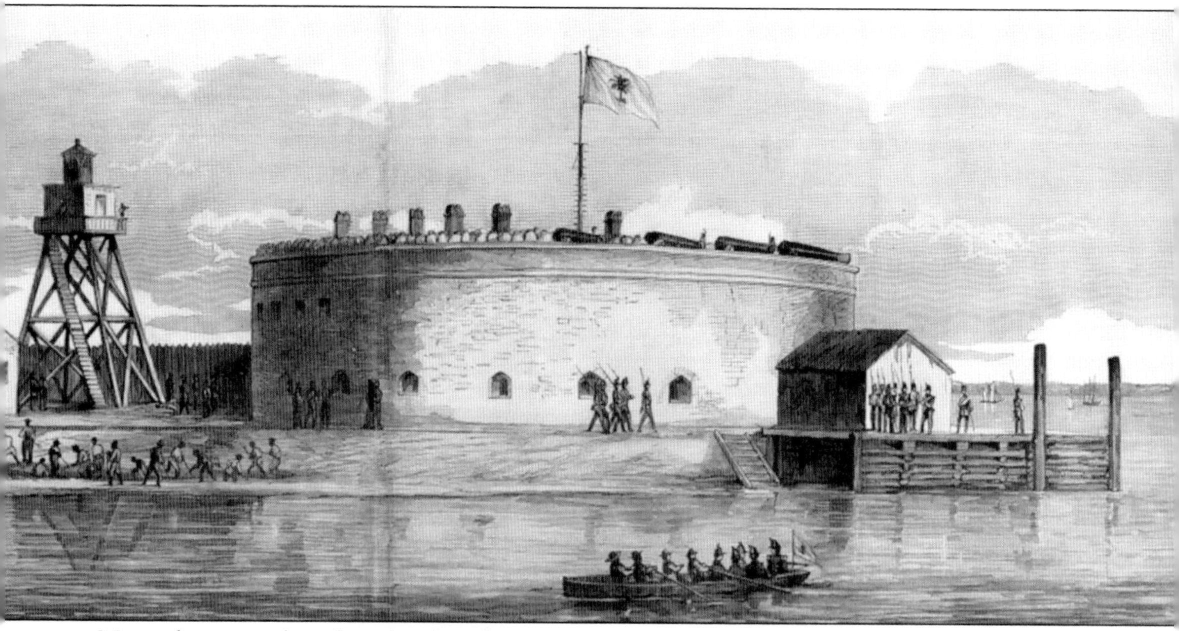

Many do not realize that this fortification is actually the first Federal fort taken over by the Confederacy. Castle Pinckney was an intriguing structure, built sometime before 1812. It saw no action during the War of 1812 and was neglected for years. It was briefly regarrisoned in response to the Nullification Crisis of 1832 during Andrew Jackson's presidency. It was later used mainly for a storehouse until the Civil War, when the Confederacy utilized it for holding prisoners, for firing on Union ships, and for the general defense of the area. After the War Between the States, it was briefly used again as a prison. Some believe that in addition to numerous other remains are the human remains of Federal prisoners executed for mutiny and buried there. Gradually, it became utilized again for storage and as a light station before eventually falling into disrepair. It is virtually nonexistent today. *The Ghosts of Castle Pinckney* by E. P. McClellan is a charming remembrance of a local boy's life on this tiny island and makes a pleasant ending to the fortification's story. (Courtesy *Frank Leslie's Illustrated Newspaper*.)

This interior shot of Castle Pinckney reveals the tidy stacks of cannonballs and the columbiads that were mounted at the fort. Columbiads were muzzle-loading cannons capable of firing shots or shells and were used in firing on targets at long range. It is not evident that Castle Pinckney was ever engaged in firing a single shot during the Civil War, however remarkable her cannons. These columbiads are actually still on the island, but weighing more than 15,000 pounds, any recovery effort would be quite an expensive endeavor. Today the island is a peaceful refuge for wildlife, picnickers, and the biting gnats known locally as no-see-ums. (Courtesy Library of Congress.)

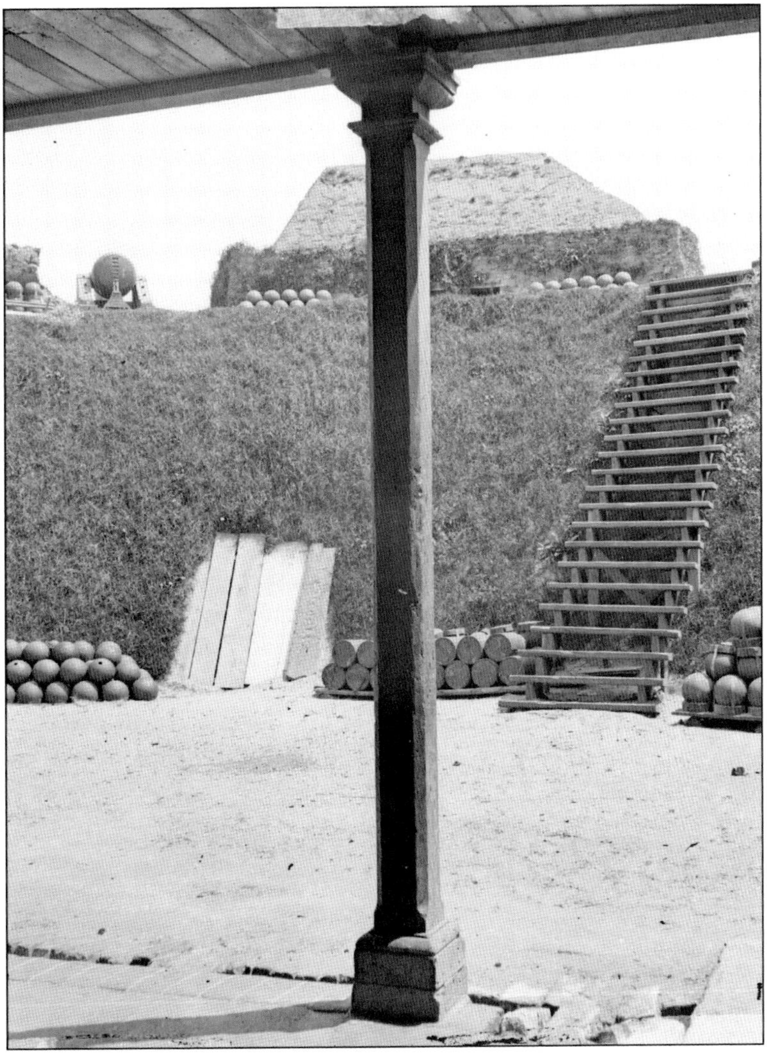

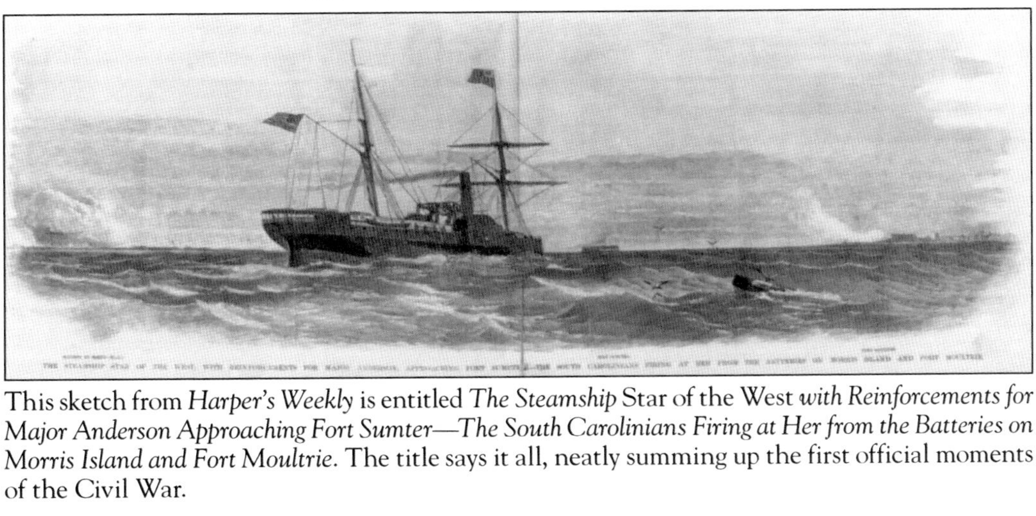

This sketch from *Harper's Weekly* is entitled *The Steamship* Star of the West *with Reinforcements for Major Anderson Approaching Fort Sumter—The South Carolinians Firing at Her from the Batteries on Morris Island and Fort Moultrie*. The title says it all, neatly summing up the first official moments of the Civil War.

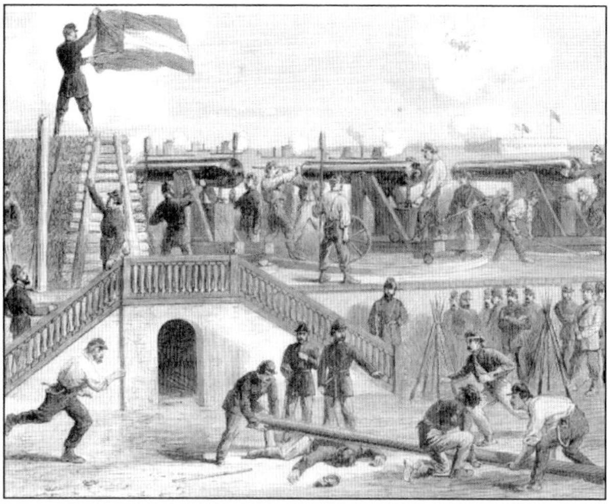

This illustration portrays the Confederates defending the fort from Federal ironclads, seen just offshore with smoke billowing from their stacks. A man is seen lying prostrate beneath the fallen flagpole, while in a scene reminiscent of Sgt. William Jasper of Revolutionary War fame, a brave soldier holds up the flag. (Courtesy *Frank Leslie's Illustrated Newspaper.*)

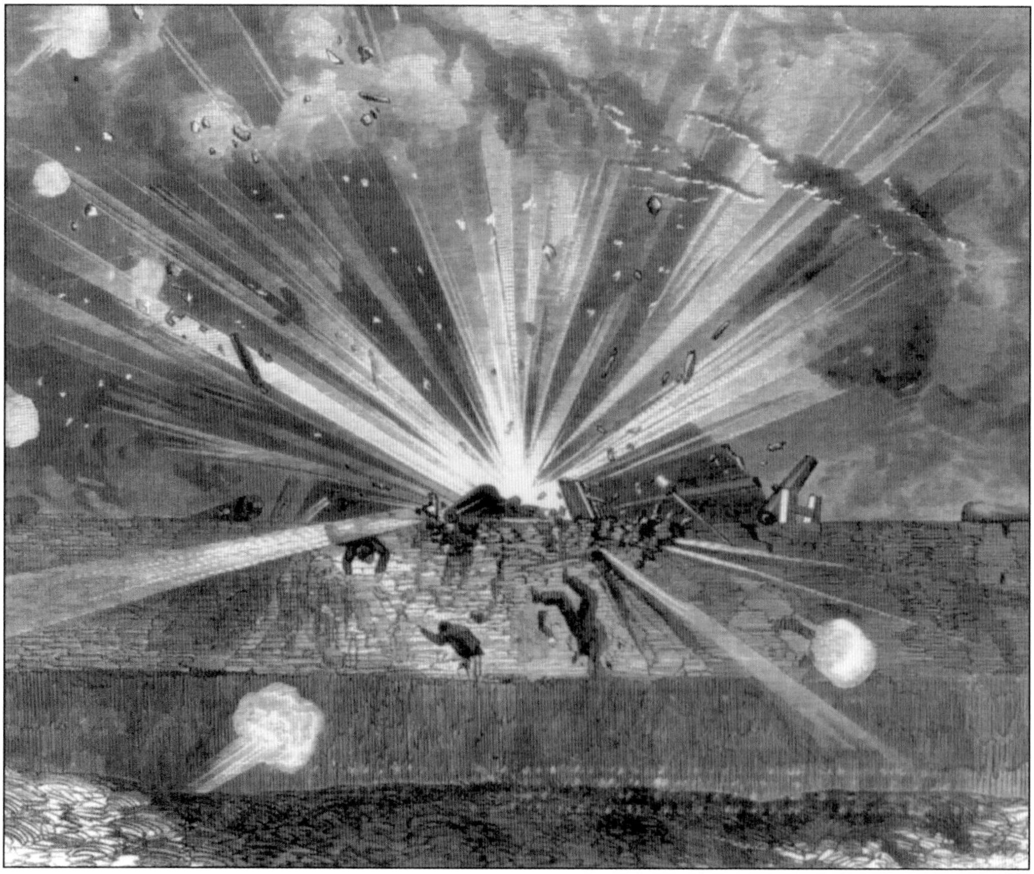

Shown here is the explosion of the magazine at Fort Moultrie from a shell fired from the USS *Weehawken*, a single-turreted monitor that had become grounded, taking on the full brunt of Confederate fire during this particular episode. Although the ship was re-floated and received a commendation from Rear Adm. John A. Dahlgren, the *Weehawken* later met a tragic end in Charleston Harbor when she sank unexpectedly, drowning four officers and 47 crewmembers. (Courtesy *Frank Leslie's Illustrated Newspaper.*)

Four

The In-Between Years

While bitter hostilities and Reconstruction wreaked havoc on the political system and culture of Charleston, life inevitably carried on. Maritime transit was restored as soon as possible, with a new steamship line beginning to ply between Charleston and New York. The Charleston, the Manhattan, and the James Adger were vessels frequently seen coming and going off East Cooper shores, and attempts at clearing the cluttered channels into the harbor, which were filled with Civil War wrecks, were fairly successful under the direction of many experts, although the sunken vessels continued to be hazardous to maritime transit.

East Cooper shores and rivers were as busy as ever after the Civil War, but not much changed in the way of maritime transportation during those years until the widespread use of motorized vessels changed the face of the waterways. Local residents were as enterprising as ever in utilizing whatever materials were available in constructing and maintaining boats, which were still the fastest and most efficient way to travel about the rural landscape. While plantations and farms were no longer wealthy, they still utilized small, coastal vessels for the transportation of goods and people from plantation to market.

Fishing and hunting were still popular pastimes, both with locals and with Northerners, who often purchased old Southern plantations for recreational purposes. These pastimes were often necessary for impoverished Southerners, both black and white. The water still provided a rich bounty to those who traversed it to hunt or plumbed it to fish, and vessels ranging from homemade boats to luxury yachts could be seen at hunting and fish camps on sea islands and riversides.

East Cooper residents continued to build pleasure craft for sailing as well, and local regattas and unofficial races were as popular as ever.

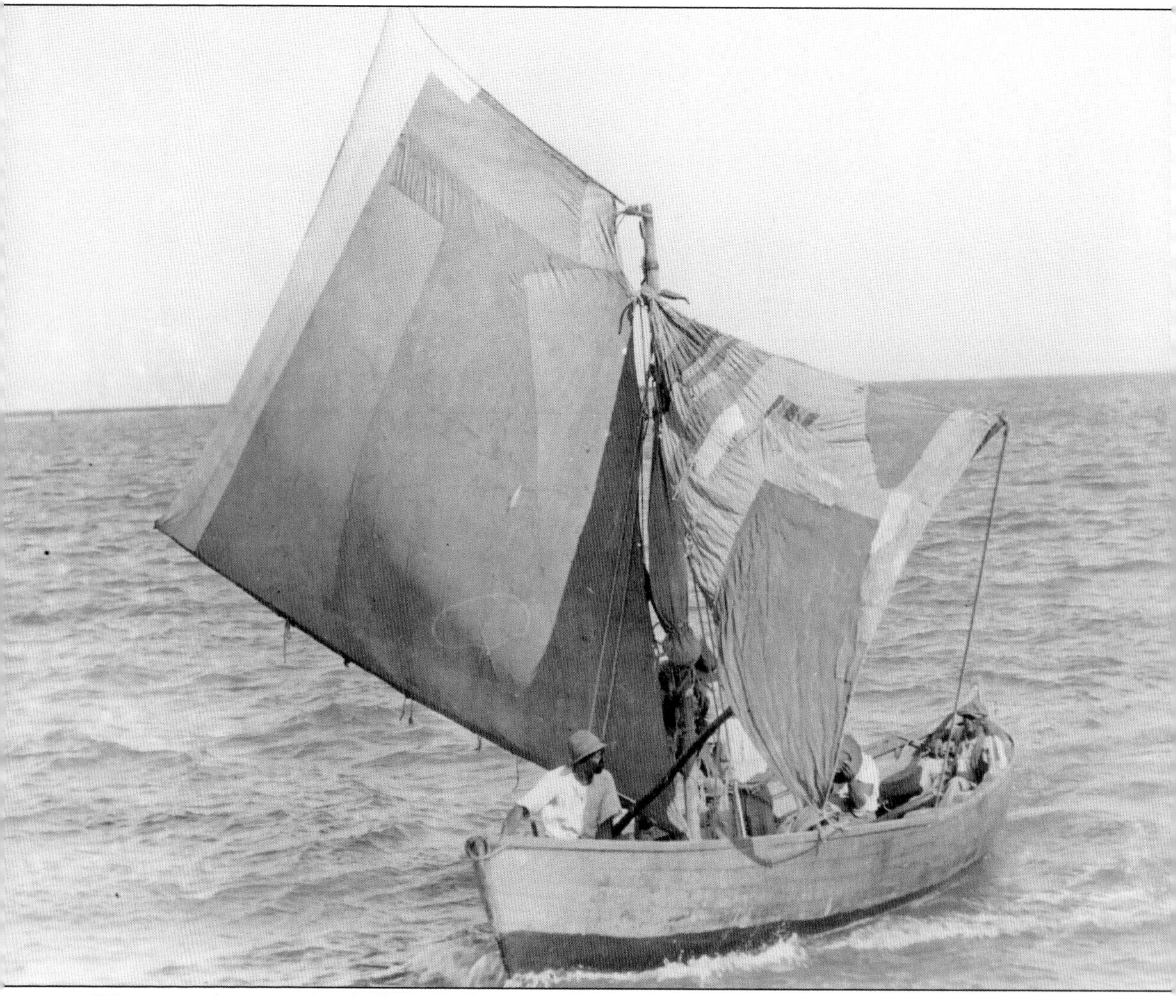

This rare photograph of what was known as a "Mosquito Fleet" vessel is charming, showing a multi-colored fabric sail ingeniously sewn by an enterprising sailor using materials at hand to create what was needed to make a living. The African American fishing fleet was well known by the mid-1800s and remained a part of the coastal and river waterscape well into the early 1900s. According to the South Carolina Seafood Heritage Timeline, in 1940, a hurricane swamped the fleet, effectively ending the era. The colorful personalities and often humorous songs and rhymes sung while peddling seafood downtown faded into Charleston's distant past, and a unique portion of African American heritage was lost with the fleet's disappearance. (Courtesy Charleston Museum.)

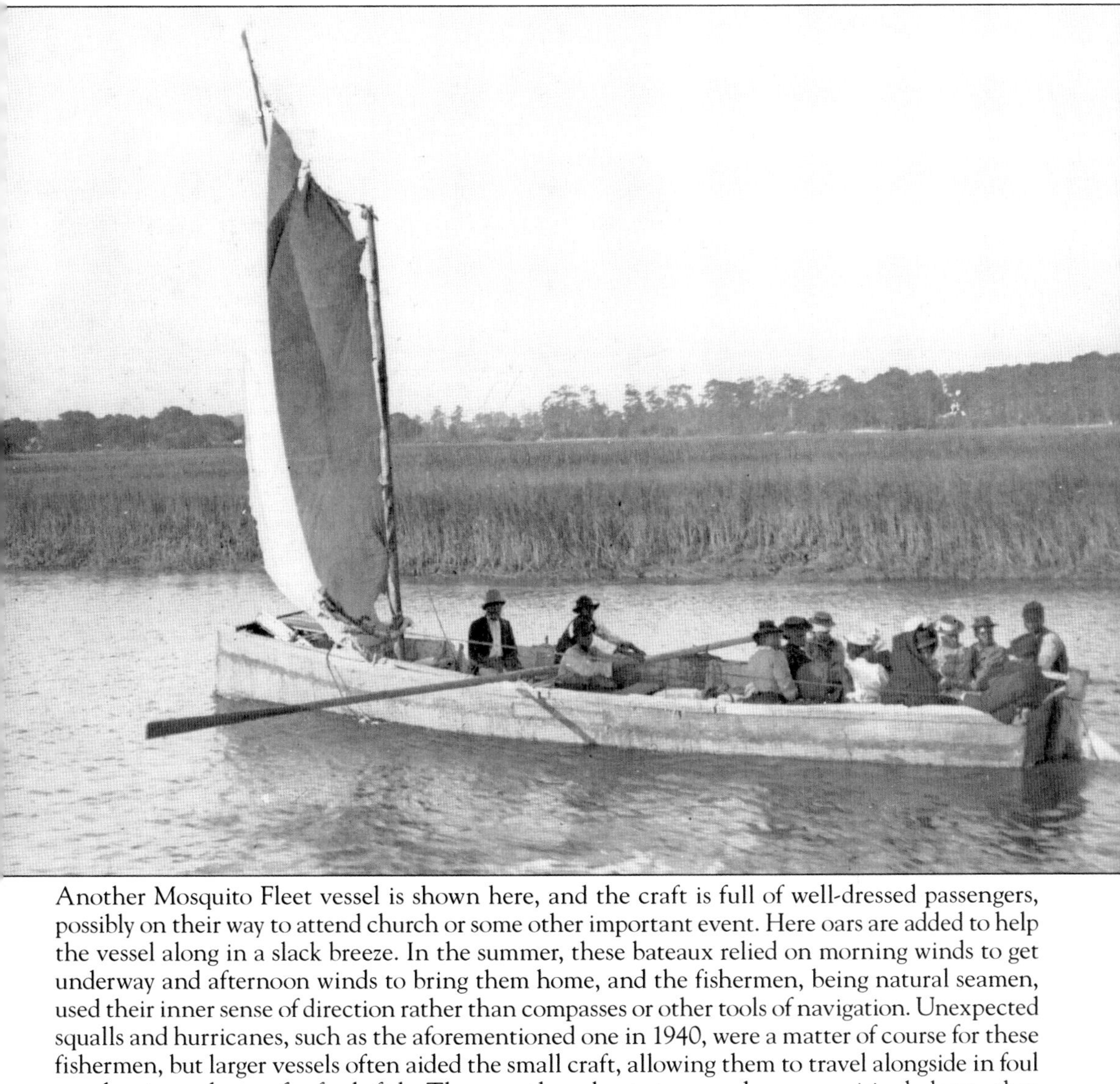

Another Mosquito Fleet vessel is shown here, and the craft is full of well-dressed passengers, possibly on their way to attend church or some other important event. Here oars are added to help the vessel along in a slack breeze. In the summer, these bateaux relied on morning winds to get underway and afternoon winds to bring them home, and the fishermen, being natural seamen, used their inner sense of direction rather than compasses or other tools of navigation. Unexpected squalls and hurricanes, such as the aforementioned one in 1940, were a matter of course for these fishermen, but larger vessels often aided the small craft, allowing them to travel alongside in foul weather in exchange for fresh fish. The area these boats traversed was surprisingly large; they plied the creeks and rivers and traveled as far as 10 to 20 miles offshore in pursuit of their bounty. In the fall, Mosquito Fleet fishermen often worked dockside in fisheries or as stevedores on the wharves. (Courtesy Charleston Museum.)

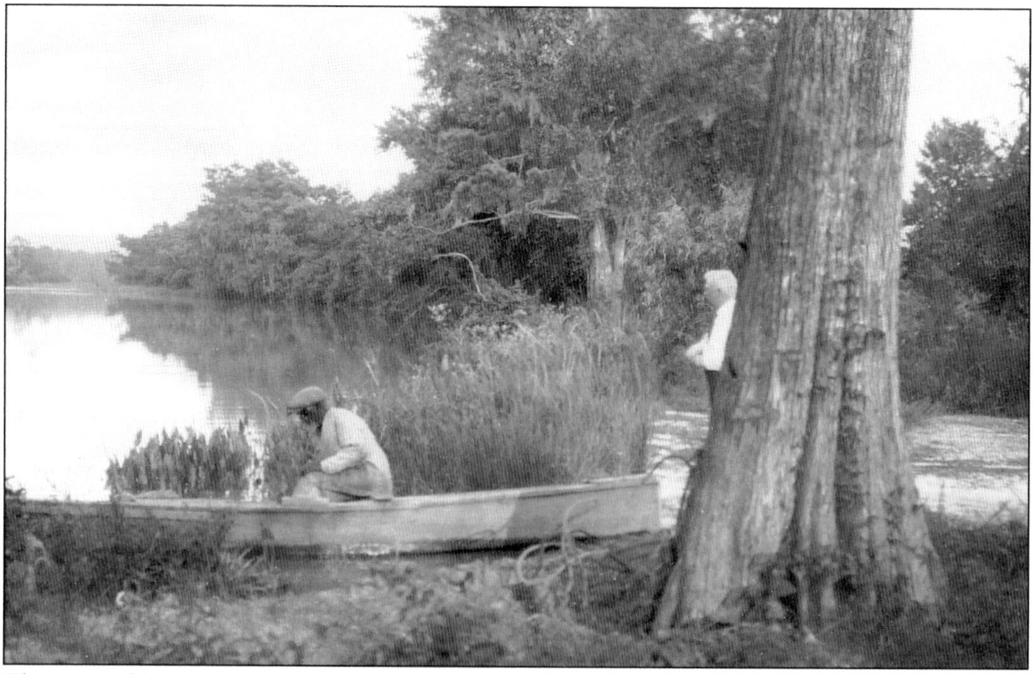

The topic of ferries in Mount Pleasant is wonderfully explained in the book *Mount Pleasant: The Victorian Village*. While larger ferries serviced the village of Mount Pleasant, many folks living in the East Cooper countryside relied on local ferrymen who were known to be at certain locations, like this one situating himself at a landing near Hampton Plantation. (Courtesy South Carolina Historic Society.)

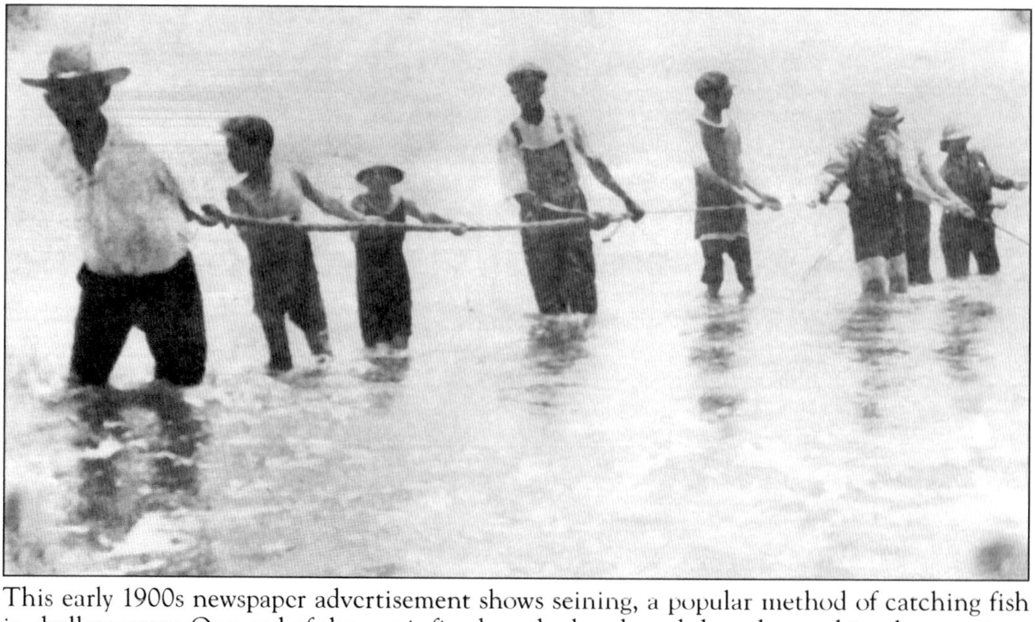

This early 1900s newspaper advertisement shows seining, a popular method of catching fish in shallow water. One end of the net is fixed on the beach and the other end is taken out into the water and then waded upstream against the current, forming a sort of half-circle. The net is hauled back to shore, capturing fish—often whole schools—in it. (Courtesy South Carolina Historic Society.)

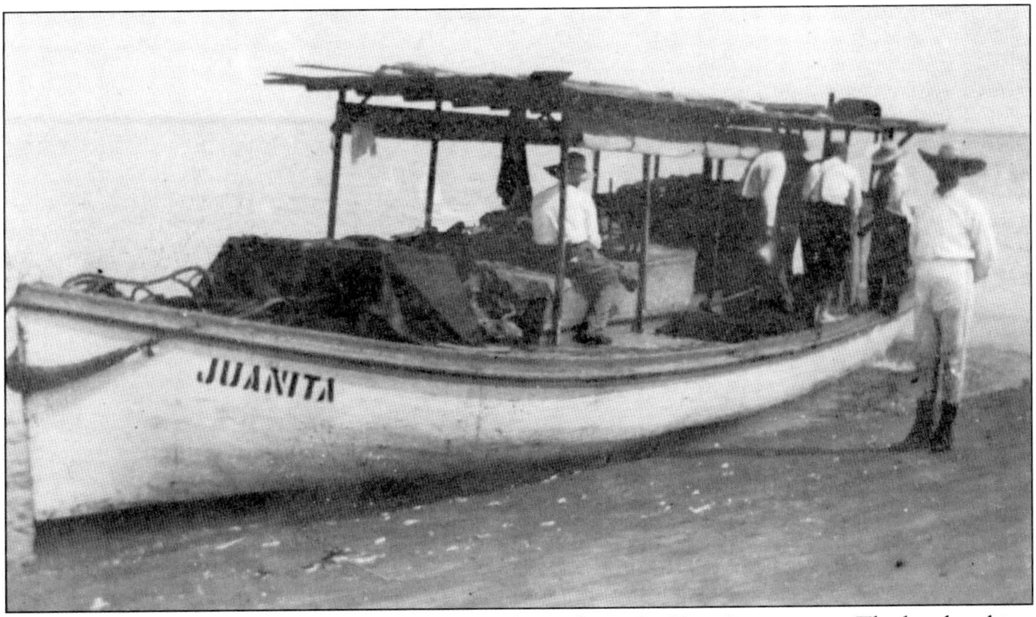

The vessel in these images, the *Juanita*, was a familiar sight in the East Cooper area. The hardworking boat was often the scene of merriment as well as enterprise, as evidenced here. She was used by locals and hired by visitors as a means of transportation to nearby sea islands, where the hunting and fishing were unbeatable. One man proudly displays the wingspan of his duck (he is wearing gartered socks, hightop shoes, and a dapper broad-brimmed hat). The clothing of the men helps date these early-1900s photographs. (Both images courtesy Andrew Magwood.)

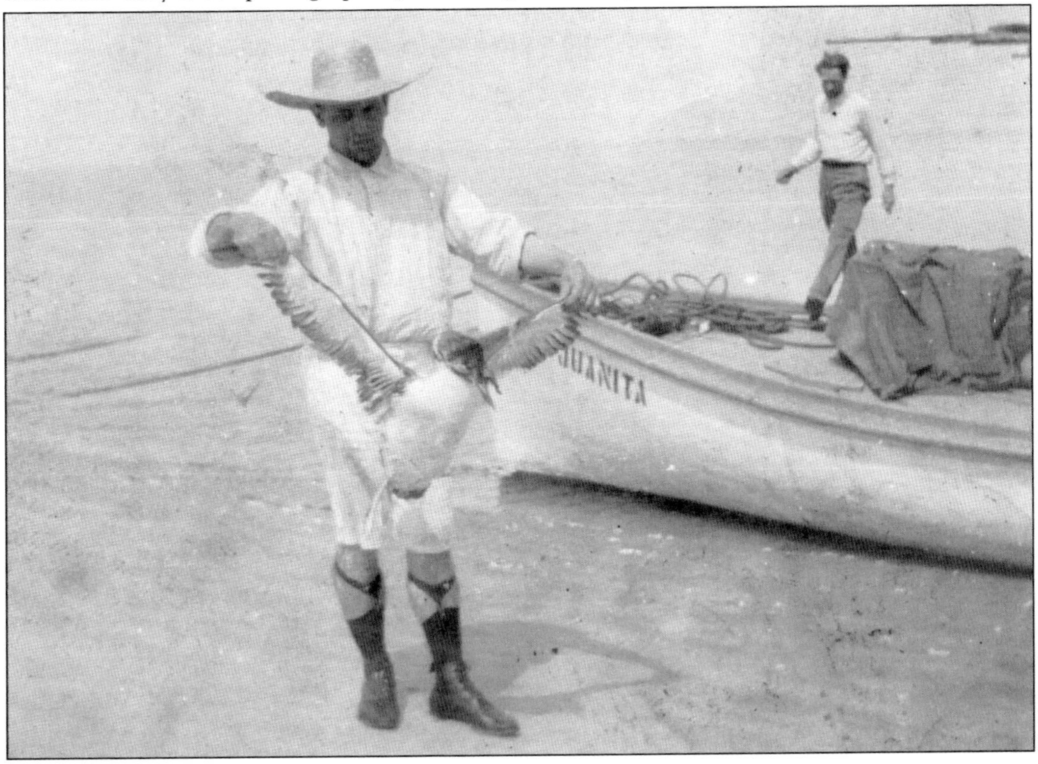

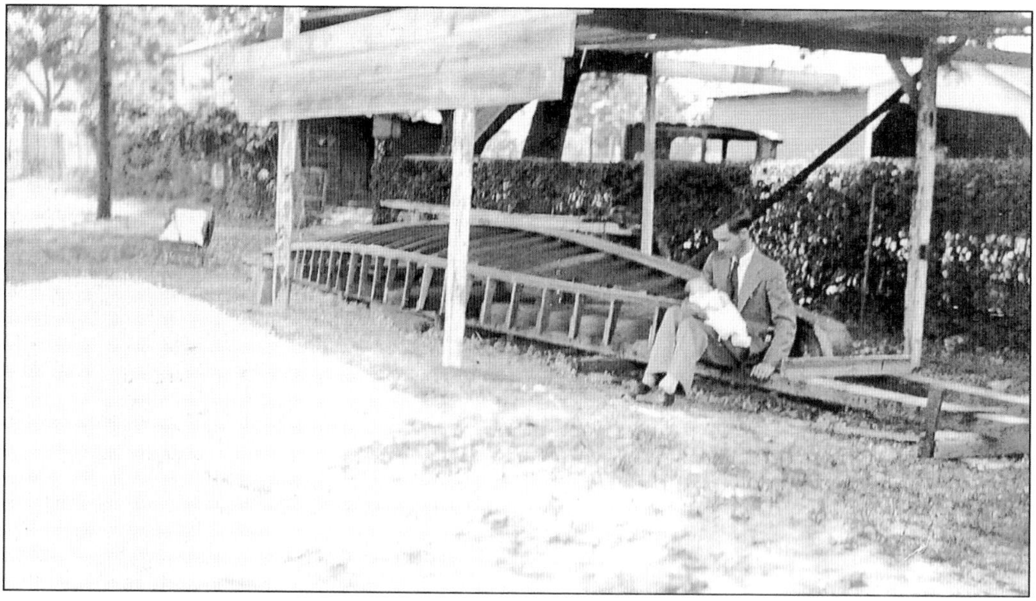

It was not just those who made their living from the sea who were extremely talented boatbuilders. The Donaldson family, seen posing here with baby Robert Donaldson Jr., was famous for boatbuilding skills and sailing prowess, as evidenced by their frequent victories in various Mount Pleasant regattas. Note the Ford Model T seen behind Catherine Donaldson in the background below. (Both images courtesy Mary Anne Hay.)

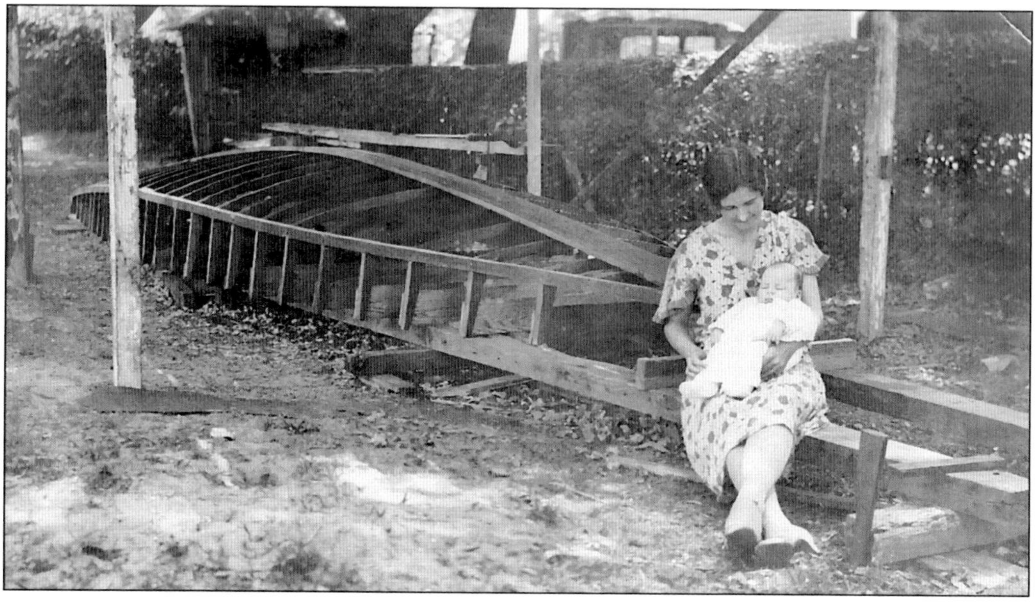

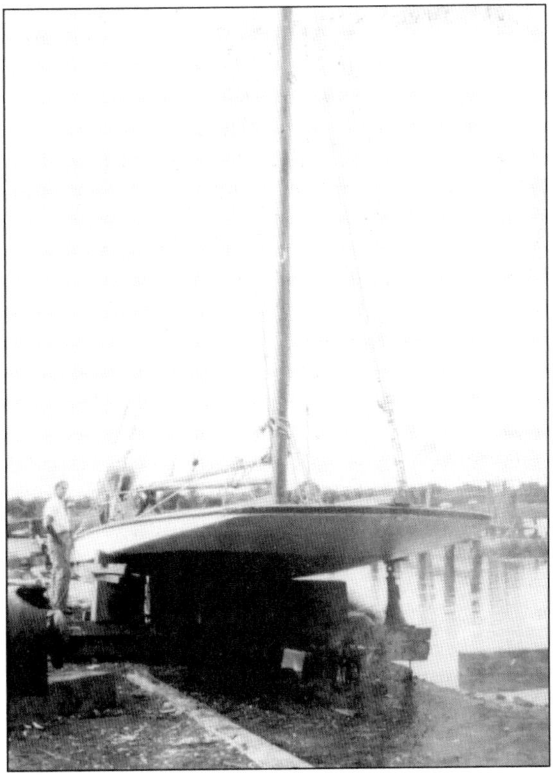

Nearby Shem Creek was often the launching place for Mount Pleasant residents and their family-built watercraft, like these sailboats. The creek was also home to official boatbuilding companies, including Mount Pleasant Boat Works and Sea Island Boat Builders. Naturally, local shrimpers and fishermen also utilized the creek for constructing vessels. Just as in the earliest days of the settlement, Shem Creek was teeming with maritime activity, with East Cooper residents and entrepreneurs taking advantage of the creek's strategic location and direct access to the Charleston Harbor. Old local families often had boathouses on the upper portion on the creek, because the property nearby was undeveloped until the 1950s. (Both images courtesy Mary Anne Hay.)

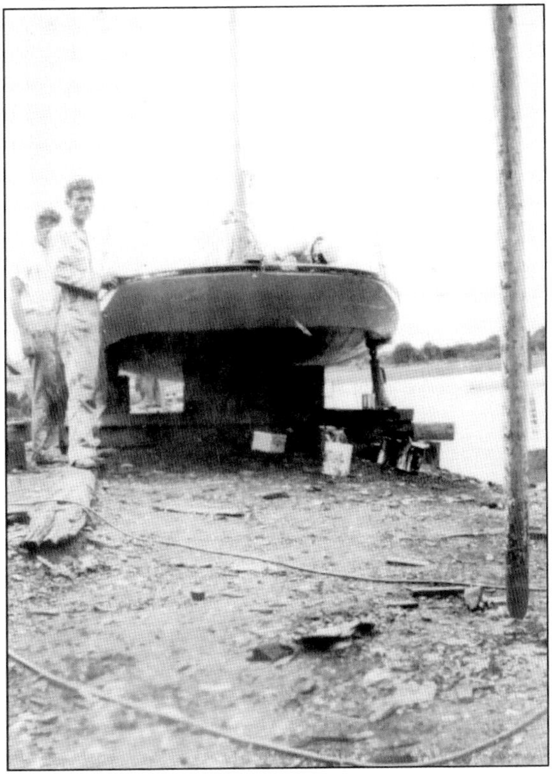

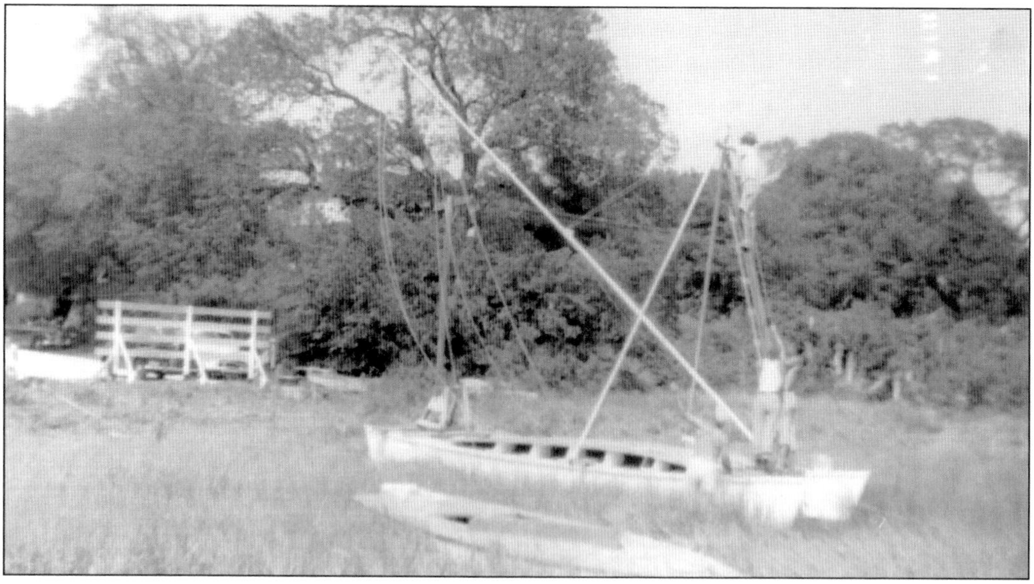

Raising the mast on a family-built craft can be a tricky business! What appears to be a typical boatbuilding scene (pictured above) shows something rather more interesting going on. In 1949, the Donaldson family, already noted for their boatbuilding talent and racing abilities, had yet another claim to fame when Malcolm Donaldson constructed what the *News and Courier* referred to as an "experimental catamaran sailboat." Donaldson got the idea for constructing the 24-foot adaptation of a Pacific rigger when reading about catamarans in a magazine. Although common today, catamarans definitely raised interest—and eyebrows—in the East Cooper area in the 1940s. Pictured below, a member of the Donaldson clan takes a break on the twin hulls at the family's landing. (Both images courtesy Mary Anne Hay.)

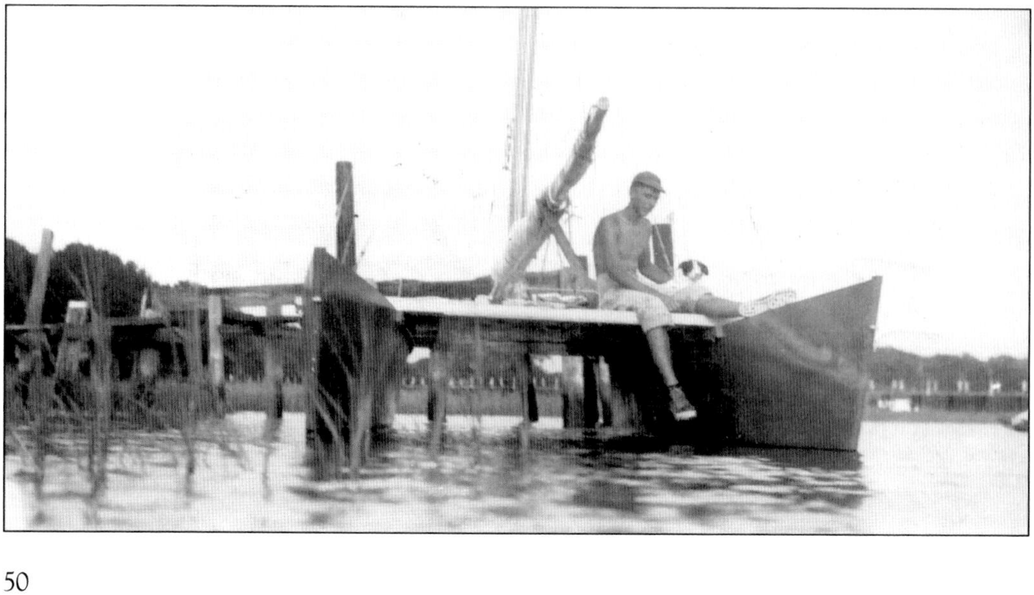

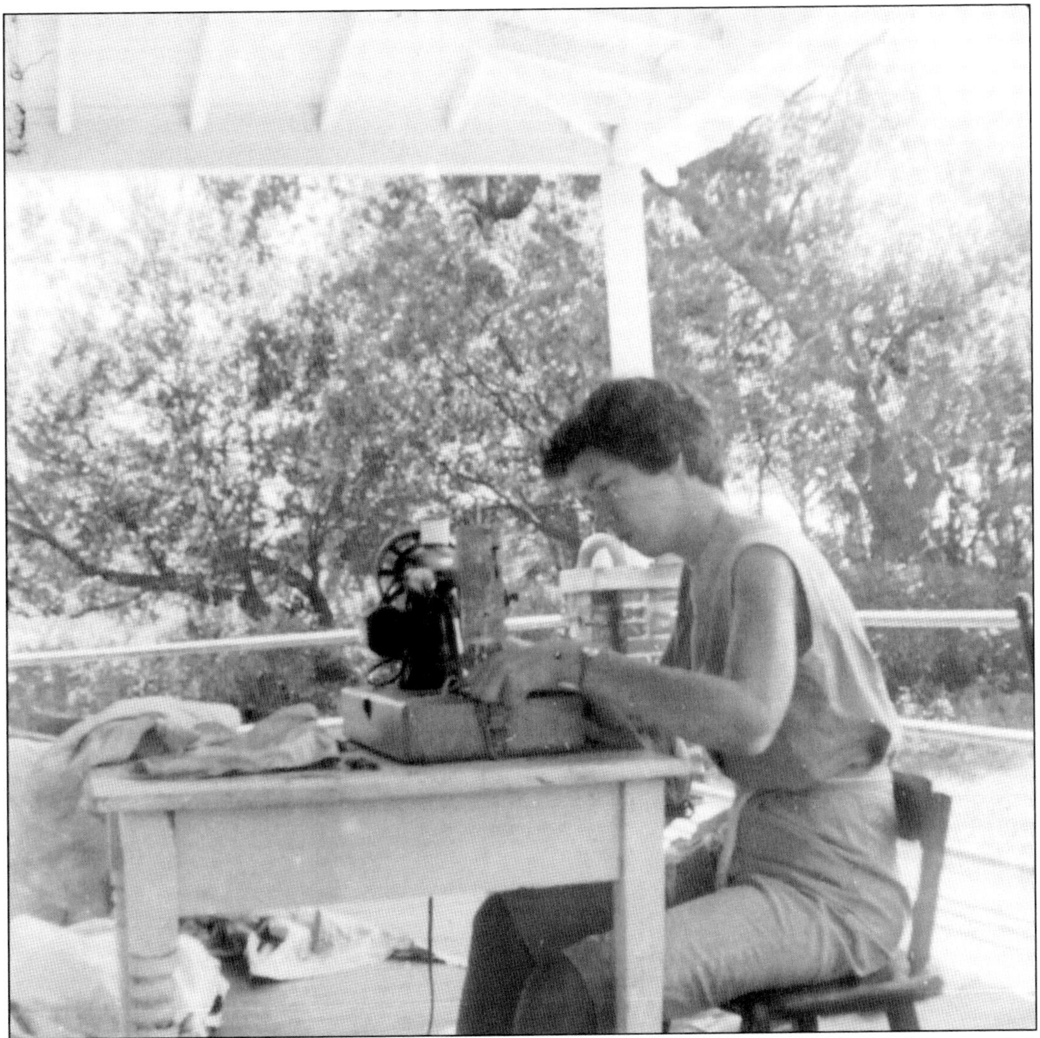

Mary Anne Hay (née Donaldson) demonstrates her skill as a sailmaker while working off the family's front porch in the Old Village. Sailcloth was used up until the 1950s or 1960s, when synthetic fabric, a war product developed by DuPont, became more widely available. The cotton in sailcloth was usually long staple, a product of the nearby sea islands as well as Egypt, with a close weave of at least 120 threads per inch. Cotton would stretch, which would alter the sail and, therefore, the sailing abilities and control. Modern sails are made from synthetic materials like Mylar and polyester, although cotton is still sometimes used in conjunction with synthetic materials in a process called lamination, during which the synthetic cloth is sandwiched in between cotton, or vice versa, and the layers are baked into a cloth. Kevlar is the fabric of choice for the sails of racing vessels. Generally speaking, nylon is the popular choice for spinnaker (or kite) sails, while polyester is the most common ordinary sailcloth. (Courtesy Mary Anne Hay.)

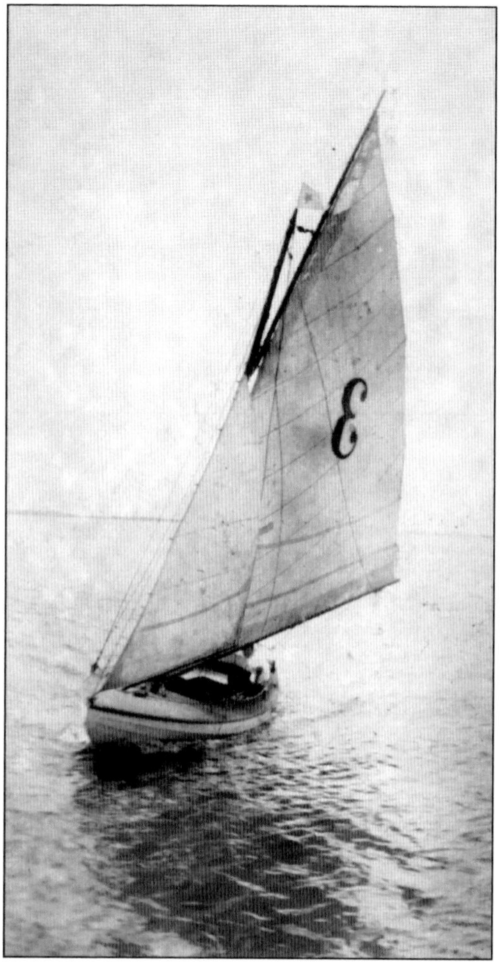

Here are two views of various Mount Pleasant Yacht Club regattas. The *News and Courier* called the Mount Pleasant course "one of the toughest in this part of the country" in an article about the 36th Annual Regatta, held in July 1950. The course was described as running around Crab Bank, a long shoal off the shore of Mount Pleasant, and the article claimed "sailboat skippers have been battling the shifting currents and limits of the bank for years." Dances kicking off and ending the three-day race were common, and judges from the Charleston Yacht Club and the Carolina Yacht Club were often in attendance, along with Mount Pleasant Yacht Club officials. (Both images courtesy Mary Anne Hay.)

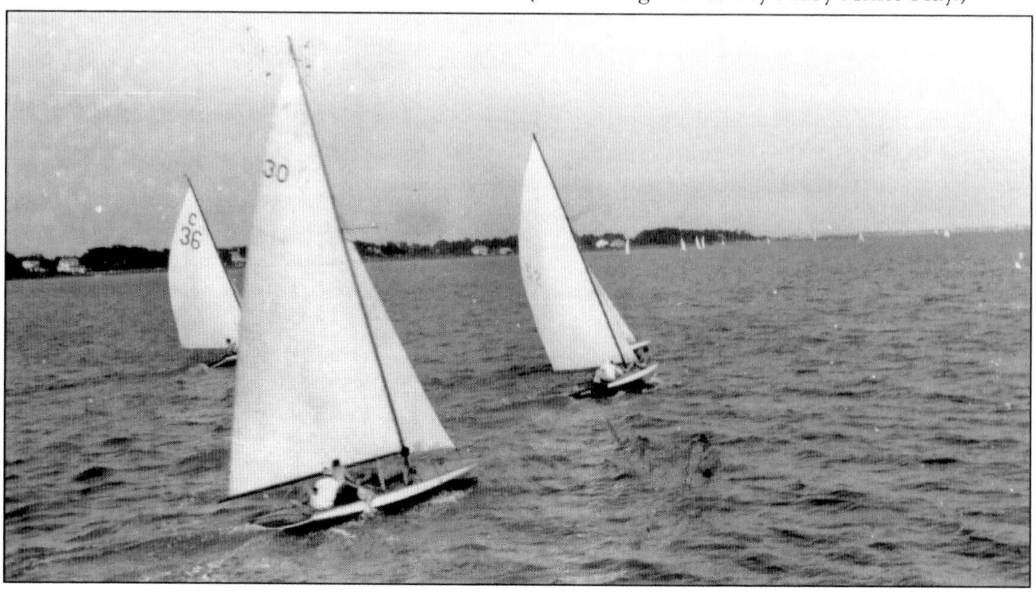

Five

East Cooper Seafood Industries and Shem Creek

While local families were using Shem Creek to launch their pleasure and racing craft, others were using the creek to outfit their seafood industry enterprises. The creek has been home to the businesses of some of the most beloved families (and characters) of the East Cooper area. A surprising variety of seafood concerns have come and gone from Shem Creek docks, representing far more than the shrimping that the creek is famous for. The creek's commercial working waterfronts have been host to net-makers, boatbuilders and craftsmen, and commercial fish houses, but in recent years, with the decline of commercial fishing industries, the creek is developing a new appearance.

Shem Creek's reputation stretches farther than her waters. The creek is famous for friendly Lowcountry faces, old-time traditions, surprisingly abundant wildlife, wonderful restaurants, a delightful nightlife, and, of course, its commercial fishing vessels, which still frame the sky and complete the view. People and vessels continue to visit this tiny yet vital East Cooper creek each year, inspired by its beauty and entranced by the combination of modern vitality and traditional maritime charm.

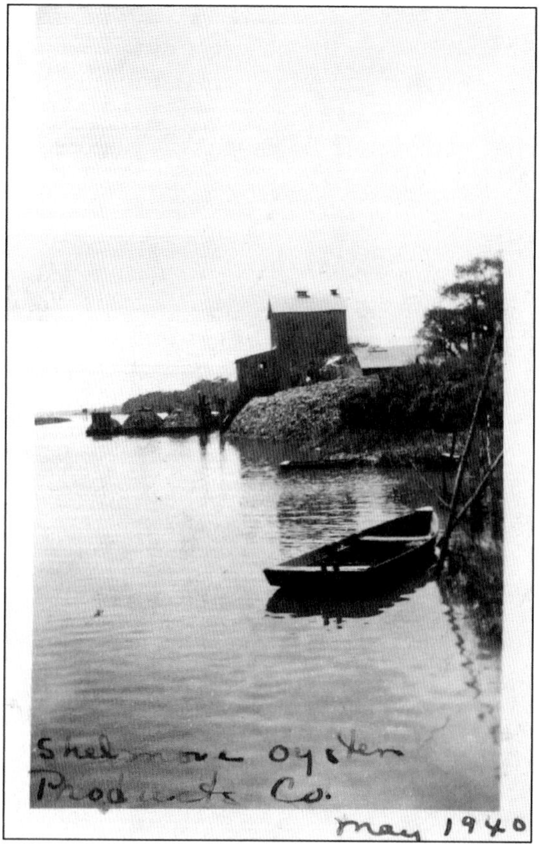

Pictured here is the Shelmore Oyster Products Company of Awendaw during the 1940s. The huge mounds of oyster shells piled along the banks of the creek tell the story of how full of activity the factory must have been during its heyday. The Shelmore Company harvested oysters on beds leased from the state and from other families in the Bull's Bay area. (Courtesy Capt. Andrew Magwood.)

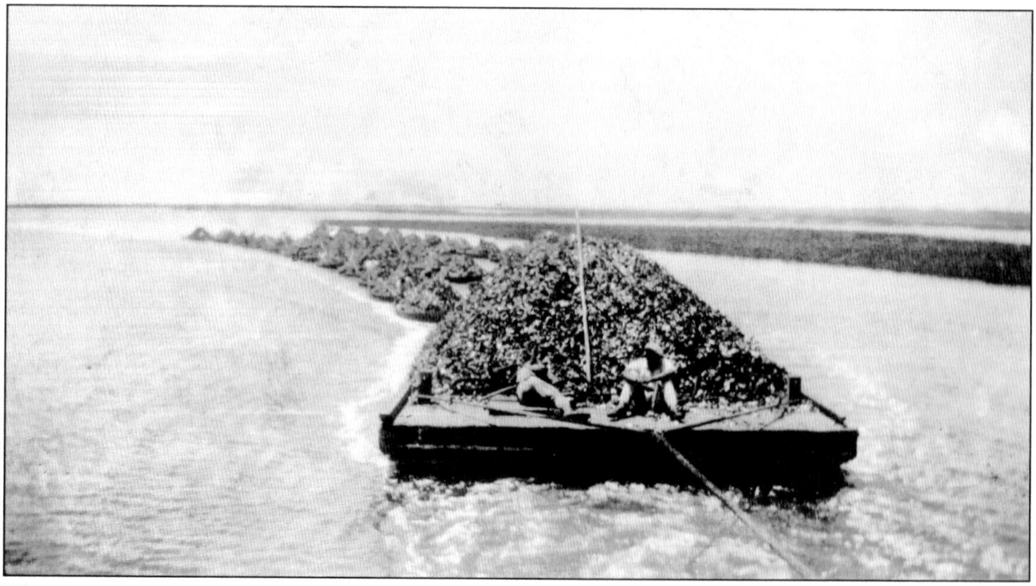

This is a unique 1940s image of oystermen sitting atop a barge laden with oysters, returning to the factory after a hard day's labor. Each bateau was pulled behind the main barge, which is loaded down with oysters as well. The men and their boats were picked up along the banks by a motorized vessel and towed back to the factory. (Courtesy Capt. Andrew Magwood.)

Capt. Earl Glines was one of the biggest seafood operators in the area. He began business as a shrimp boat worker in 1950, eventually acquiring his own oyster and clam beds, the oyster boats *Katherine* and *Nee-Ree*, the shrimp boats *Tommie* and *North Winds*, the Glines Seafood Restaurant, and later the Shelmore Oyster Products Company. Now residing at a local retirement home, Captain Glines continues to weave crab nets and hammocks by hand. (Courtesy Capt. Earl Glines.)

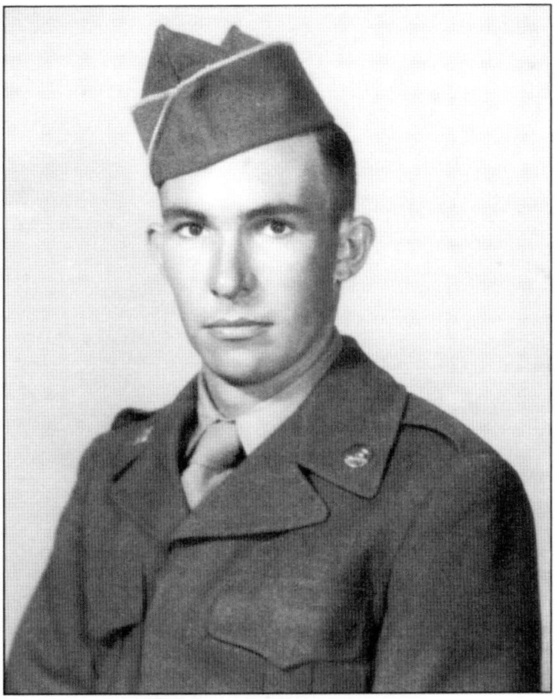

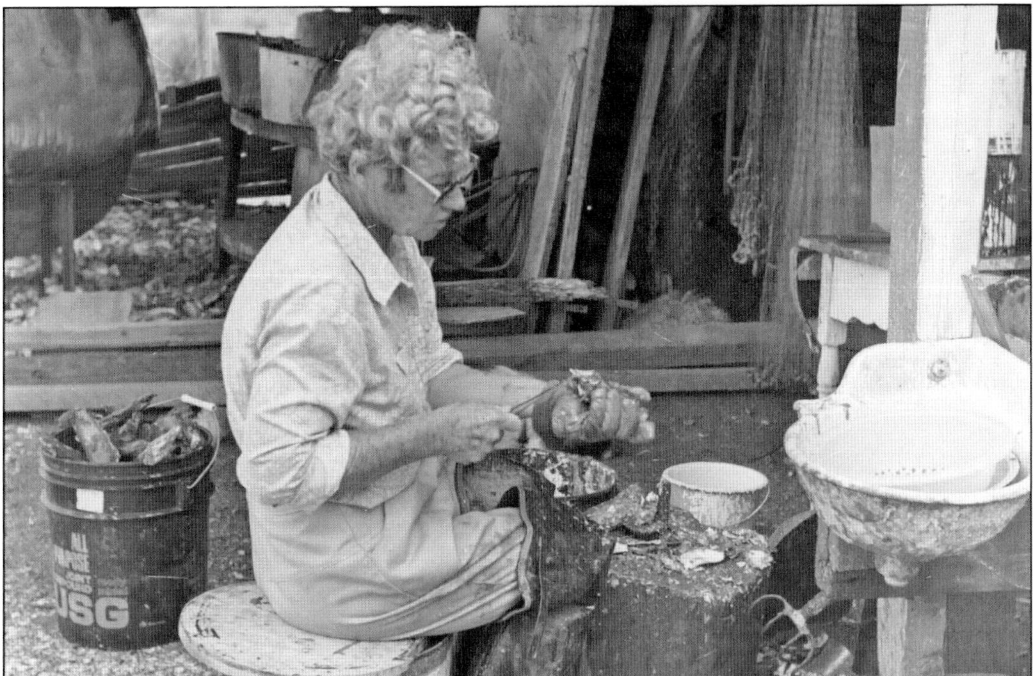

The Magwood family of Little Bull Island has been harvesting oysters and selling them for generations. Here Ethel Magwood sits at an oyster block, where she places the oyster across the file and strikes it, breaking the shell and accessing the meat. After shucking 10 to 12 gallons, she would sell them downtown for 50¢ a quart, walking down Broad Street with her oysters in mason jars or waxed cartons. (Photograph by Martin Puckhaber; courtesy Capt. Andrew Magwood.)

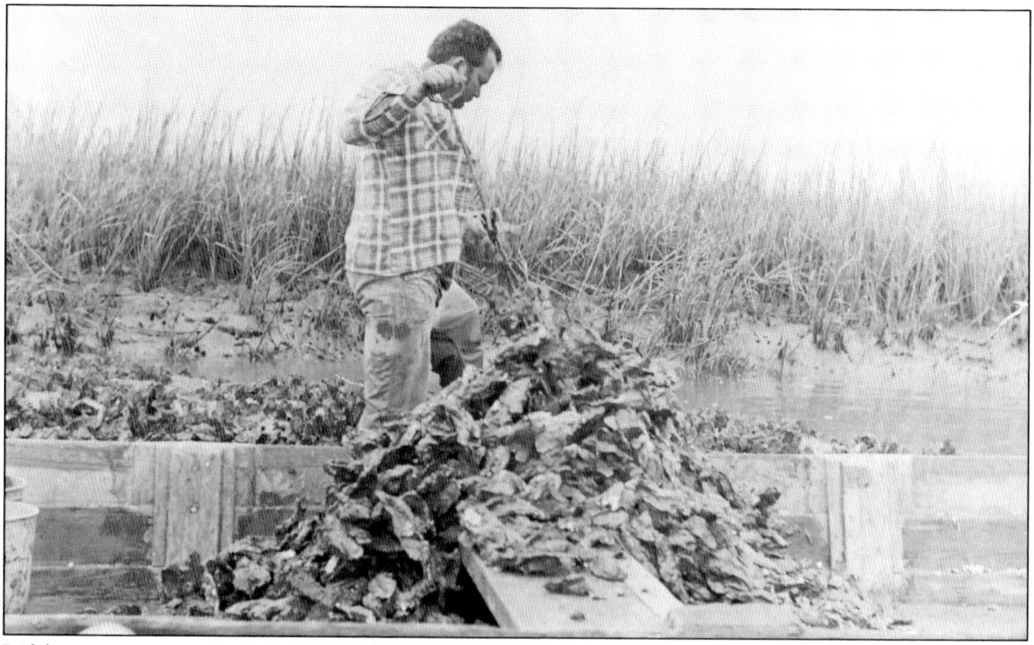

Lifelong commercial shrimper and oysterman Capt. Andrew Magwood picks oysters that are growing on the banks at low tide with an oyster grab and loads them into his homemade bateau. Captain Magwood owned and operated the trawler *Playboy* from Shem Creek before retiring from the shrimping industry. He is a highly respected mentor for many in the seafood industry. The oysters in the 1970s image are large and plentiful. (Photograph by Martin Puckhaber; courtesy Capt. Andrew Magwood.)

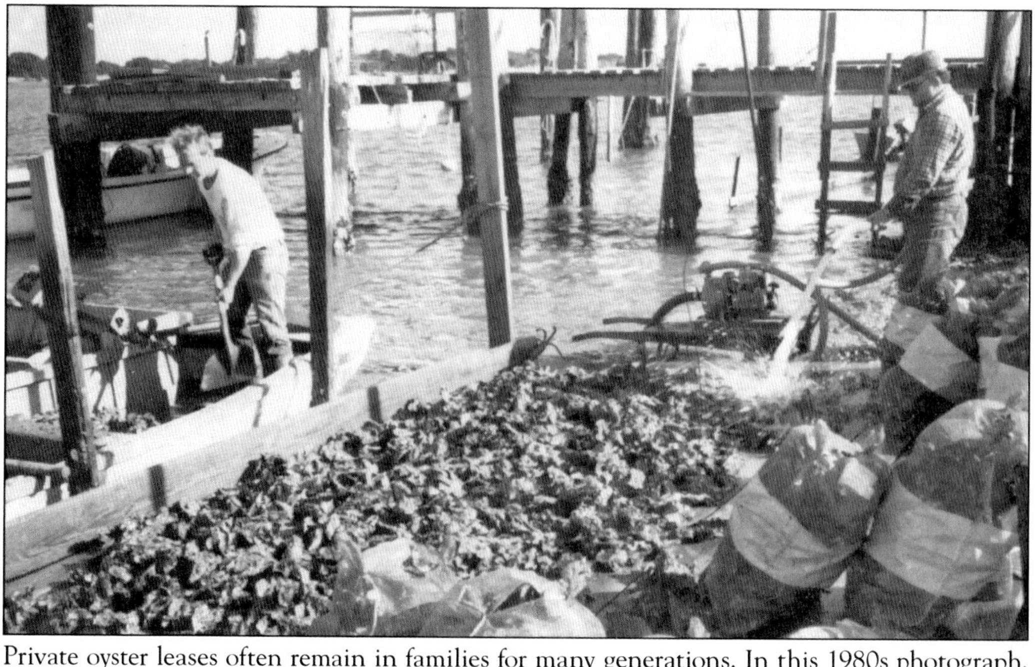

Private oyster leases often remain in families for many generations. In this 1980s photograph, harvested oysters are shoveled out of the boat onto oyster boards, washed with a portable pump, graded, placed into bushel sacks, and sent to market.

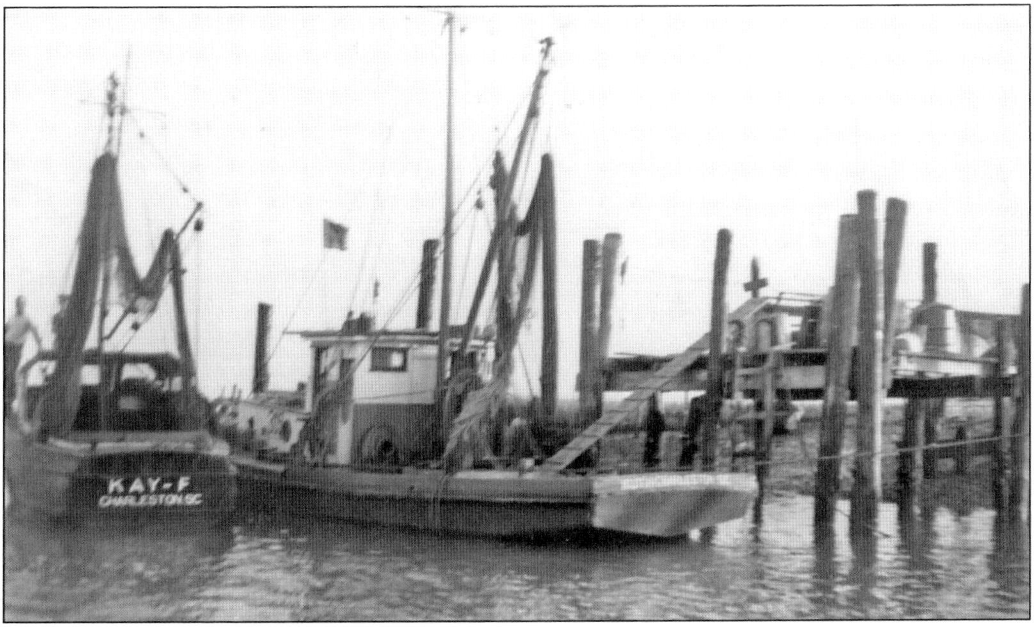

Early trawlers were limited by a lack of technology and size, were rigged with a single net, and were powered by dangerous, potentially explosive gasoline engines that were often difficult to crank. In this 1940s image, two trawlers let their nets dry in the sun.

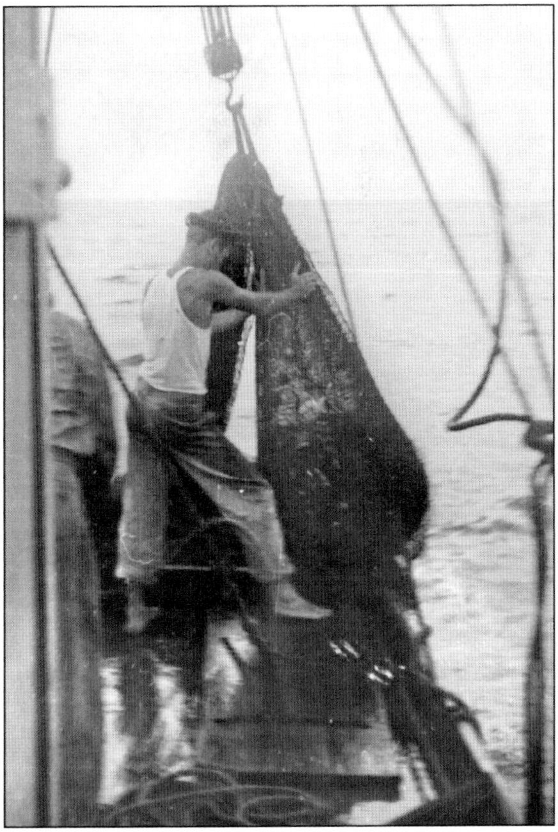

This 1940s image shows a net being pulled aboard one of the first-generation trawlers. Tar-dipped cotton nets like this one were approximately 40 to 45 feet long and were easily torn as they dragged the ocean floor. Nets were hauled in by hand and were then hoisted aboard with the aid of block and tackle before mechanical wenches evolved.

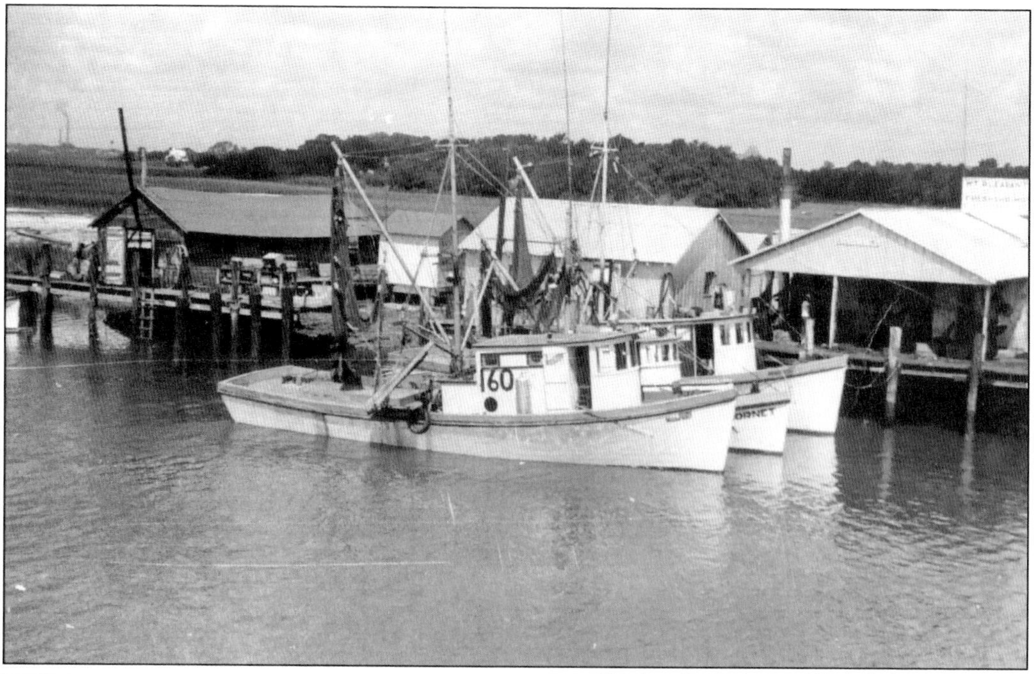

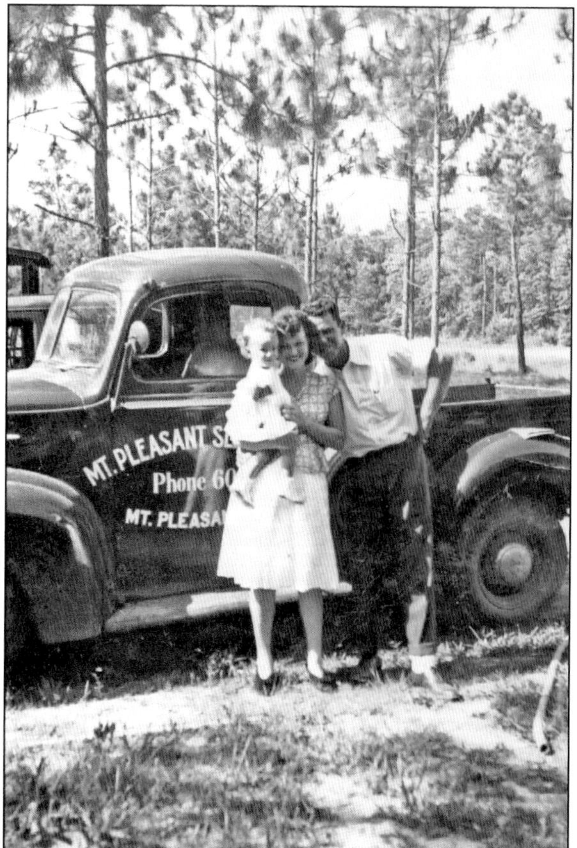

Walter D. Toler and his father, Walter G. Toler, established Mount Pleasant Seafood in 1945. Capt. W. D. Toler began with a small, 26-foot boat, the *Captains Gig*, but his fleet soon grew to include the *Hornet*, the *Florence*, the *Miss Nell*, the *Miss Norma*, the *Miss Judy*, the *Peggy Ann*, and the *Miss Donna*. The boats pictured above at dockside at Mount Pleasant Seafood are the *Miss Judy*, the *Hornet*, and the *Miss Norma*. Pictured at left, young Captain Toler poses proudly with his wife, Lillian, and daughter Peggy next to his first truck, which was purchased for the family business. (Courtesy Toler family.)

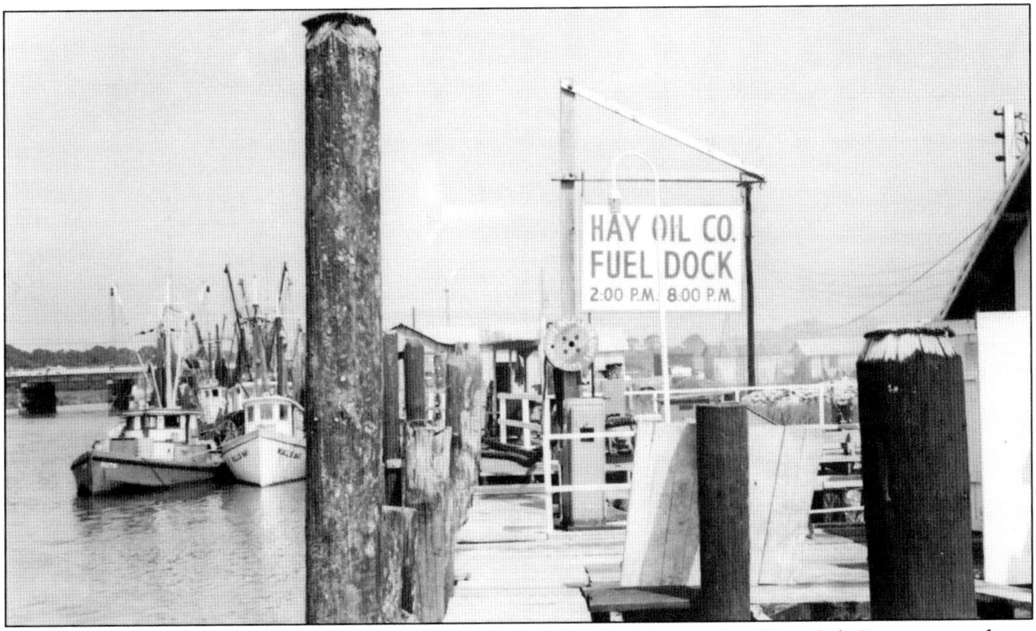

This 1950s image looking toward the Shem Creek Bridge shows the Hay Oil Company, where boats could purchase fuel and block ice. Capt. William Magwood owned the dock at the end of Magwood Lane in the Old Village of Mount Pleasant, now simply referred to as Geechie Dock. He also owned and operated the *Skipper*, the first shrimp trawler in Shem Creek. The two boats in the background are the *Bulls Bay* and the *Ruth*. (Courtesy Capt. Andrew Magwood.)

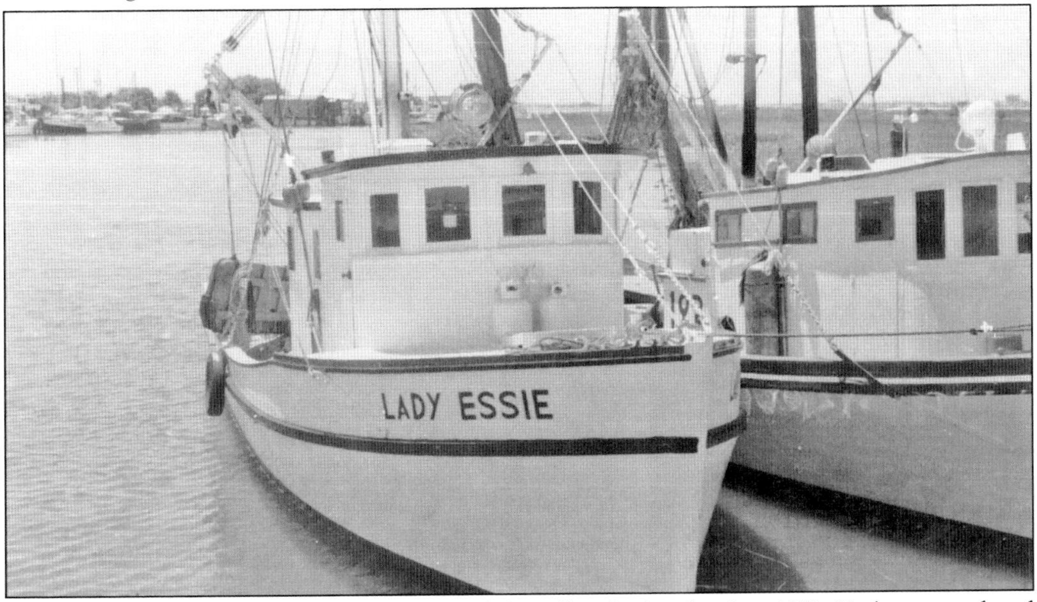

Capt. Barry Wilson acquired his first boat while still in high school in 1951. He has owned and operated the vessels *Speed Ball*, *Lady Essie* (pictured here), *Grey Ghost*, and *Flying Cloud*. He is a 45-year veteran in the Shem Creek shrimping community and captained the U.S. Coast Guard cutter *Comanche* for Patriots Point before retiring. Revered in his industry, Captain Wilson served on the South Carolina Shrimpers Association board for many years. (Courtesy Capt. Barry Wilson.)

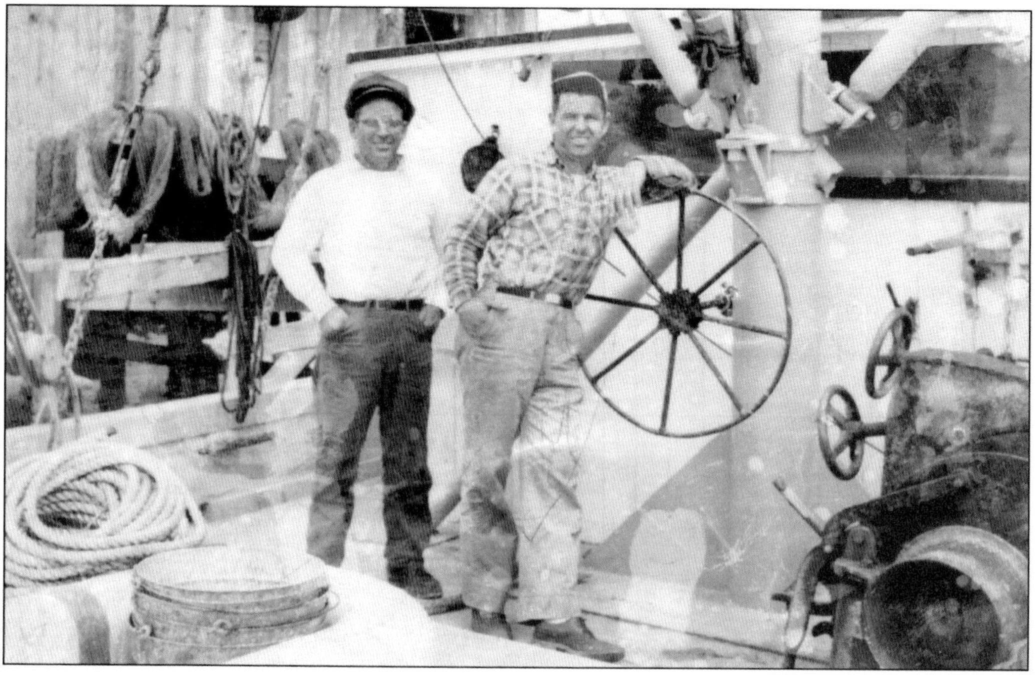

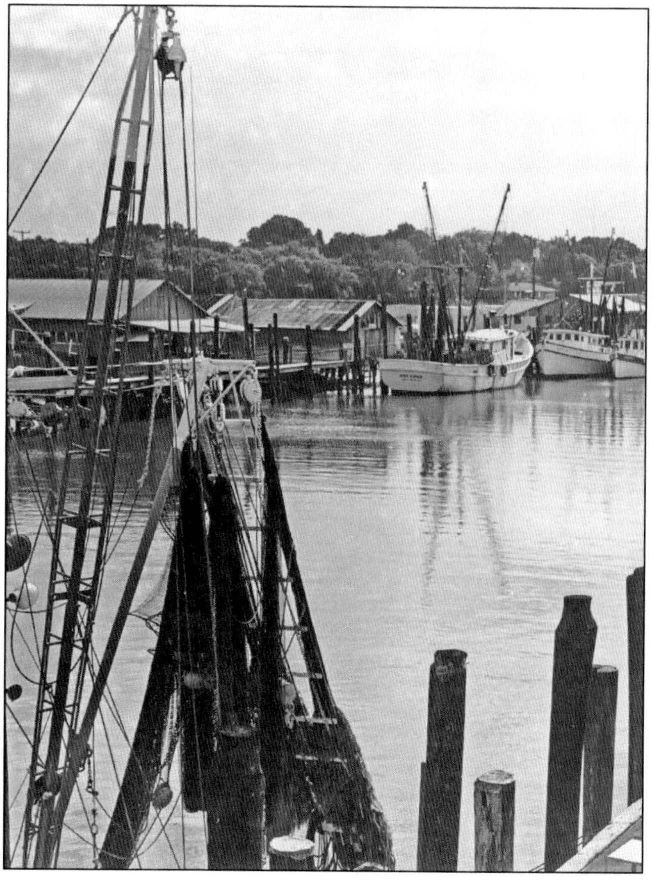

Walter D. Toler and W. D. Coons (left) pose on the deck of the *Miss Norma* dockside at Mount Pleasant Seafood in 1950. Coons was a talented diesel mechanic, building and repairing engines out of his shop on the corner of Mill and Church Streets. He is credited with keeping many vessels running over the years and is remembered fondly by many on the creek as a generous, friendly person. (Courtesy Toler family.)

This 1960s image from the top of the Shem Creek bridge shows Moultrie Fisheries, established in 1957 by the Simmons family; Shem Creek Fisheries, owned by the Ruddock family; and Bulls Bay Fish Company, established in 1949 by Robert Elliott Magwood Sr. The working waterfronts along Shem Creek were typically connected by docks, but sometimes boards were thrown down between them for traveling from dock to dock or from boat to boat.

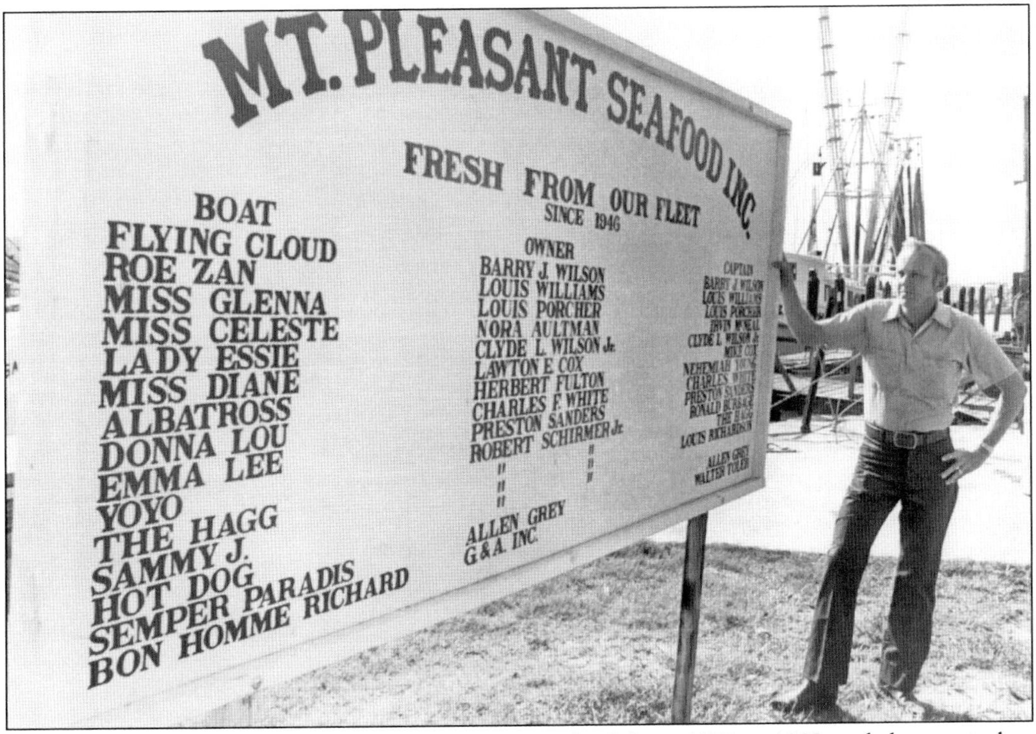

Buddy Sturgis, the manager of Mount Pleasant Seafood from 1974 to 1982 and the son-in-law of Walter D. Toler, stands in front of the company sign. This historic image lists boats, owners, and captains that were unloading at the seafood house in November 1979. (Photograph by Dick Burbage; Courtesy Toler family.)

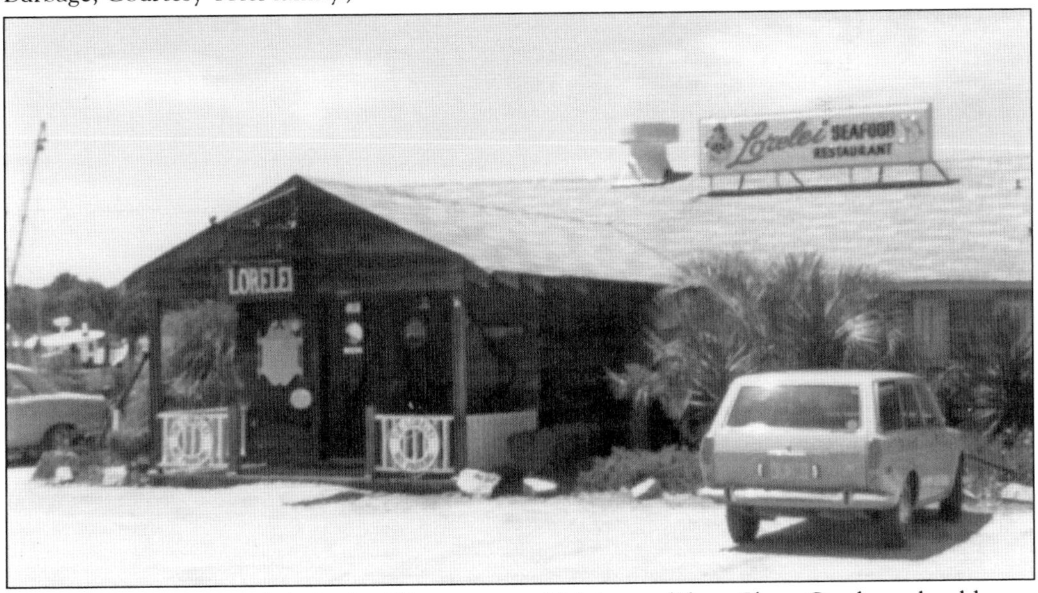

Here is the popular Lorelei's Seafood Restaurant, which began life on Shem Creek as a bunkhouse for fishermen. It was owned by the Toler family and was leased to several different local families over the years. Locals remember the walls of the restaurant inside being adorned with hand-painted murals by artist Taffy Stratton. (Courtesy Toler family.)

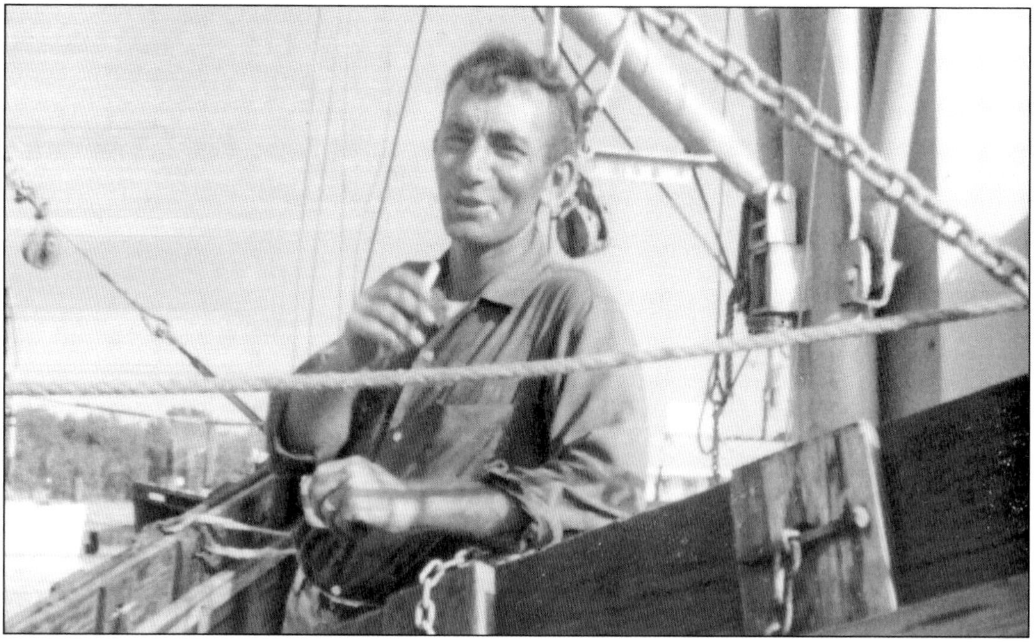

Here Capt. Louis Williams, a near-50-year-veteran commercial shrimper on Shem Creek, poses aboard one of his vessels, the *Roe Zan*, in 1963. It was named after his children, Rose Marie and Zandie. He named a later vessel the *Mar-Lou* after his grandchildren. During the off-season in the 1980s, Captain Williams trawled for military mines offshore, receiving an honorary certificate from the U.S. Navy for his contribution. (Courtesy Williams family.)

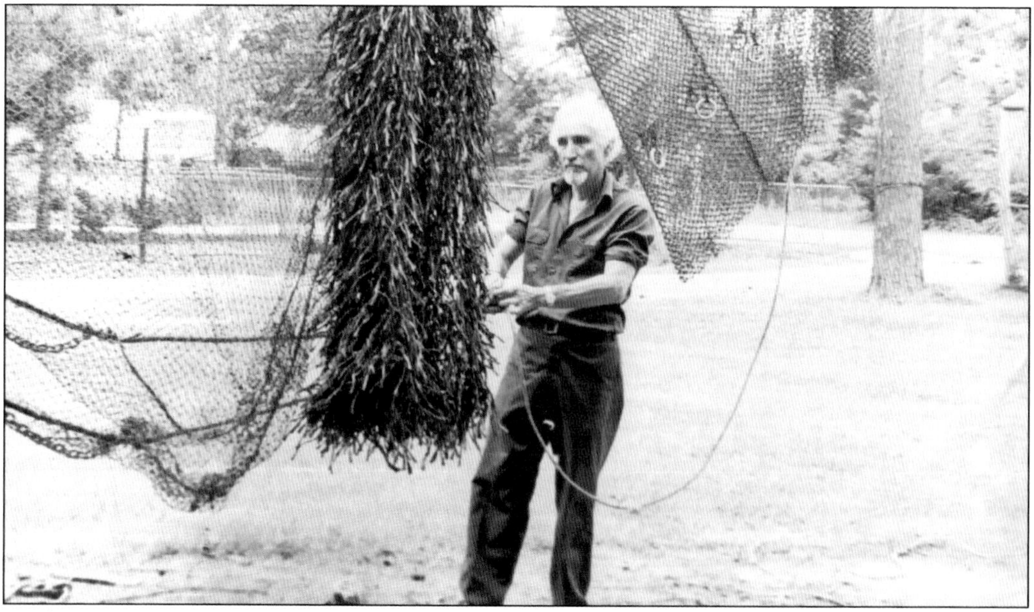

Hugh Missroon, a net-maker extraordinaire, has been an indispensable member of the commercial shrimping community from North Carolina to Key West. After repairing nets with his brother in the 1930s, he realized there was a demand for his specialized skill. Hundreds of nets have been sold from Missroon's Net Shop on Highway 17, and he is revered as the best in the business and has patented his own design. (Courtesy Hugh Missroon and family.)

Pictured at right, the late Capt. Thomas Chandler, known as Captain Tom and the "Gentleman Shrimper," was one of the original shrimpers out of Shem Creek. A 25-year veteran of the industry, he trawled the waters of the Atlantic Ocean from North Carolina to the Yucatan Peninsula. He built his famous, handcrafted vessel, the 60-foot *Mary Elliott*, himself at Chandler's Boatyard on Coburg Creek in 1951. The vessel was greatly admired by fishermen everywhere not only for her fine wood and superior craftsmanship, but also because of her state-of-the-art equipment. Famous for introducing, manufacturing, and distributing the Seward Stabilizer (a marine anti-roll device) to Southeastern shrimp boats, the East Cooper native served as vice president of the South Carolina Shrimpers Association and was greatly revered in the industry. The *Mary Elliott* is pictured below in all her glory. (Both images courtesy MaeRe Chandler Skinner.)

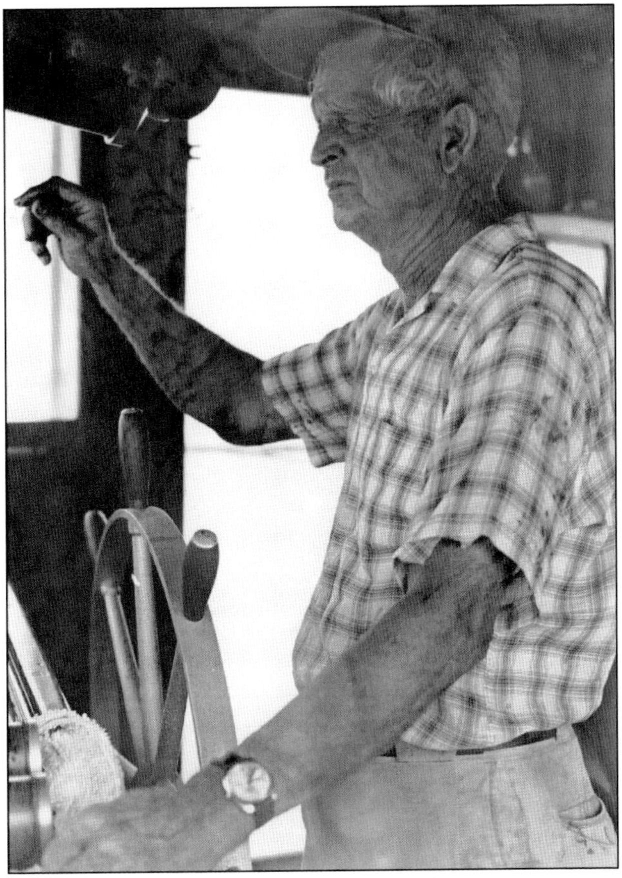

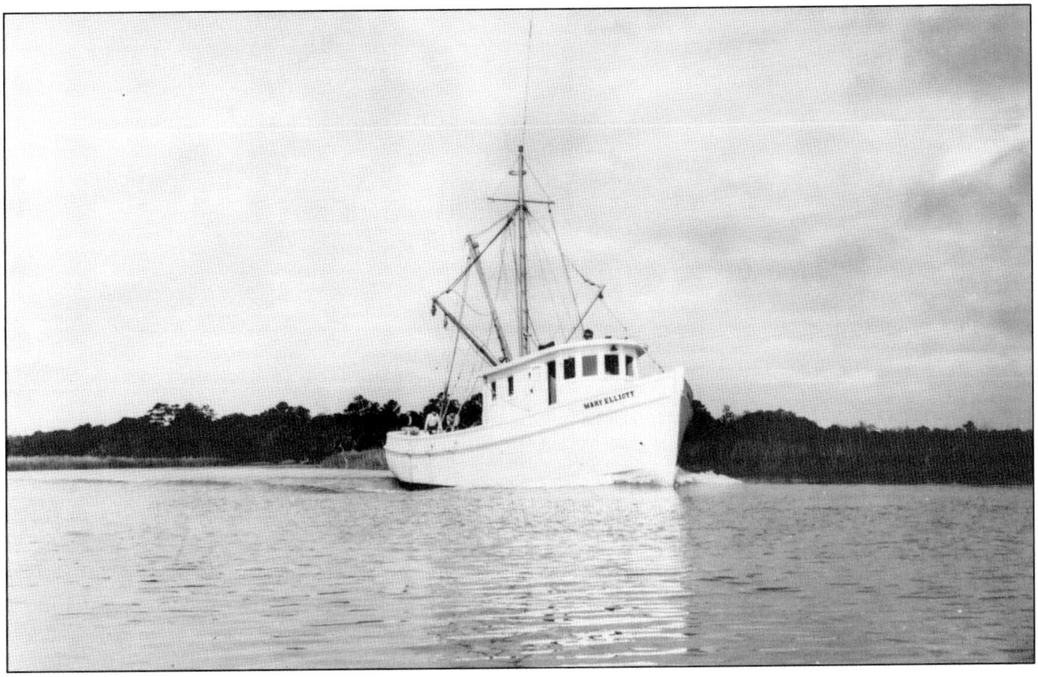

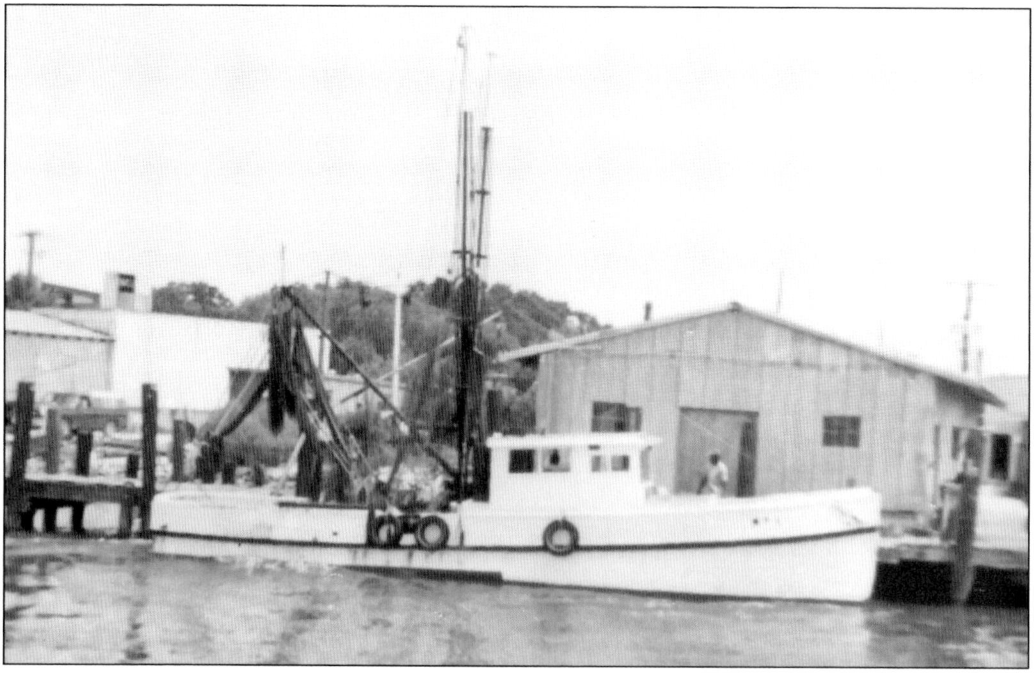

Here the *MTL*, owned and operated by the Hills family, rests dockside at the Wando Shrimp Company. Purchased for $83 from the Army Transportation Corporation at an auction in the early 1950s, the unique, deep-hulled vessel was 46 feet long but only 10 feet wide. (Courtesy Hills family.)

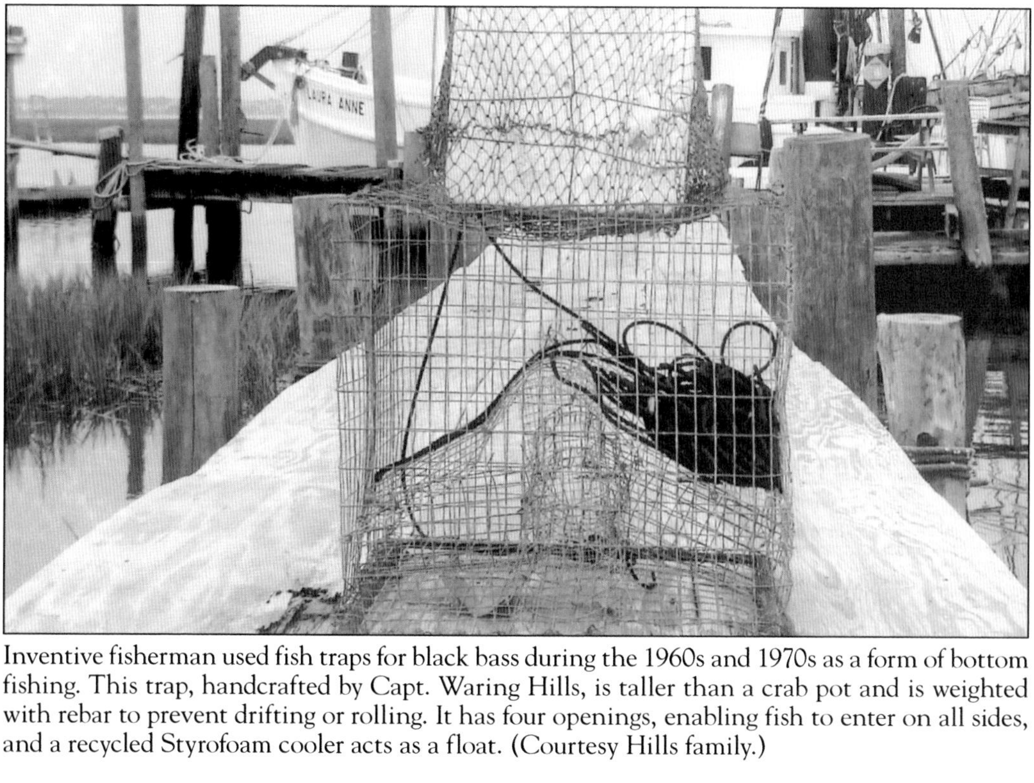

Inventive fisherman used fish traps for black bass during the 1960s and 1970s as a form of bottom fishing. This trap, handcrafted by Capt. Waring Hills, is taller than a crab pot and is weighted with rebar to prevent drifting or rolling. It has four openings, enabling fish to enter on all sides, and a recycled Styrofoam cooler acts as a float. (Courtesy Hills family.)

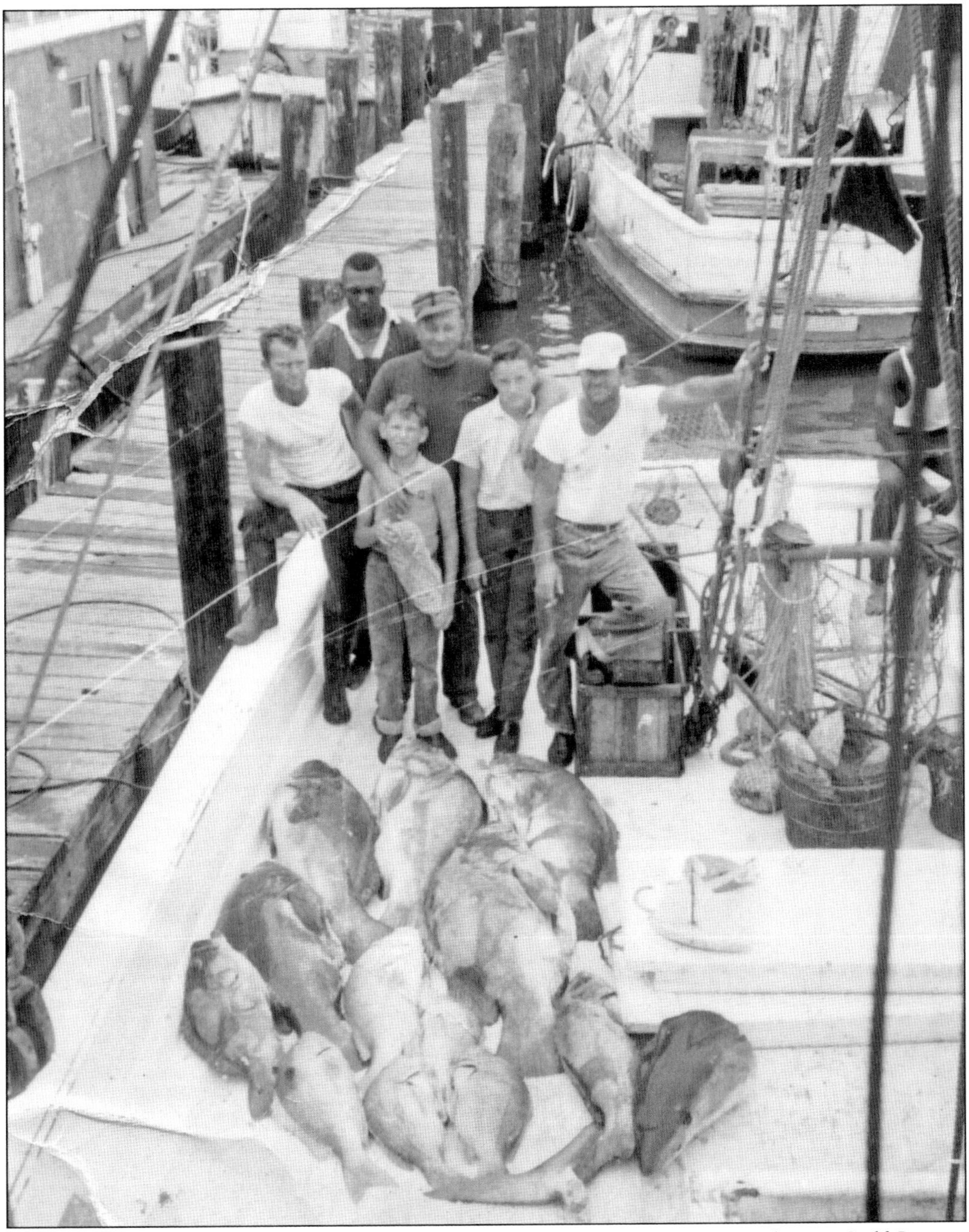

In this beloved 1960s image of the Magwood family, a proud crew returns from a Gulf Stream fishing trip with large snapper, grouper, and even a shark on deck. The passengers and crew of the *Skipper and Wayne* would travel to the Gulf Stream for five to six days at a time to "hand-line" fish. This type of fishing was labor intensive, with each man handling two lines with up to four hooks, each line being tied off of the boat and literally pulled in by hand. Fisherman using hand lines tell tales of hands being cut by fish lines and immobilized for days afterwards. Pictured from left to right are Andrew Magwood, Harold White, Junior Magwood embracing his sons Skipper and Wayne, and Dan Magwood.

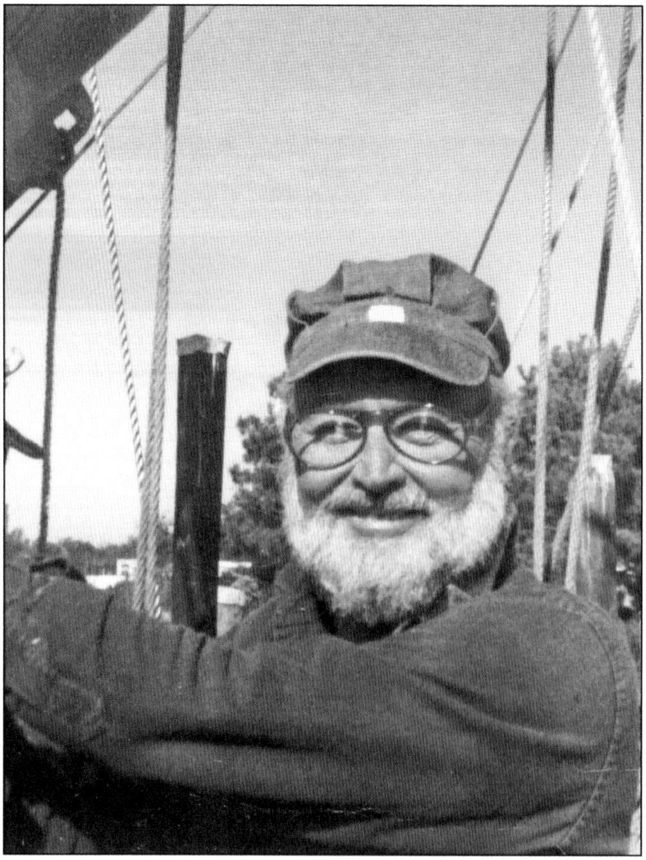

Pictured at left, the late Capt. Walter L. Shaffer, known as Capt. Wally, began shrimping in the 1950s. In his 38-year career, he owned and operated the vessels *Daw-Daw*, *Christeen*, *Little Lady*, *Phyllis Mae*, *Carol El*, and *Pardner*. Capt. Wally was an honored member of the seafood industry, serving four terms as president of the South Carolina Shrimpers Association and being a trustee for the Gulf and South Atlantic Fisheries Development Foundation. He was also commended by the South Carolina Department of Natural Resources (SCDNR) Board for "courage and dedication in preserving the long-term health of the marine resources of South Carolina." A good captain needs a good crew; pictured below is Capt. Wally's valued friend and crewmember Georgie Nesbitt. The two fished together for 32 years. (Courtesy Phyllis Shaffer.)

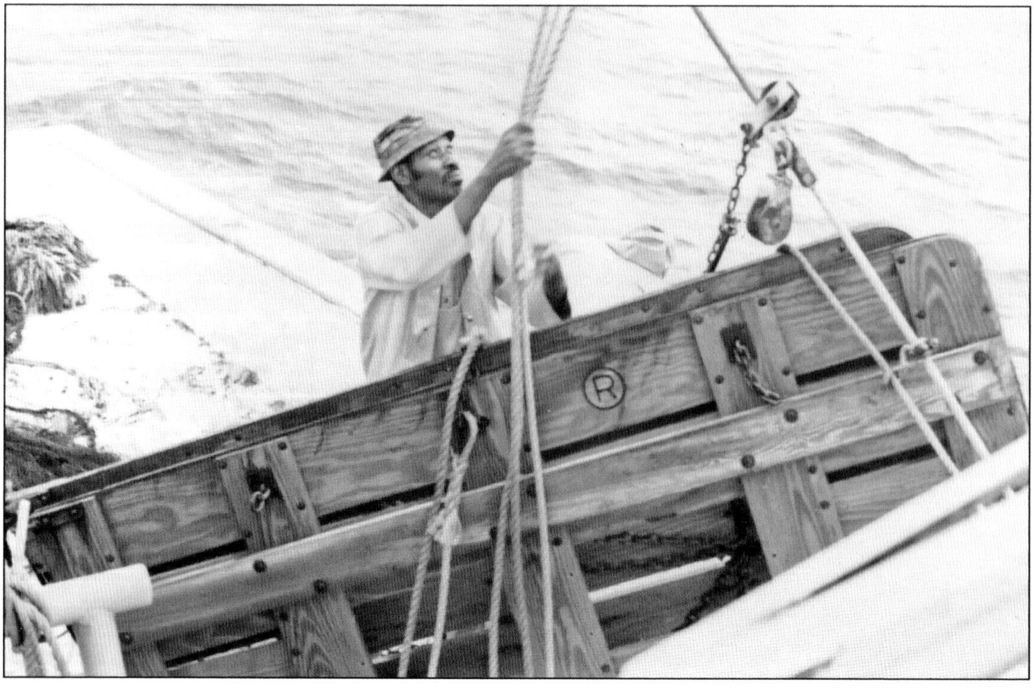

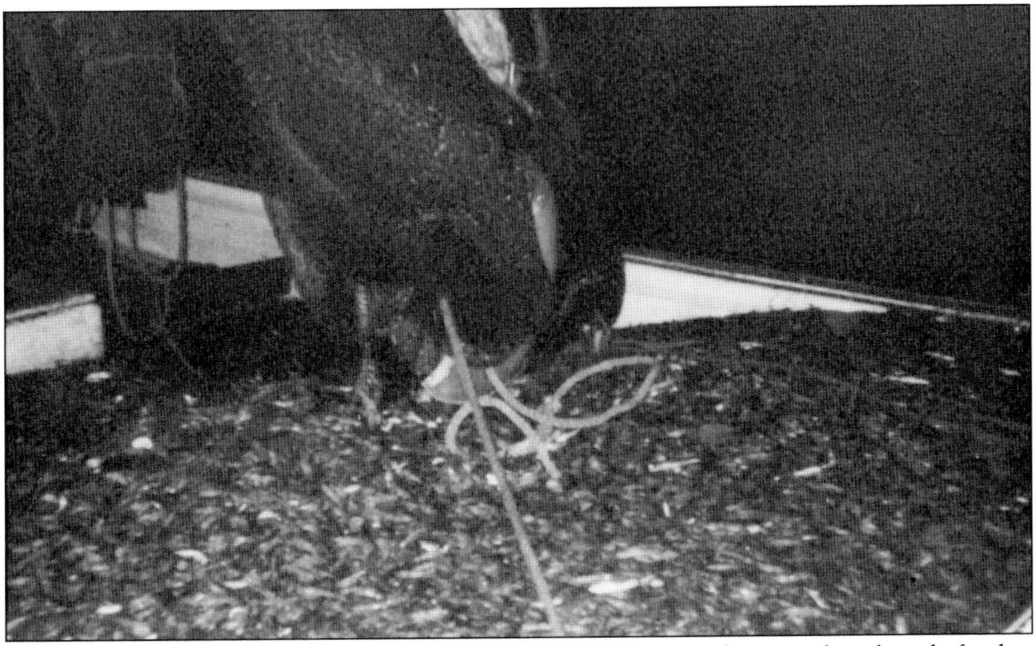

These exciting, record-making catches would thrill any captain and are nearly unheard of today. In December 1968, the back deck of the trawler *Skipper and Wayne* (above) is loaded down with shrimp—the haul was 6,300 pounds of tails! Pictured below, Capt. Wally Shaffer stands proudly with his own impressive catch that same winter, with only one crewmember, Roy Jenkins, to help. Trawling for shrimp requires skill and great knowledge of local waters, including issues such as depth, water temperatures, and bottom environments. Weather patterns and seasons also affect quantities and locations of shrimp. (Above courtesy Magwood family; below courtesy Phyllis Shaffer.)

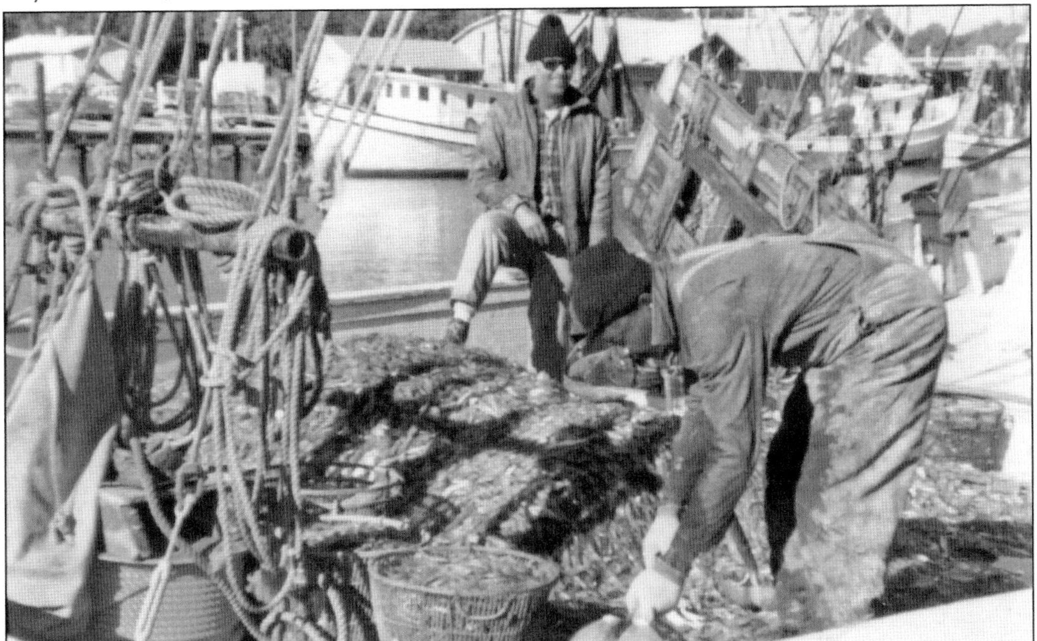

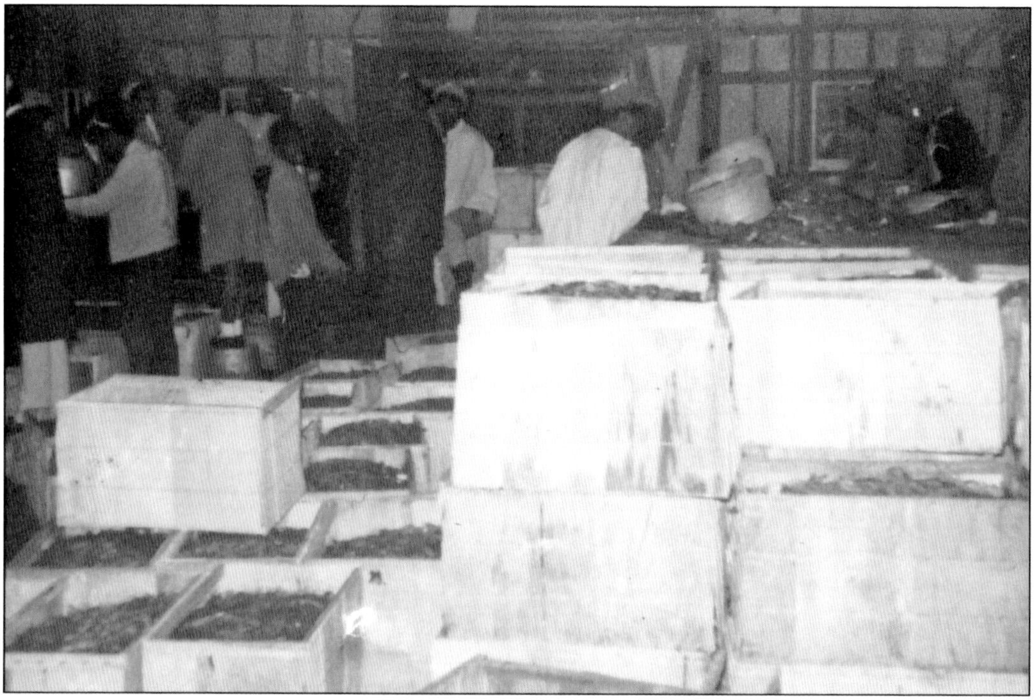

This historic image taken inside Moultrie Fisheries shows boxes filled to capacity and stacked up, waiting to be processed. Capt. Wally Shaffer unloaded these shrimp on his record-breaking day in December 1968. Wooden boxes this size are capable of holding 100 pounds of shrimp. (Courtesy Phyllis Shaffer.)

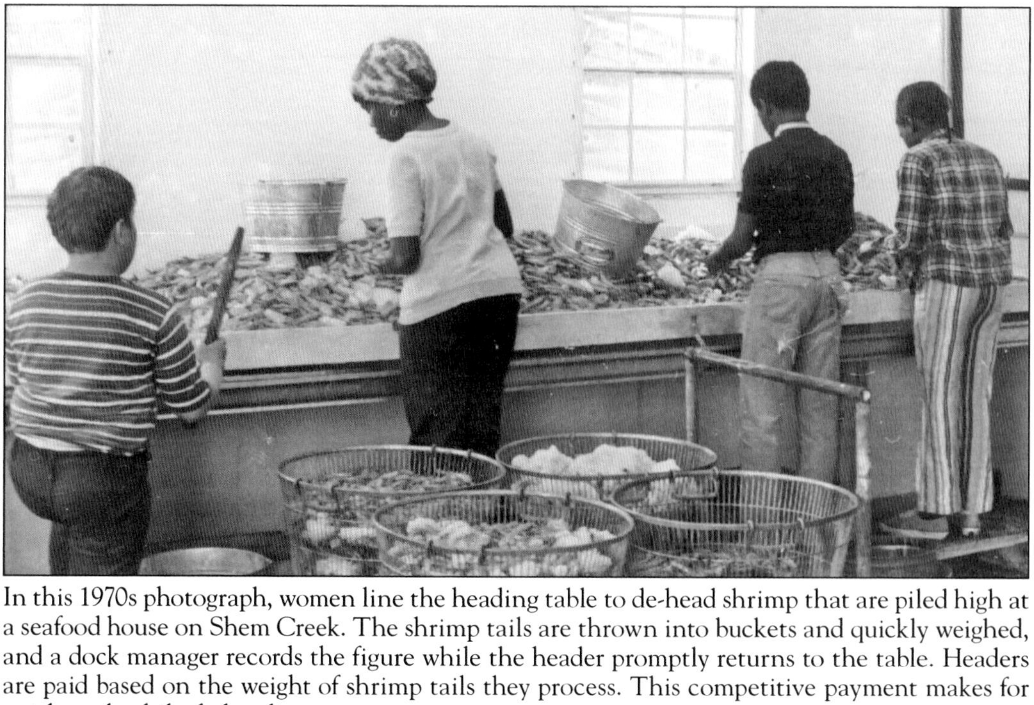

In this 1970s photograph, women line the heading table to de-head shrimp that are piled high at a seafood house on Shem Creek. The shrimp tails are thrown into buckets and quickly weighed, and a dock manager records the figure while the header promptly returns to the table. Headers are paid based on the weight of shrimp tails they process. This competitive payment makes for quick work while de-heading.

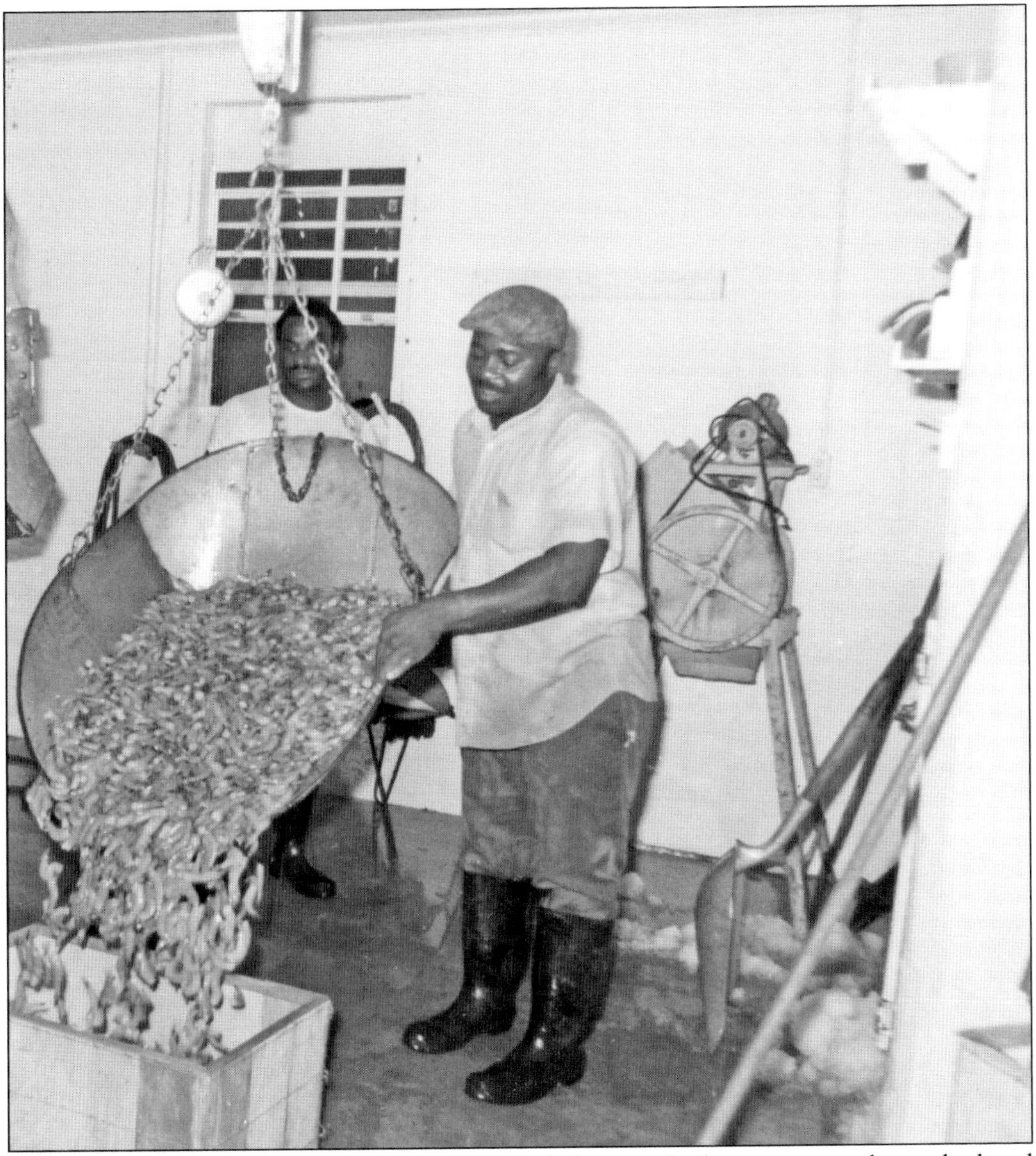

Shrimp unloaded off Shem Creek boats are loaded into a fresh water vat to be washed and rinsed. They are then moved out of the vat via a metal conveyer belt and dumped into a large scale. They are weighed in 50- and 100-pound quantities, placed into wooden boxes, and iced and stored in a refrigerated cooler before being sold locally or for shipment. When catches are too great to be consumed by the local market, the perishable delicacies are purchased by freight trucking companies and driven to processing factories located on the Gulf Shore and in Florida via large refrigerator trucks. In this image, William Bailem (right) and Joe Manigault, longtime employees of Magwood Seafood, process a fresh catch.

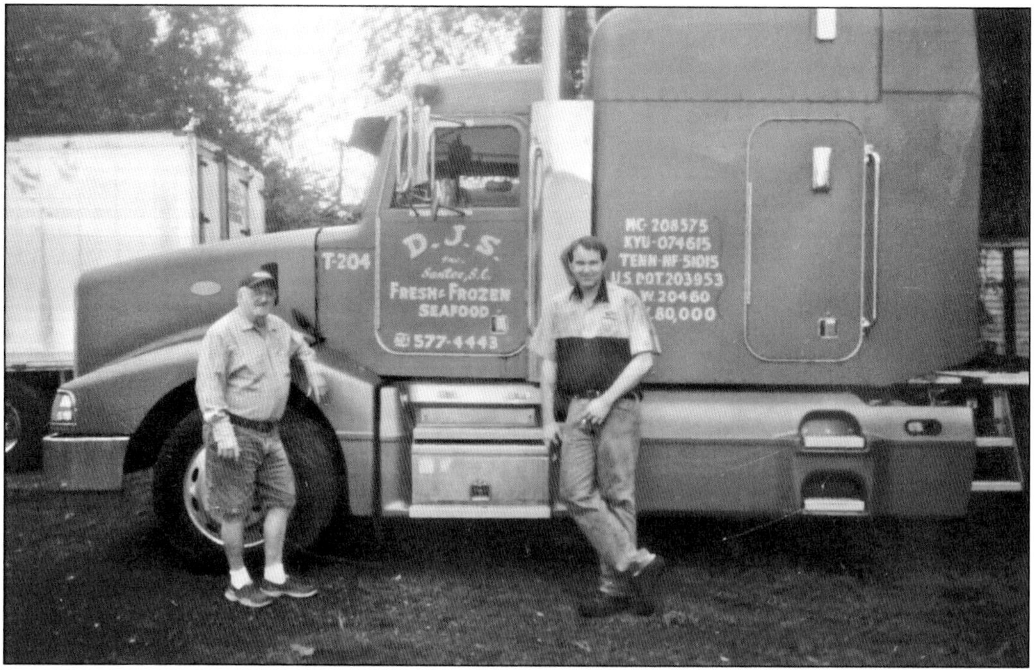

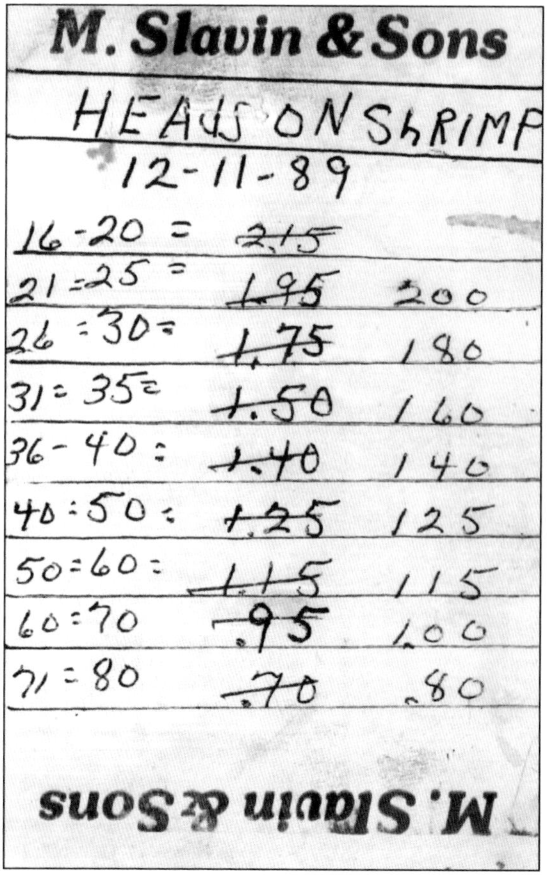

M. Slavin & Sons

HEADS ON SHRIMP

12-11-89

Size		
16-20 =	~~2.15~~	
21=25 =	~~1.95~~	200
26=30=	~~1.75~~	180
31=35=	~~1.50~~	160
36-40 =	~~1.40~~	140
40=50 =	~~1.25~~	125
50=60 =	~~1.15~~	115
60=70	~~.95~~	1.00
71=80	~~.70~~	.80

M. Slavin & Sons

David Jones of David Jones Seafood and Trucking Company was one of the oldest buyers of seafood from Shem Creek, operating for more than 50 years. He is pictured above with his grandson Steve. Taking seafood as far north as New York, as far west as Texas, and as far south as Florida, Jones recalls picking up loads of seafood as large as one thousand 100-pound boxes twice a week during Shem Creek's heydays. Headers would de-head shrimp literally all throughout the night for him to pick up a shipment in the morning. At left is a card kept by Jones that listed the wholesale prices of shrimp in December 1989. The first column lists sizes, and the second and third columns list wholesale market prices. (Both images courtesy David Jones.)

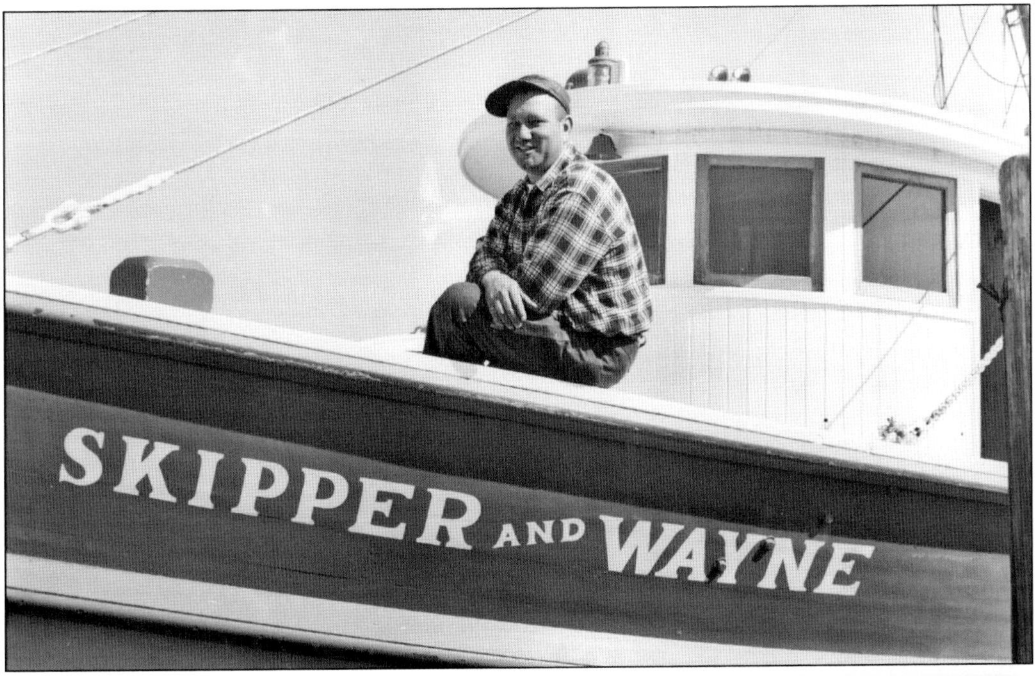

The late Capt. C. A. Magwood Jr. established the family business, C. A. Magwood Jr. and Sons, in 1972. Raised on Little Bull Island as the eldest of 11 children, Captain Magwood worked with his cousins to learn the business of trawling. Building his first vessel in 1958, he helped his two brothers and later his three sons acquire boats of their own, eventually growing the business into a fleet of six vessels. He was active in the industry, lobbying at the local, state, and federal levels, and he received many commendations and awards. He is fondly remembered for his hard work ethic, colorful personality, and passion for his industry. Pictured above, Captain Magwood sits aboard his first vessel, the *Skipper and Wayne*. The front door of Magwood's Seafood proudly displays the family motto (below).

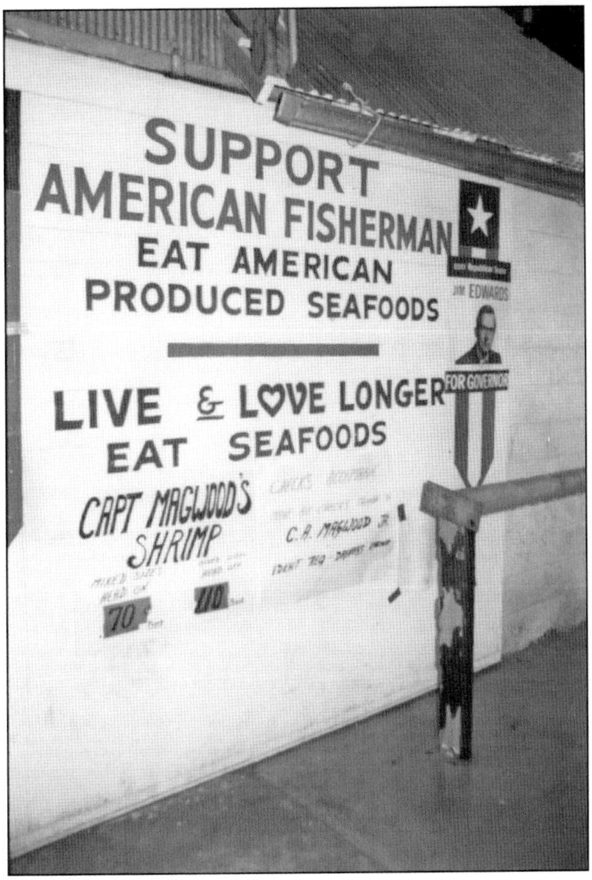

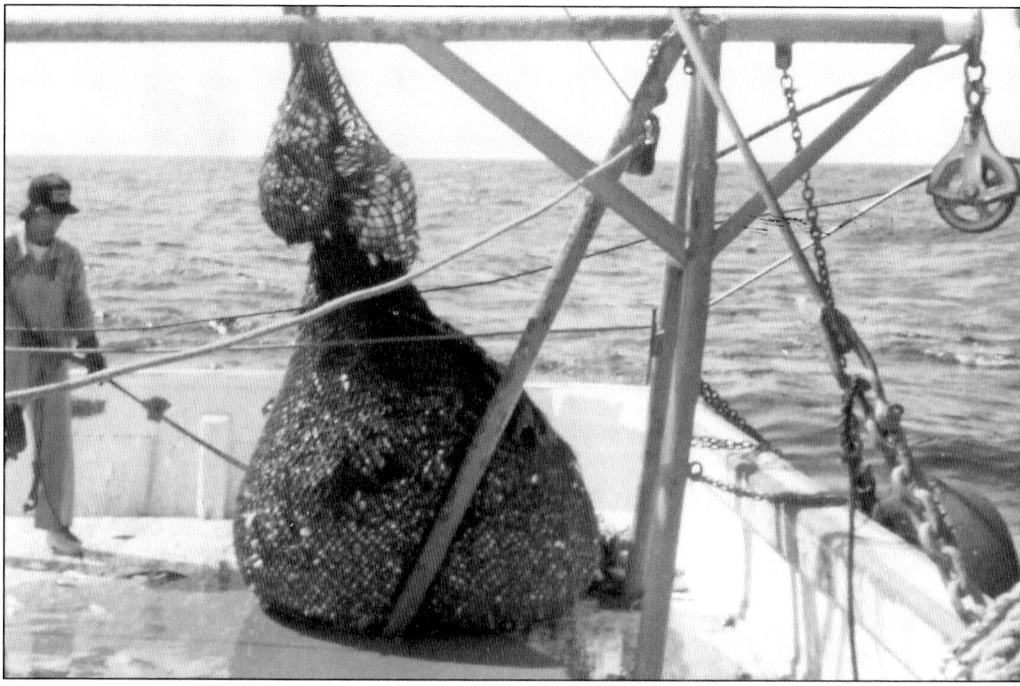

The "gallows rig" seen in this image was used while dragging for fish in the 1980s. Boats pulled one net, approximately 80 feet in length, with steel doors. Doug Richardson (above) prepares to open up the bag, while the fish are spread out over the deck (below). Vermillion, snapper, and grouper make up the majority of the catch, while squid, cigar minnow, occasional spiny lobster, black bass, and white and pink porgies make an appearance as well. All of these were processed and sold to both local and Northern fish markets, including Fulton Fish Market and the Blue Ribbon Fish Market, both in New York City.

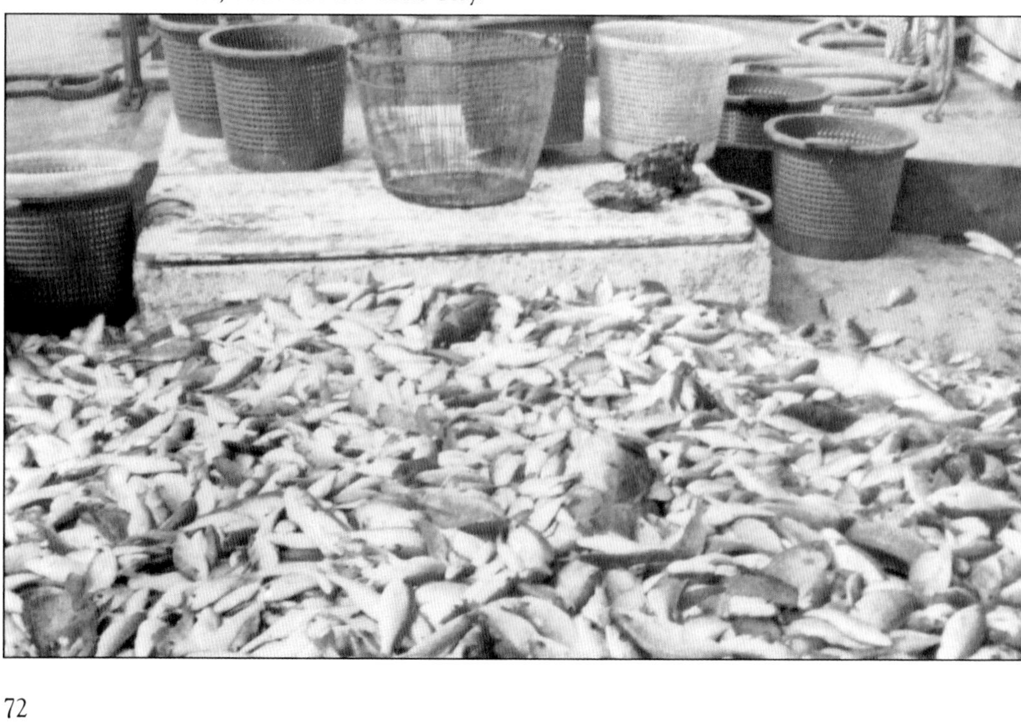

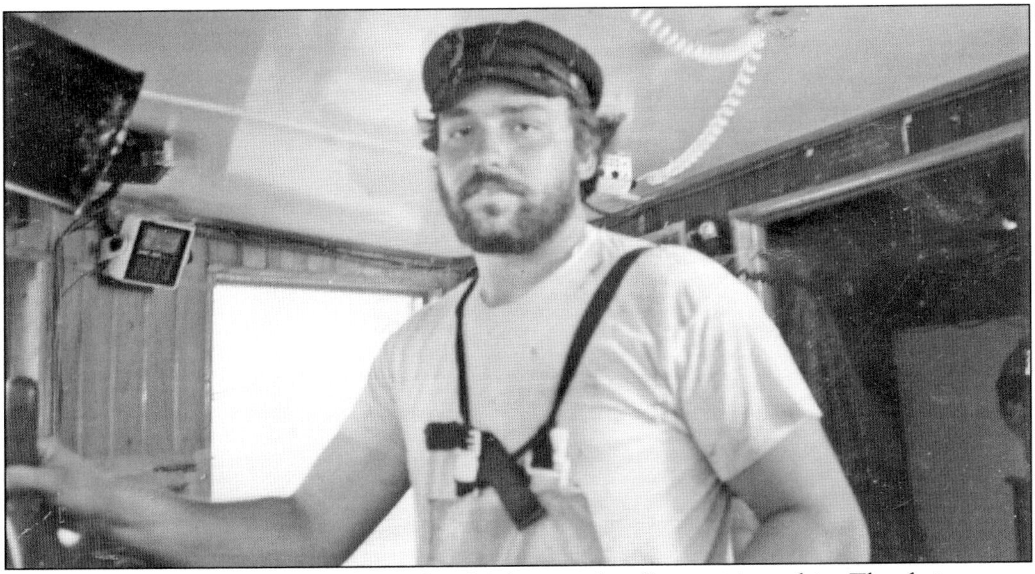

Rock shrimping was another industry local fishermen briefly participated in. The shrimp were located offshore from Charleston in 120 to 250 feet of water. The smaller boats of the 1970s relied on ice to preserve their catches, and the trip could only last as long as the ice, usually three to five days. Rock shrimping lasted for five to eight years before the species migrated south; they are still caught in Florida waters today. Pictured above, Capt. Donnie Brown is shown *c.* 1980 at the helm of the *Ethel and Clarence*. Capt. Wayne Magwood (below) stands in front of a pile of large rock shrimp. Rock shrimp are covered by a rock-hard shell and are quite difficult to peel, but the taste is well worth the effort. Local catches were unloaded at fish houses and sent to factories for further processing. (Above courtesy Capt. Donnie Brown; below courtesy Capt. Wayne Magwood.)

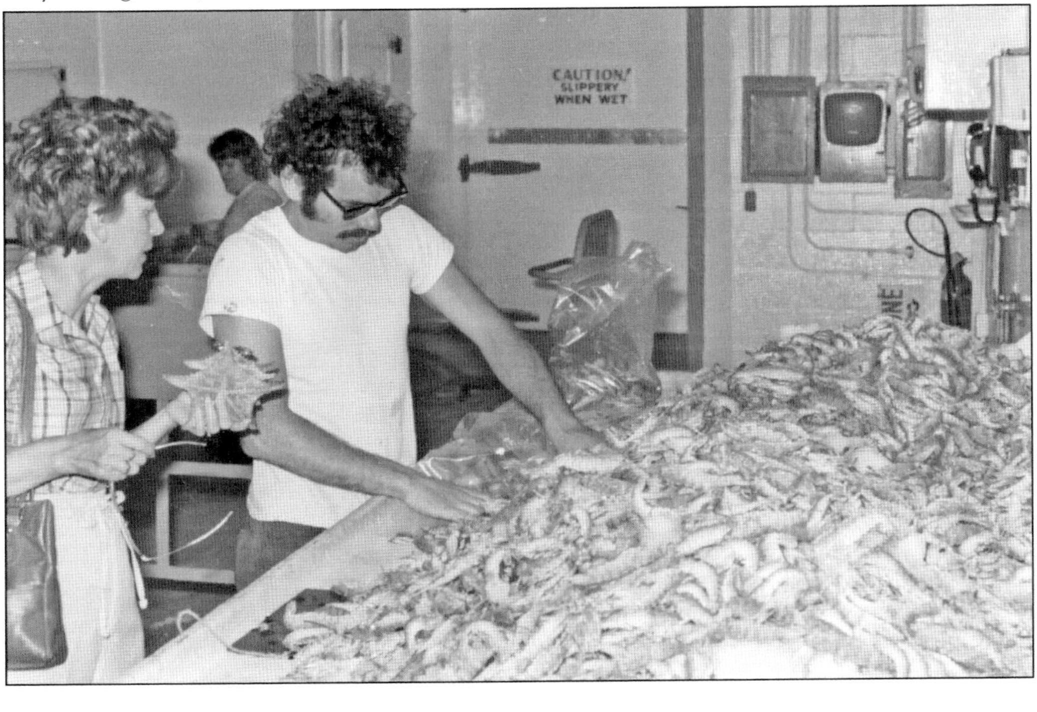

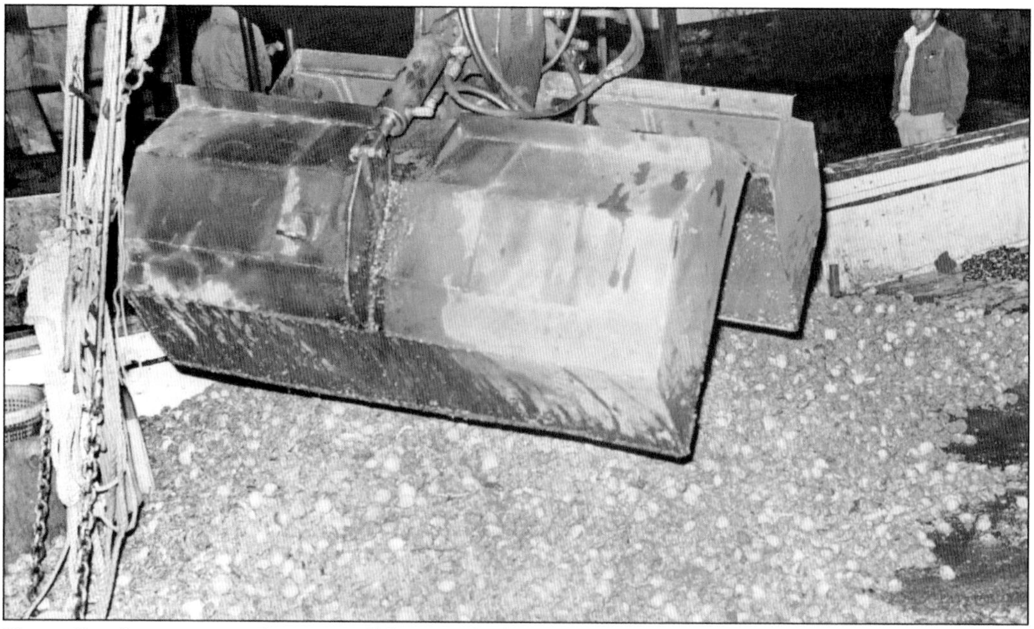

Shem Creek participated in a small but profitable sea scallop industry in the late 1980s. Vessels had to be seaworthy in order to venture the 40 miles offshore in 140 to 160 feet of water. In good conditions, most trawlers travel about 10 miles per hour on calm seas, but winter months are rough in the Atlantic Ocean, making for slower travel. A boat would journey six or eight hours to its destination before setting out nets. It would then trawl for about 12 hours, making 20- to 40-minute drags before making the return journey. Unloading as soon as they reached the dock, the crews would refuel and add ice to make the journey straight back out to sea, weather permitting. The captain and crew slept only a few precious hours with alternate watches at the helm on the journeys to and from the destination site.

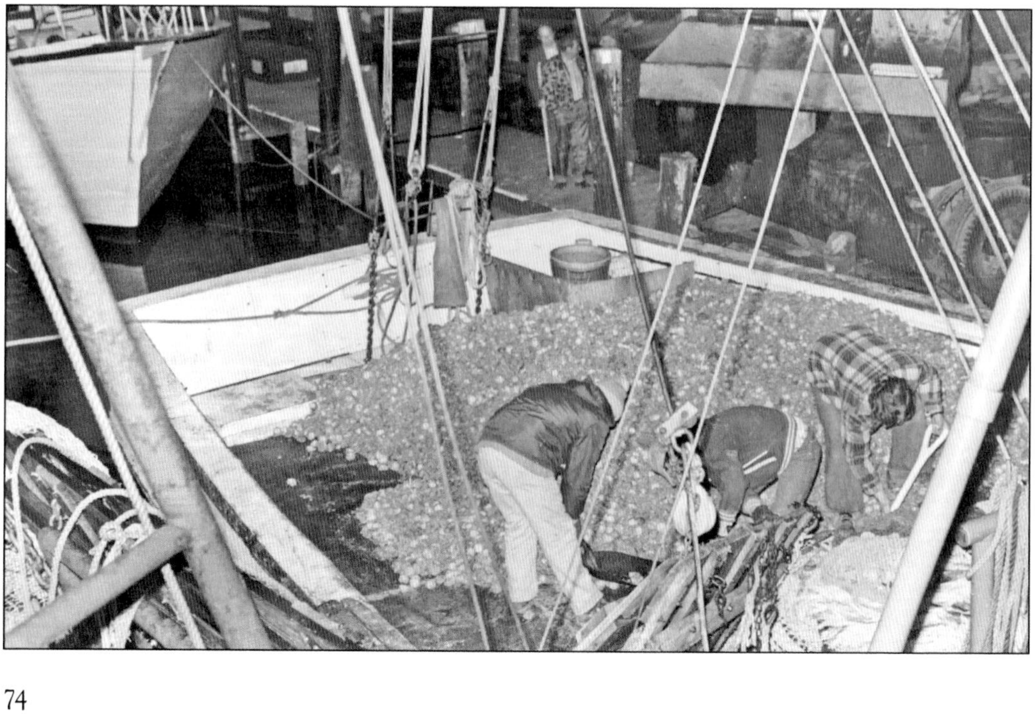

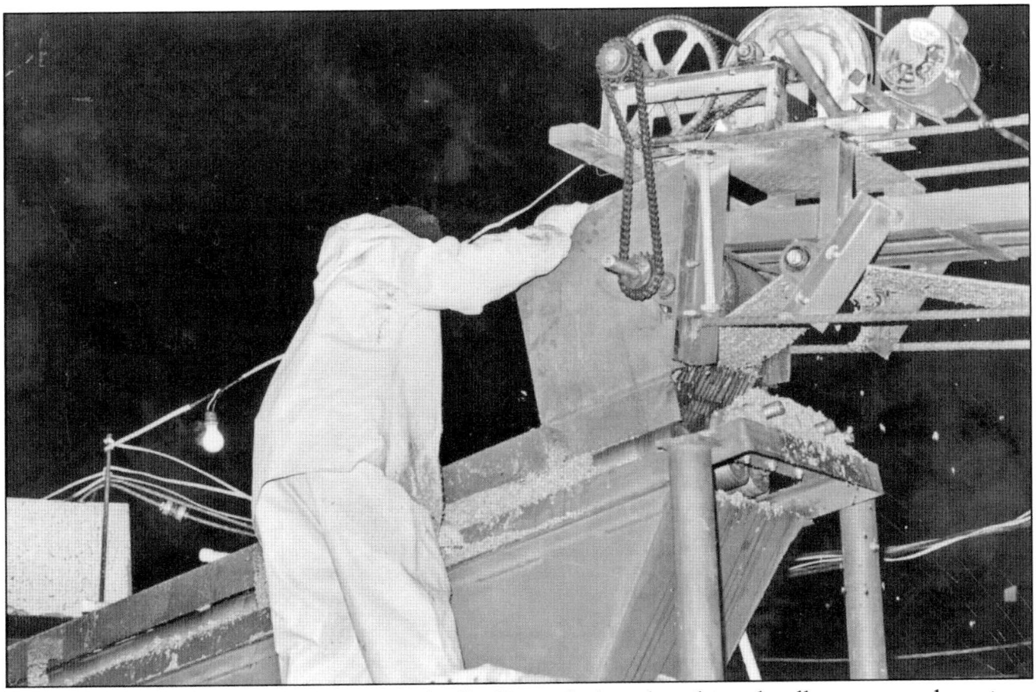

At first, scallops were shoveled by hand off of boat decks, placed in wheelbarrows, and put into trucks for transport. Later a hydraulic clam bucket was used to take them off the boat and place them into a hopper that washed and conveyed them to refrigerated trucks for transport. Scallops unloaded at Shem Creek were shipped to North Carolina or Florida for processing. The scallops were shucked by machines and hand-packed into gallon containers for retail distribution to seafood markets, grocery stores, and restaurants. Pictured below, the *Mary Rena*, captained by Ferrell White, unloads scallops at Mount Pleasant Seafood. (Courtesy Capt. Warren Rector.)

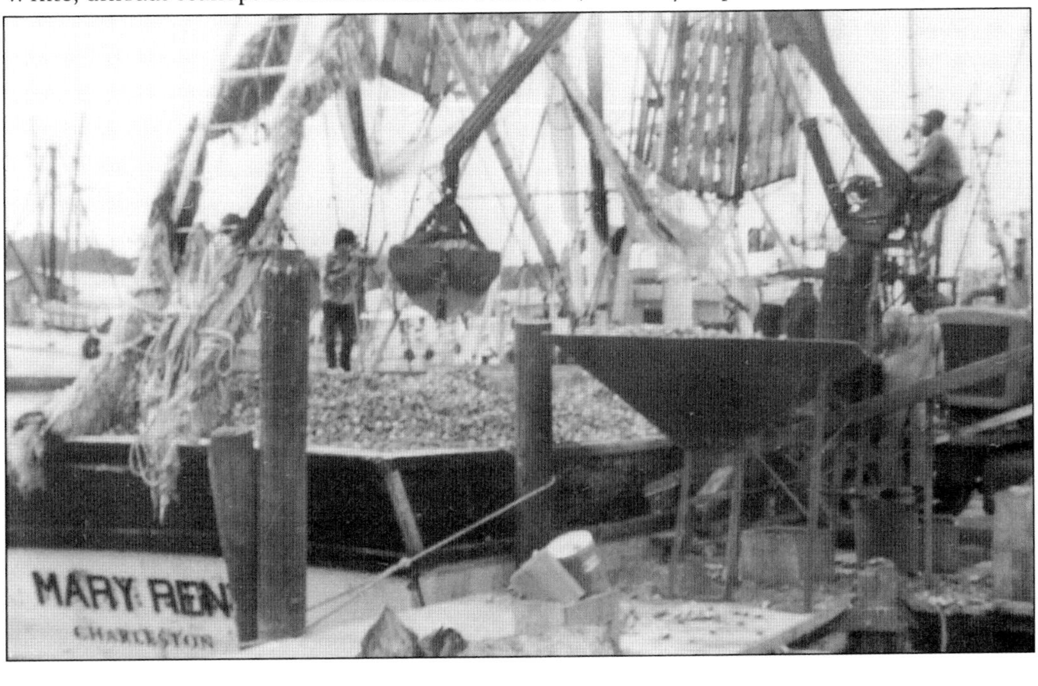

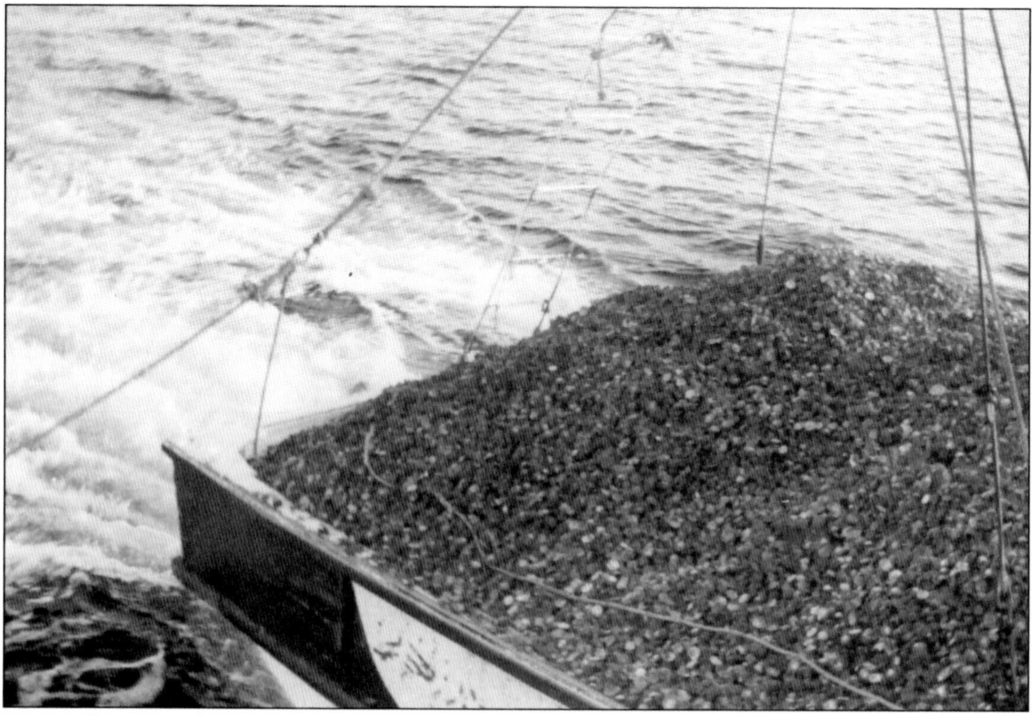

Here a Shem Creek vessel is precariously weighted down to its waterline on a return journey from an offshore scallop endeavor.

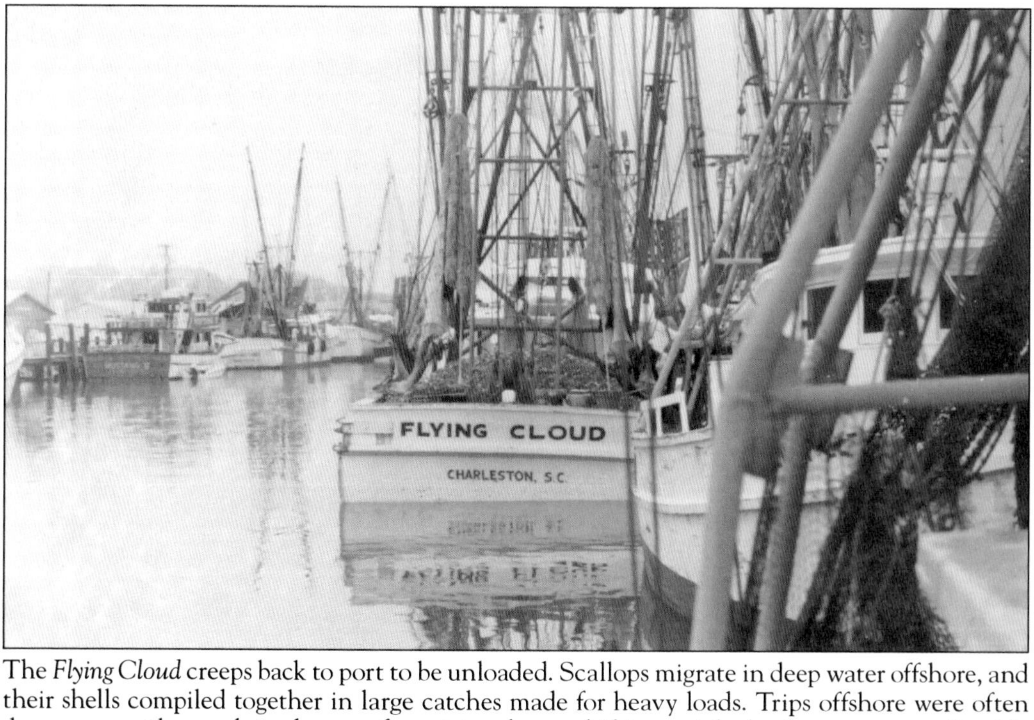

The *Flying Cloud* creeps back to port to be unloaded. Scallops migrate in deep water offshore, and their shells compiled together in large catches made for heavy loads. Trips offshore were often dangerous, with vessels in danger of capsizing due to shifting weight loads on an unpredictable sea. (Courtesy Capt. Barry Wilson.)

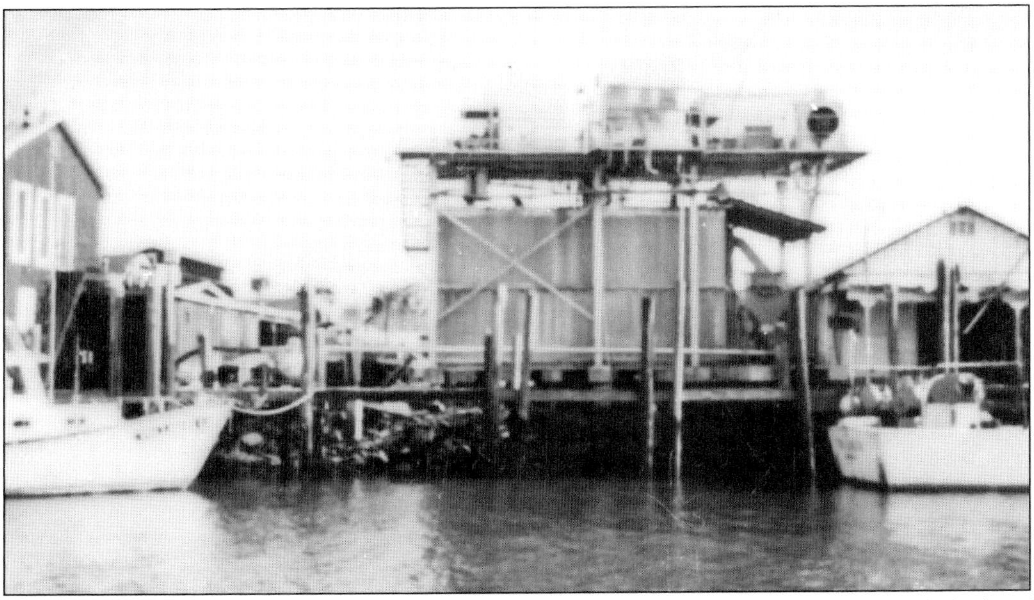

Moultrie Fisheries established an ice business in the early 1960s, hauling in 300-pound blocks of ice that were broken down and crushed on-site. In the 1970s, the family's machines and freezers were capable of making 100 tons of ice per day, providing a valuable service to the growing commercial fleets of Shem Creek. Closing in the 1990s, Moultrie Fisheries is now the site of a local restaurant, Red's Ice House. (Courtesy Billy Simmons.)

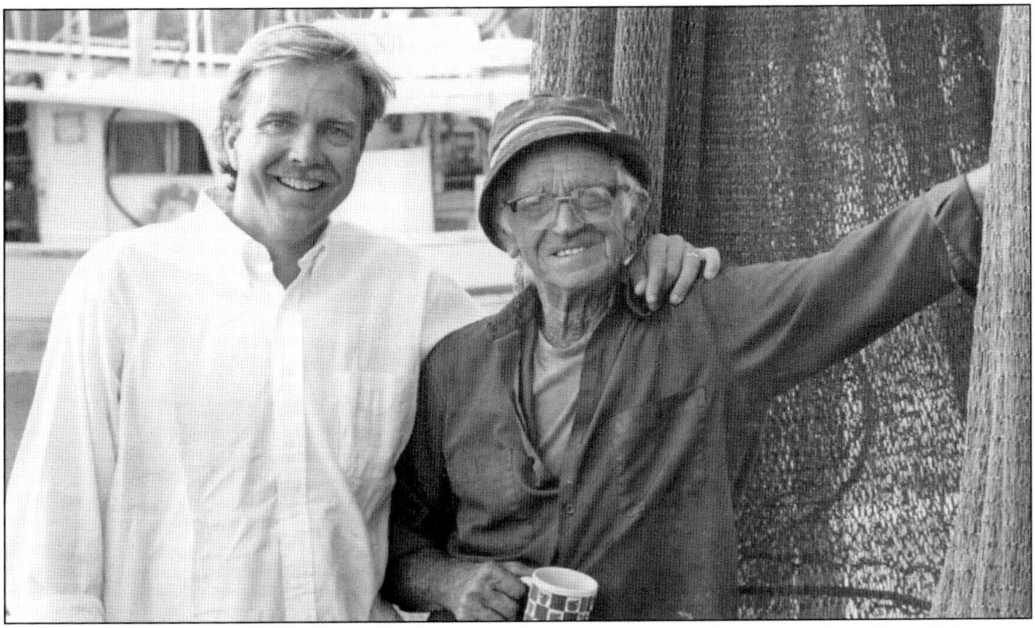

Capt. Robert Schirmer Jr. is pictured here with his son, Sam. Also known as the "Hagg," Captain Schirmer started shrimping on Shem Creek in 1966. During his career, he owned and operated six vessels, retiring at age 75. The vessels included long-liners and trawlers the *Hotdog*, the *Yo-Yo*, the *Miss Charleston*, the *Hagg*, the *Miss Diana*, and the *Sammy J.* Beloved and modest, Captain Schirmer can be found on any given day holding court at Geechie Dock. (Photograph by Anne Darby Parker; courtesy Schirmer family.)

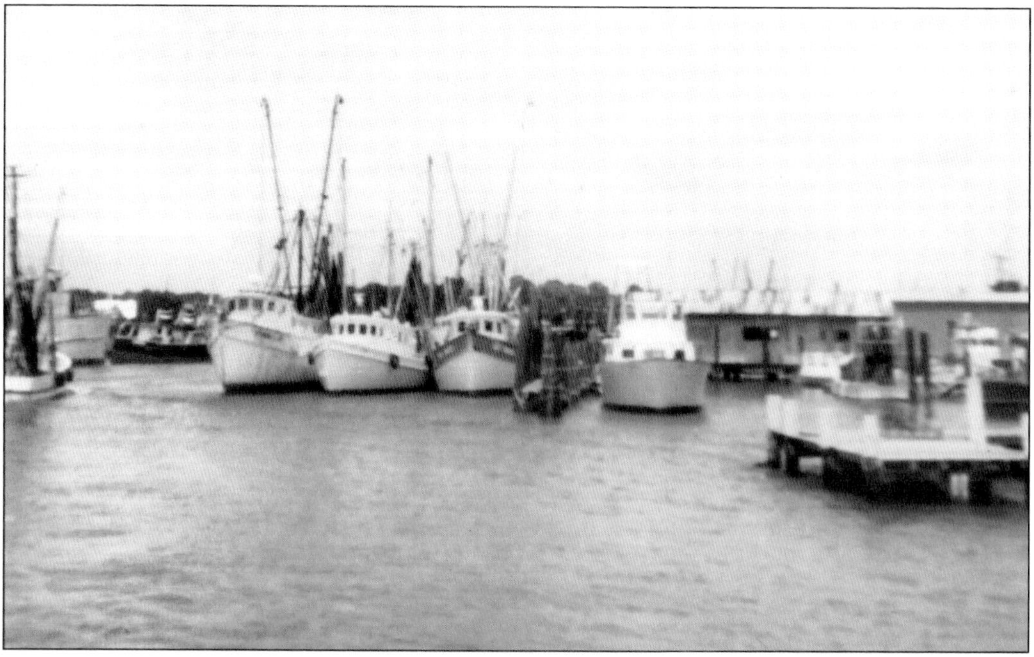

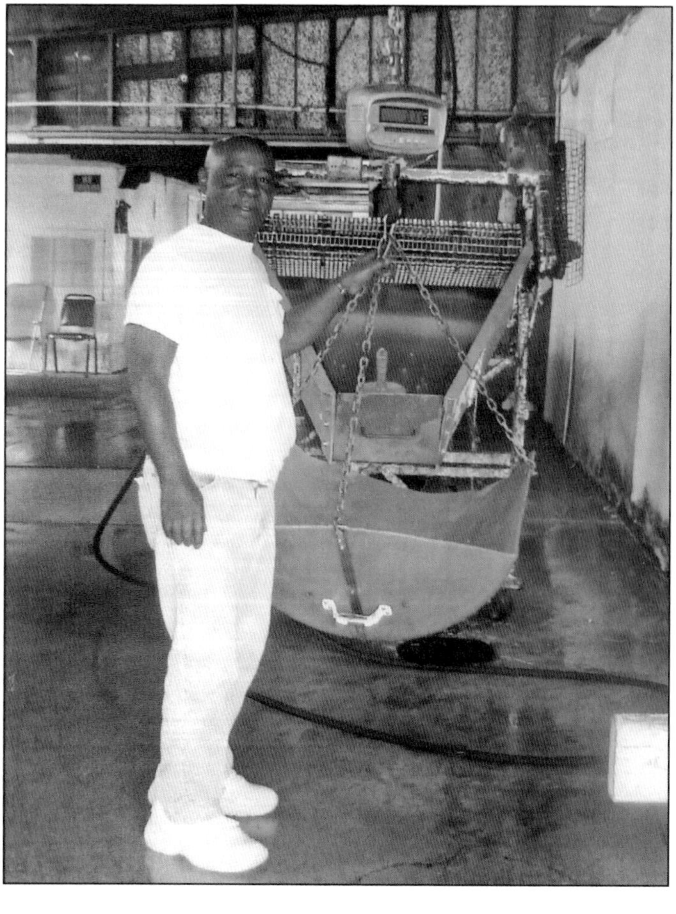

Pictured above in the 1980s is the Wando Shrimp Company, located at the mouth of Shem Creek. Alec W. Smalls, known as "Hambone," (pictured at left) has worked for the Thelning family since he was 17 years old. In the early 1960s, Smalls recalls days of working with a large, wooden vat, having to hand-dip shrimp with a net into scales, and hand-chipping ice. There were times that boats came back to the docks so overflowing with shrimp that they had to be iced on the spot so they would not spoil before being unloaded. He also recalls working at processing shrimp and packing them into trucks until three and four o'clock in the morning. Smalls continues to manage the Wando Shrimp Company and is a beloved member of the creek family.

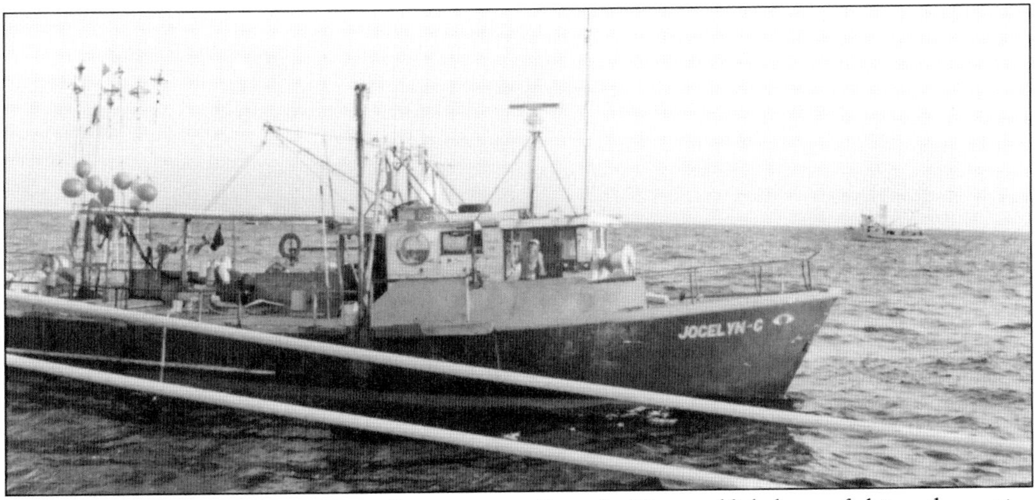

Renowned fisherman Capt. Tony Geisman recalls only 15 swordfish boats fishing the entire eastern seaboard in the late 1970s. With primitive radar and loran for navigating, fishermen relied on water temperatures and visual aids, such as the colors of colliding water masses, weed lines, and current rips, to locate fish. While fishing in the Gulf Stream off Charleston in 1976 with Capt. Sten Carlson aboard the *Jocelyn C*, they came upon the catch of a lifetime—8,000 pounds of swordfish in one set— while also locating what is now called the Charleston Bump. Shem Creek was the closest pack-out facility, so the *Jocelyn C.* came there to unload, becoming the first boat to unload swordfish in South Carolina. Pictured above is the *Jocelyn C.* Pictured below is one of the *Jocelyn C.* crews in the 1970s. From left to right are Jack Kline, Tony Geisman, Michael Craven, and Ronnie Kline. (Courtesy Capt. Tony Geisman.)

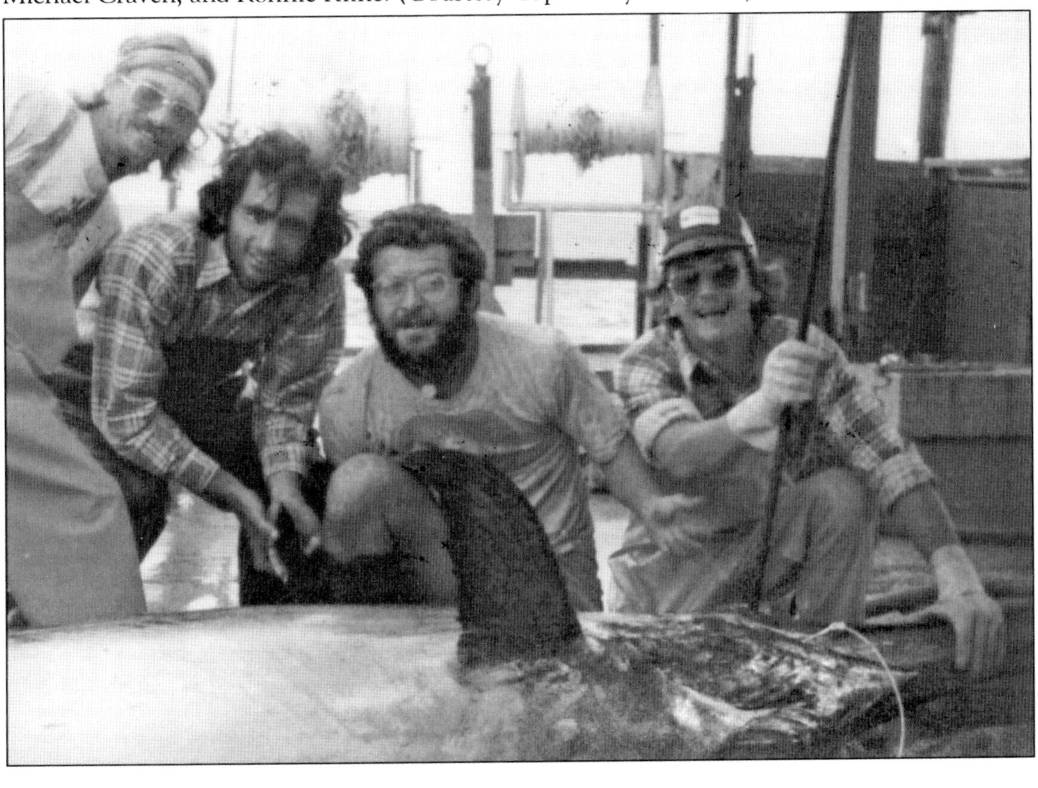

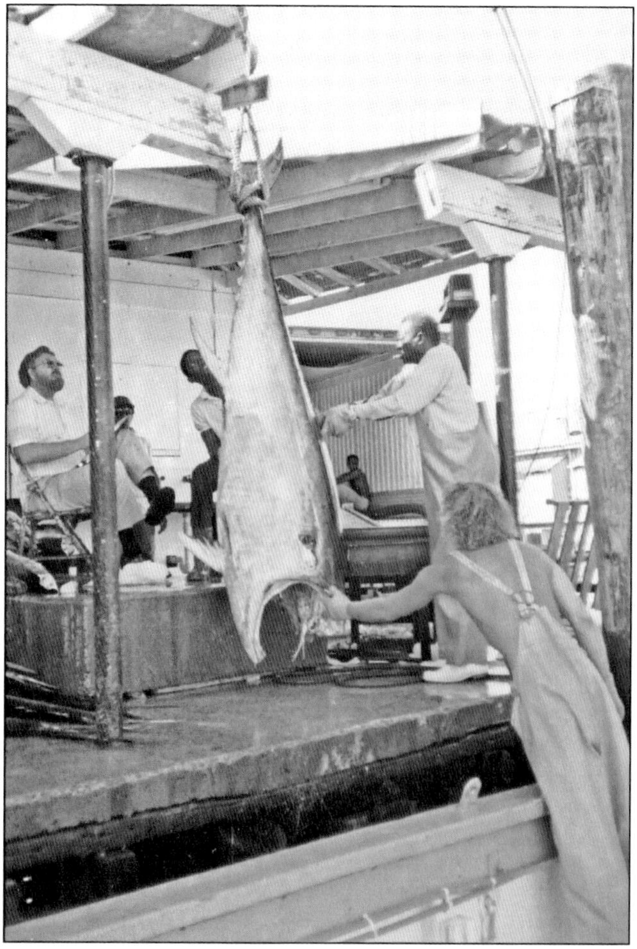

A large bluefin tuna is being unloaded at Moultrie Fisheries. The highly regarded, late Red Simmons records the weight of the fish before they are placed in the truck for shipment. Pictured below, boats dockside in the late 1970s include the *Adventuress* from Cape Canaveral, Florida; the *Olympic Javelin* from Massachusetts; and the *Trade Winds*, which was owned by Red Simmons. The original Trawler restaurant is visible in the background. (Both images courtesy Capt. Tony Geisman.)

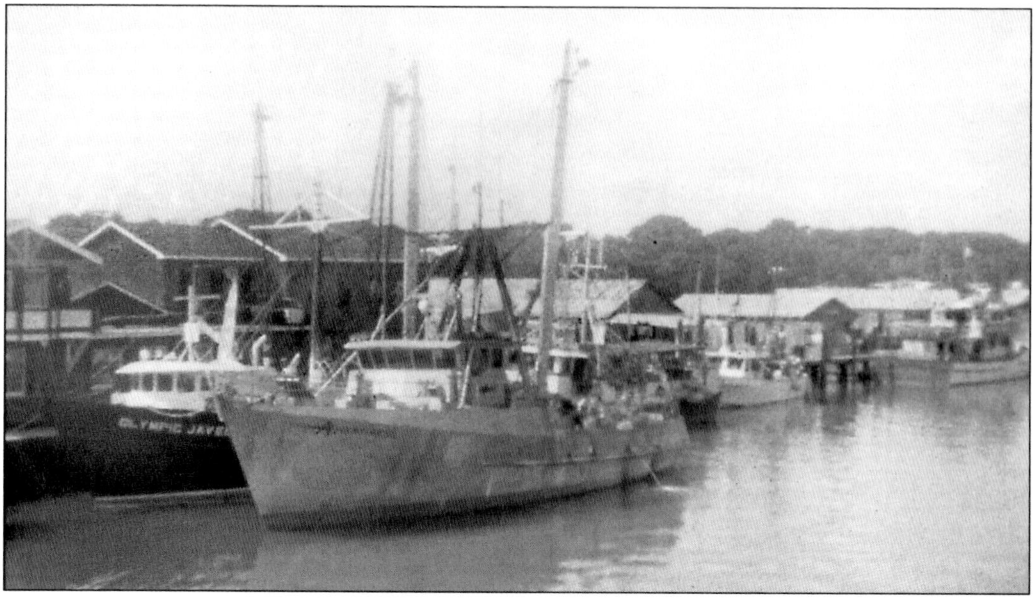

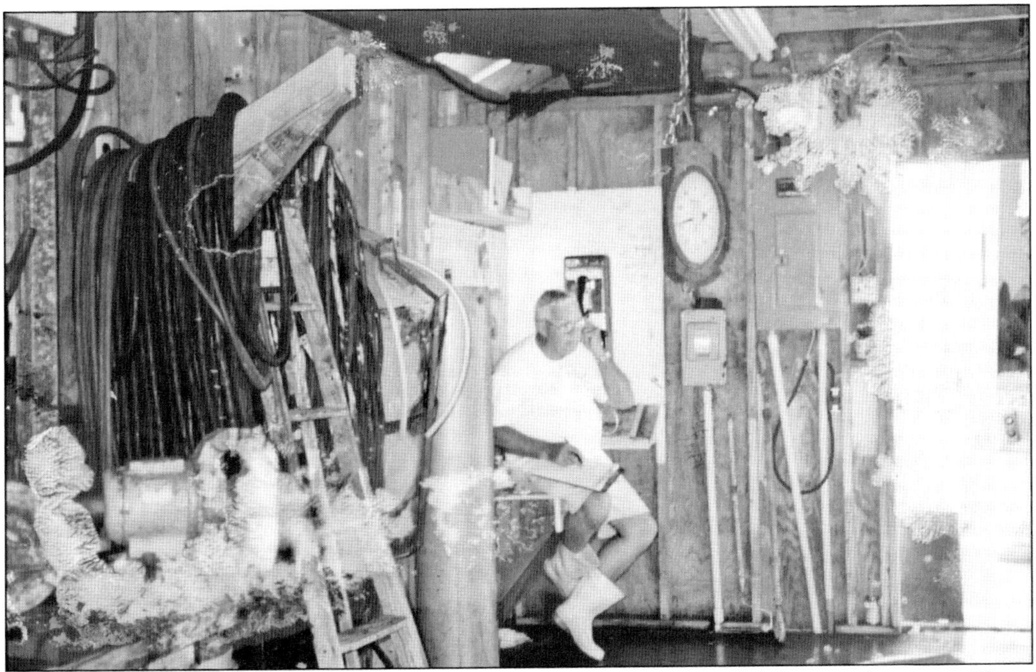

Capt. Robert "Bobby" Santos, a 30-year veteran of the commercial fishing industry on Shem Creek, worked on several different vessels before commissioning his own boat, the *Betty Boop*. He has fished the waters of the Caribbean, the Gulf of Mexico, and the Southeastern seaboard. Pictured here in the 1980s conducting business at Geechie Dock, Captain Santos is currently retired and is a beloved member of the local seafood industry. (Courtesy Capt. Robert Santos.)

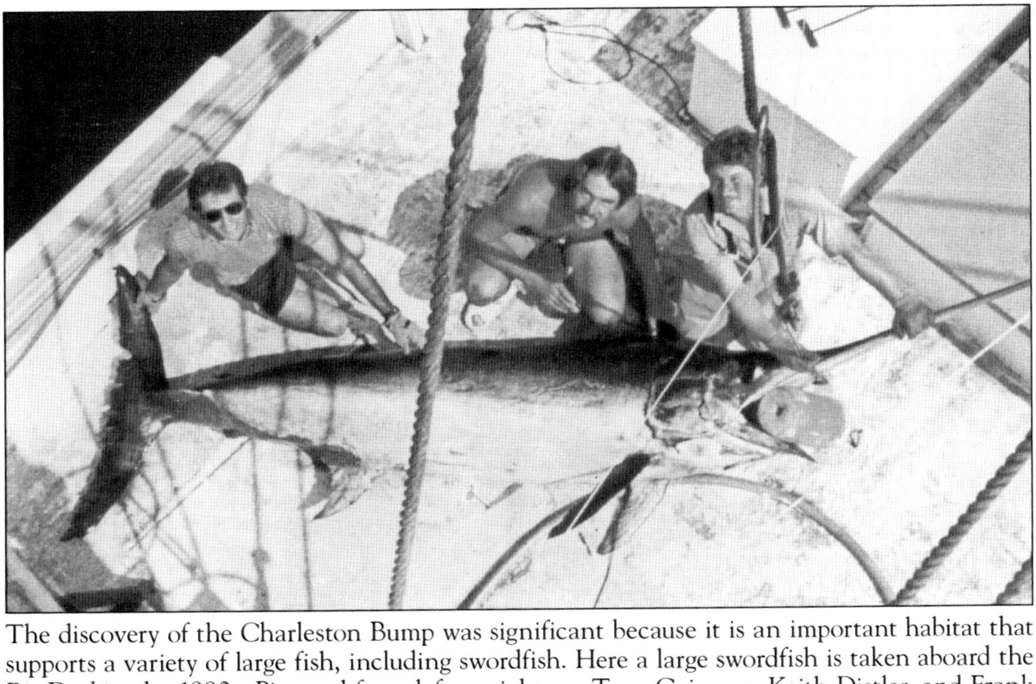

The discovery of the Charleston Bump was significant because it is an important habitat that supports a variety of large fish, including swordfish. Here a large swordfish is taken aboard the *Big Deal* in the 1980s. Pictured from left to right are Tony Geisman, Keith Distler, and Frank Kanapaux. (Courtesy Capt. Tony Geisman.)

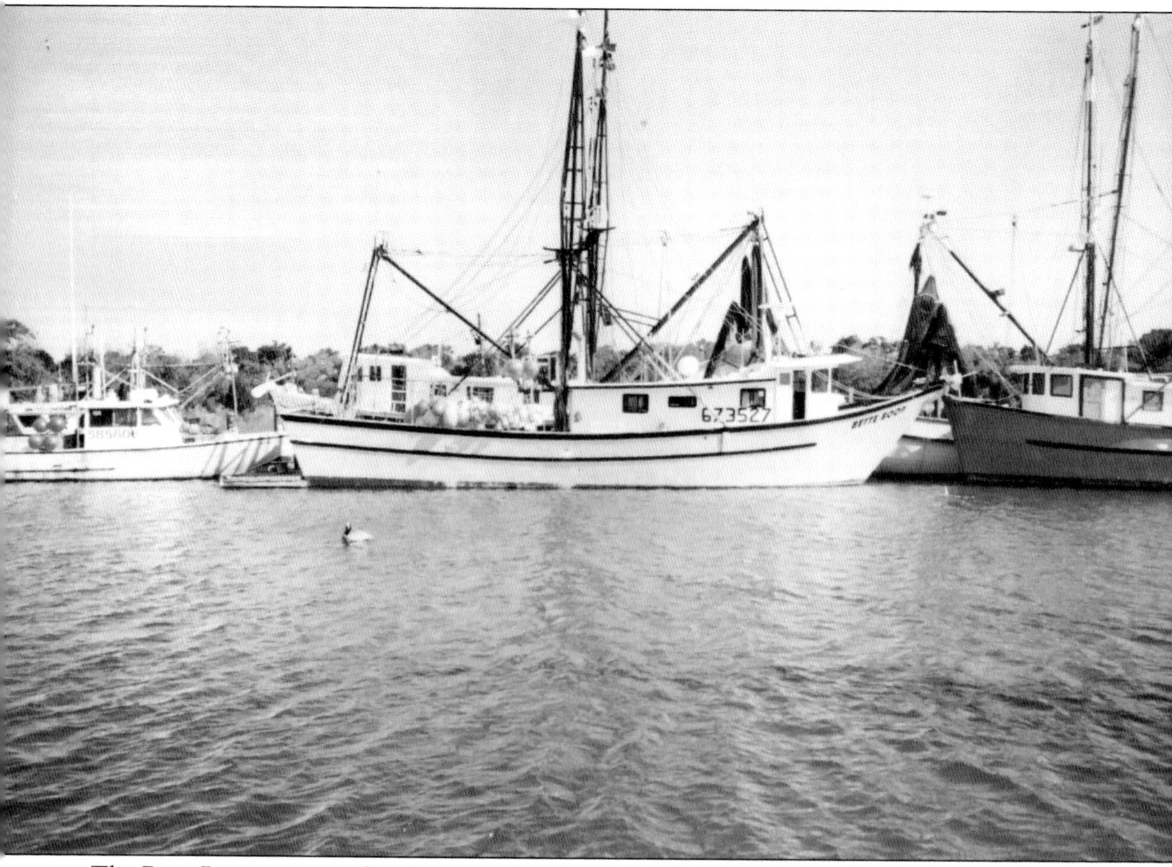

The *Betty Boop* was owned and operated by the Santos family for more than 20 years. Boatbuilder John Bridges constructed this fine 72-foot vessel, which was commissioned by the family, of hand-laid fiberglass in Thunderbolt, Georgia. While based out of Shem Creek, the *Betty Boop* fished deep water for swordfish, traveling to destinations as distant as the Yucatan Peninsula, the Caribbean, and the Gulf of Mexico. She now resides in and fishes the waters of Trinidad. (Courtesy Capt. John Santos.)

An extraordinary catch by Capt. John Santos—a bluefin tuna weighing 740 pounds—is being pulled from the hold of the *Betty Boop*. It was caught approximately 120 miles offshore. A local restaurant chain purchased the tuna. (Courtesy Kimberly Morales.)

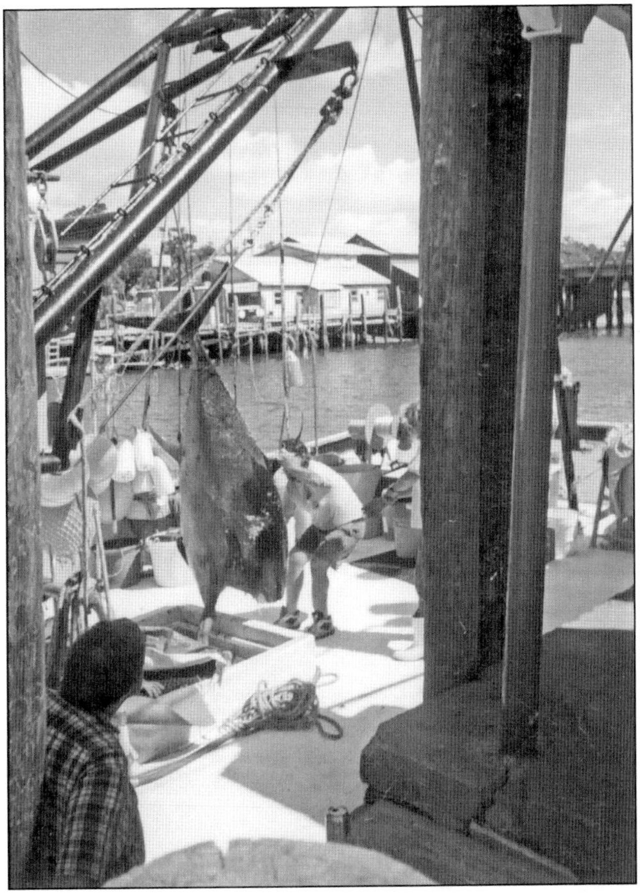

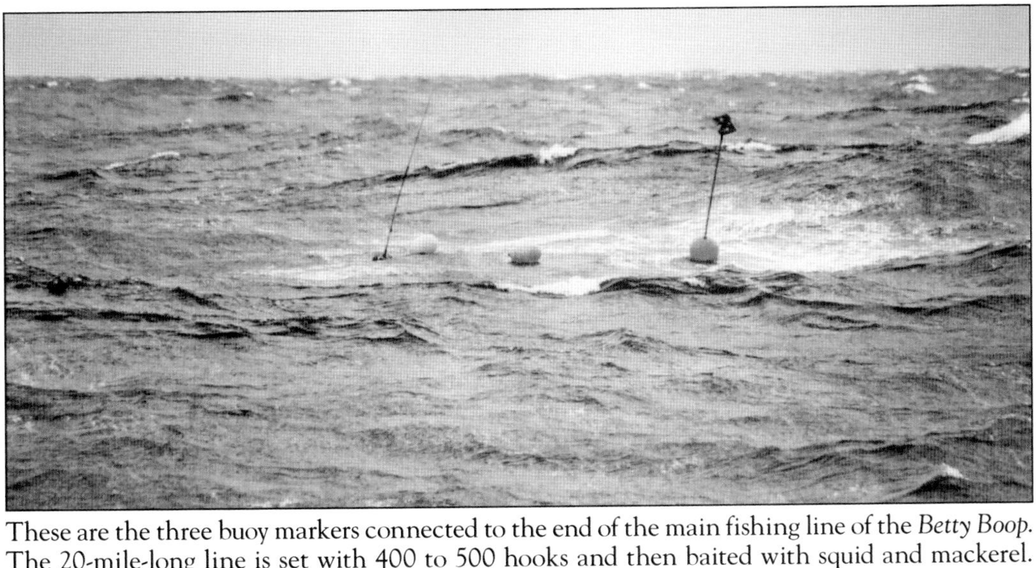

These are the three buoy markers connected to the end of the main fishing line of the *Betty Boop*. The 20-mile-long line is set with 400 to 500 hooks and then baited with squid and mackerel. The line is set at sundown and disconnected from the boat, remaining adrift. The high flyer, the poley ball, and the beacon buoy are easily retrieved at sunup and then hauled back onto the vessel. (Courtesy Capt. John Santos.)

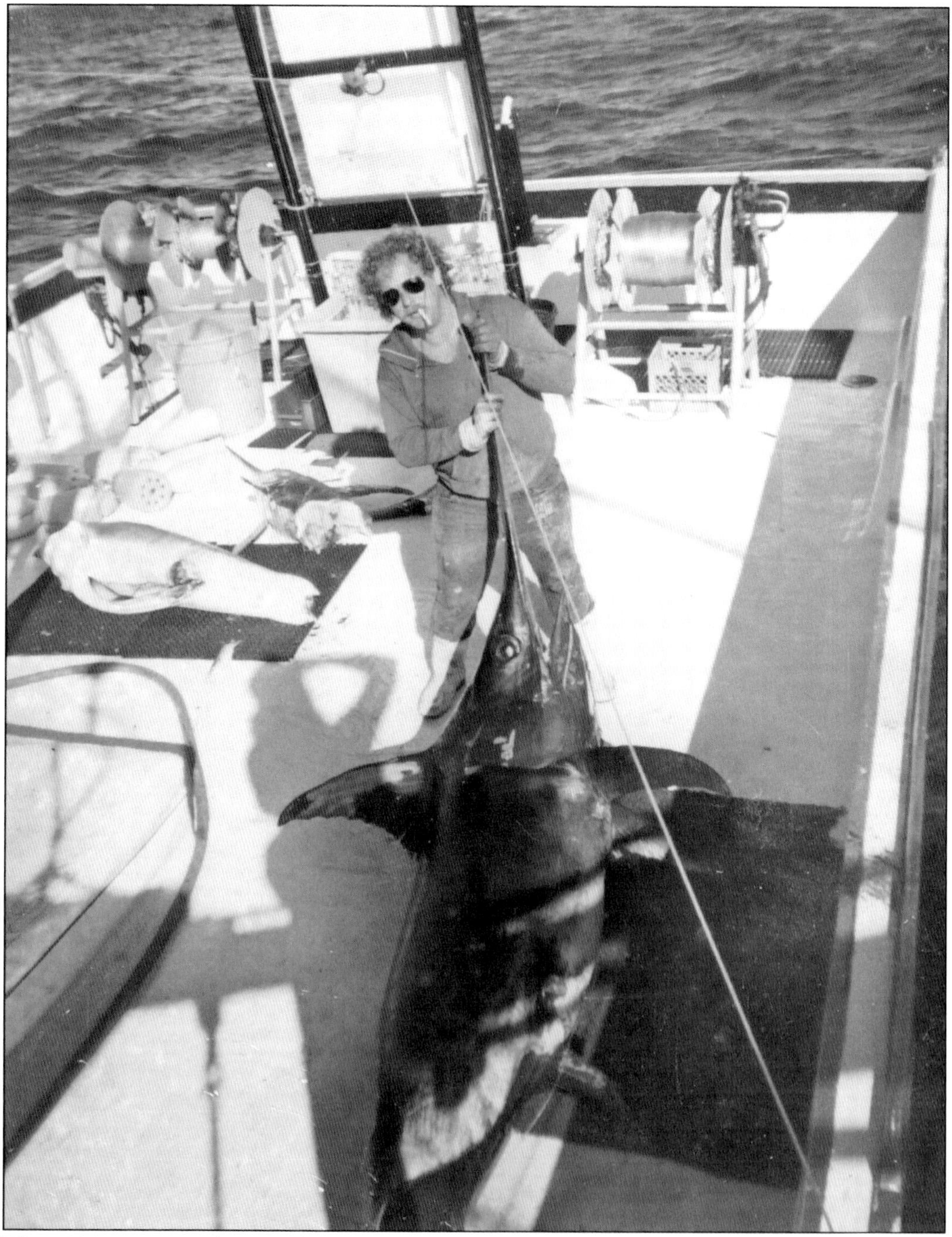

This 1980s image is of Capt. John Santos, a second-generation fisherman, aboard the *Betty Boop*. He is holding onto an extraordinary catch, a 150-pound swordfish. In the background, lying on the deck, are a mako shark carcass and a swordfish that has been bitten in half by a large shark. While swordfish were the target, other fish such as tuna, dolphin, wahoo, and shark were caught as well. These fish were cleaned and gutted on the trip and off-loaded for markets in the local area or transported by truck to Northern states for further processing and distribution. (Courtesy Capt. John Santos.)

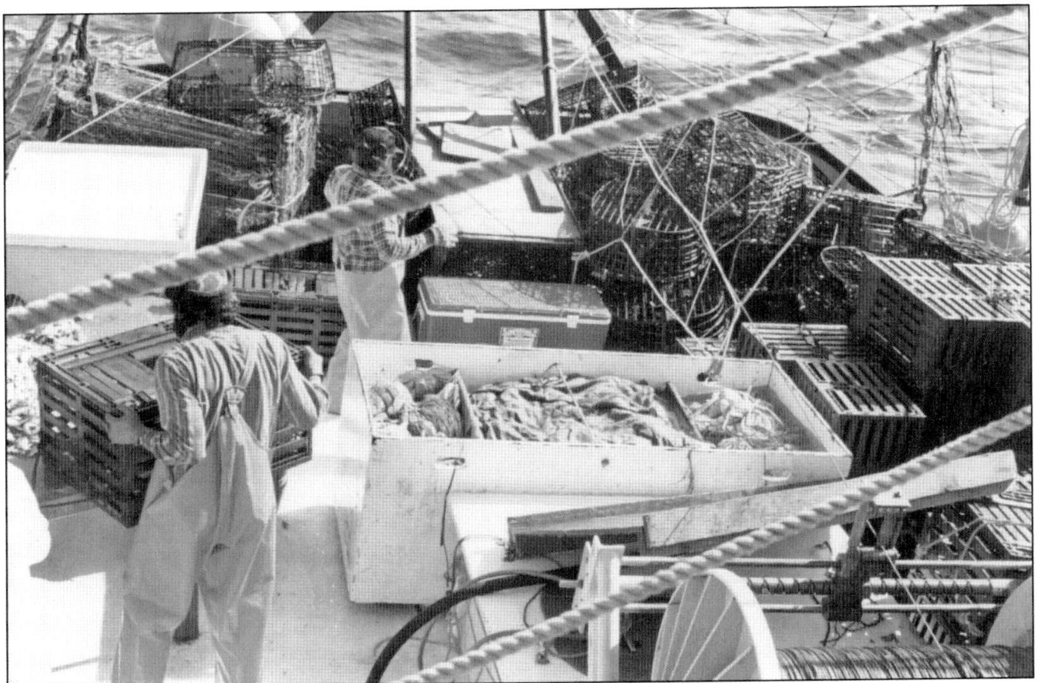

A little-known industry fishermen of Shem Creek were briefly involved in was the quest for golden crab. Fishermen say these large, tasty bottom-dwellers can grow as large as five pounds. Capt. Tony Geisman and Capt. Jim Bussey of the *Heavy Duty II* found these crabs 60 miles offshore in 1,500 to 1,800 feet of water in the 1980s. The *Heavy Duty II* (above) has a deck littered with different styles of crab pots the crew experimented with. The crew would bait and set 10 miles of line with 800 pots attached to it. Pictured below, a gold crab's body, claws, and legs are full of edible meat. (Both images courtesy Capt. Tony Geisman.)

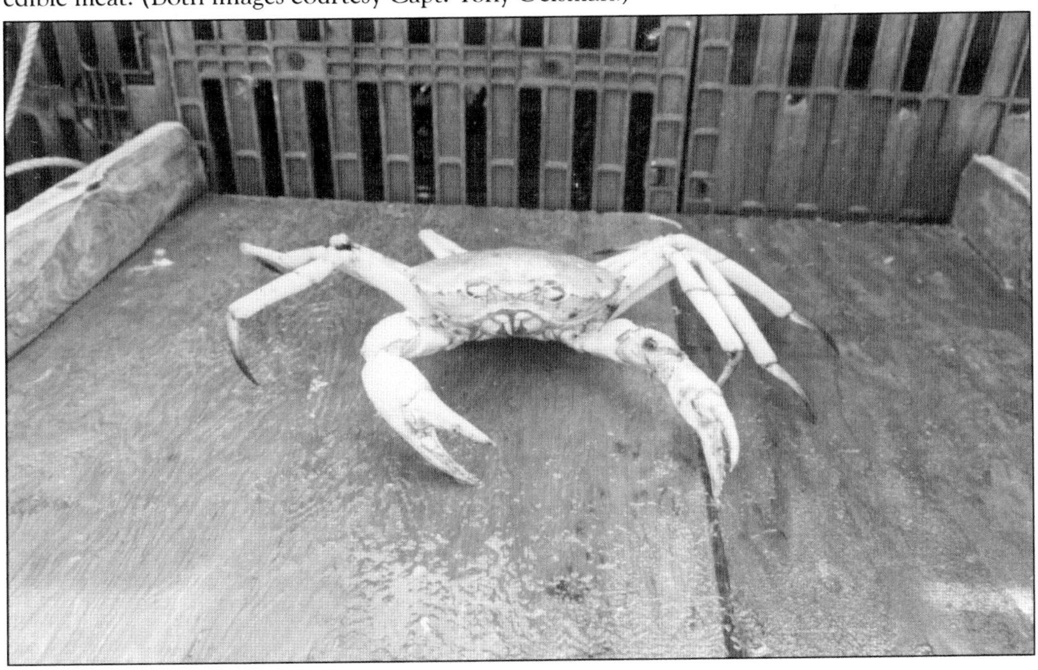

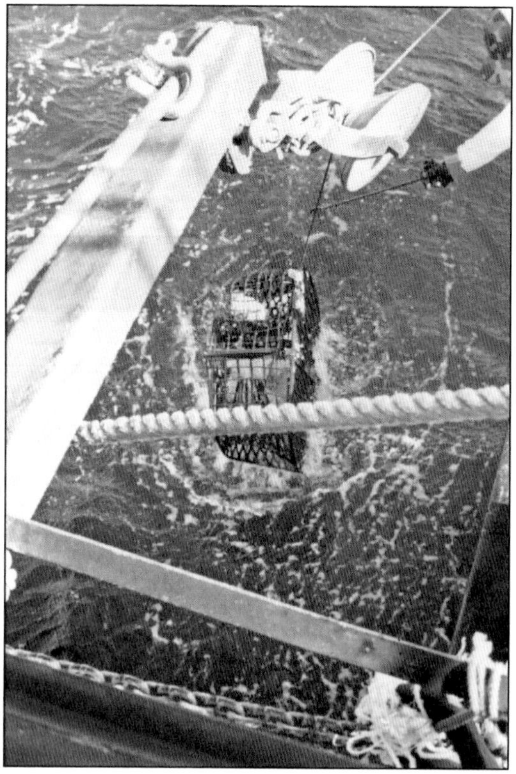

The long-liner, outfitted for fishing, is redesigned for hauling crab pots back. Pictured at left, pots connected to long cables are hoisted out of the water via a mechanical wench. The crab is then dumped and graded. The five-man crew could keep crabs alive in the hole for up to a week if they layered them with burlap sacks on top of a layer of salt-water ice produced by the vessel. Within four or five months, the captain abandoned the enterprise because of problems in processing and distribution. Pictured below, Tony Geisman and Woody Underwood bait traps. (Both images courtesy Capt. Tony Geisman.)

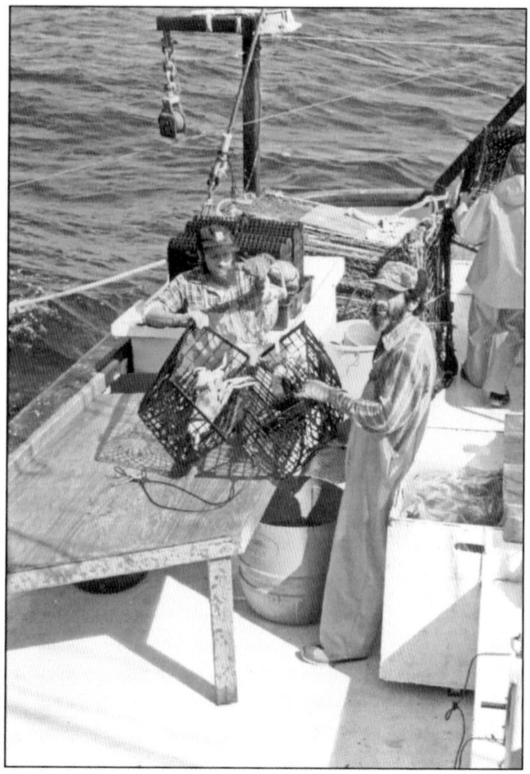

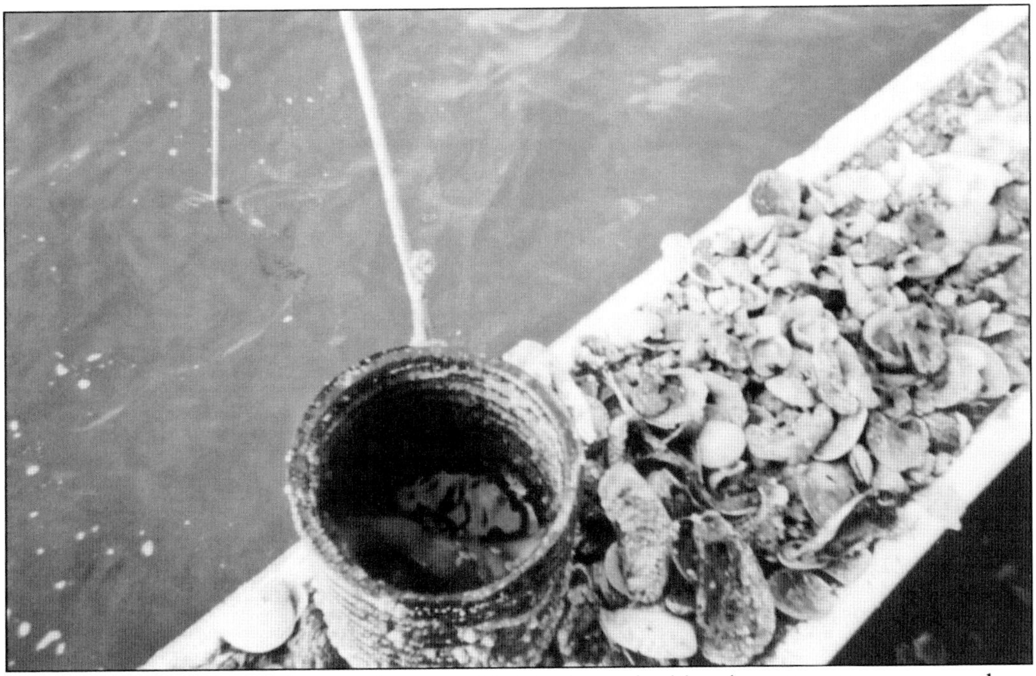

Octopus fishing can be a slippery business. This industry had local participation as recently as the year 2000. Capt. Tony Geisman of the 35-foot *Answered Prayer* reminisces about fishing for the octopus using black corrugated pipe with concrete poured into the bottoms to act as a weight and floor for the octopus den. Traps are set in 40 to 60 feet of water and left on the ocean floor for approximately two weeks. Pipes are pulled out of the water and checked for octopus. No bait is required because the octopus will freely take up residence in this cozy hole. Bob North, also known as "Grouper Bob," shows off a good haul from the traps. Pictured above, an octopus sits inside a trap; the shells on the rail have been gathered by the octopus and retrieved from the traps as well. (Both images courtesy Capt. Tony Geisman.)

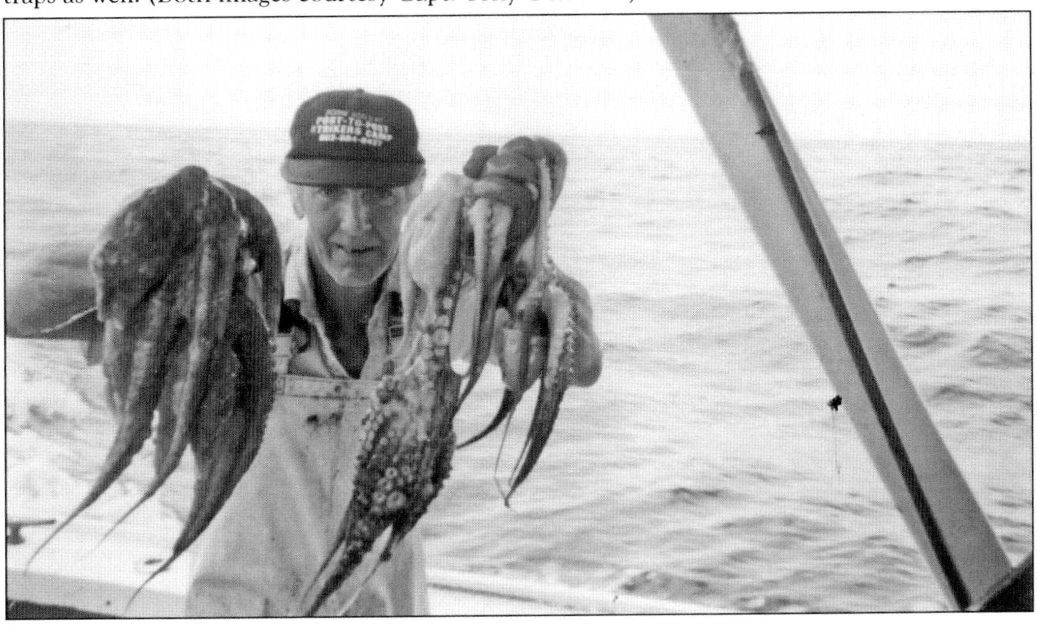

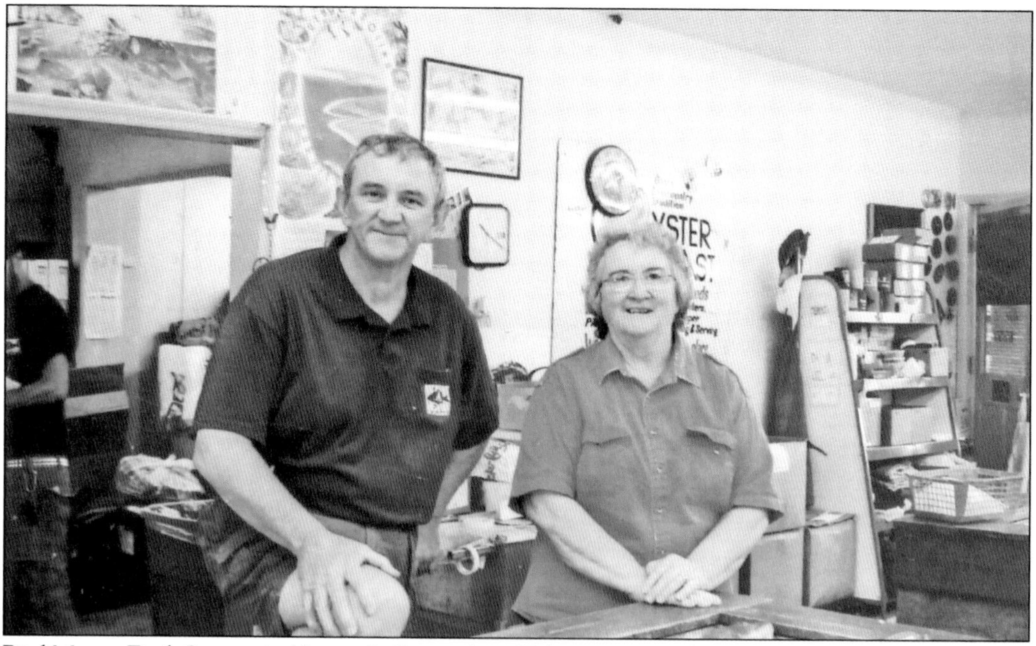

Rial Moore Fitch Jr. married his wife, Peggy Ann Toler, in 1975. The two currently operate Mount Pleasant Seafood Retail and have been the owners since 1976. The store continues to sell a wide variety of fresh and frozen seafood and also offers catering services. Here Rial Fitch poses with Kathy Whray, who has been an employee of Mount Pleasant Seafood for 23 years.

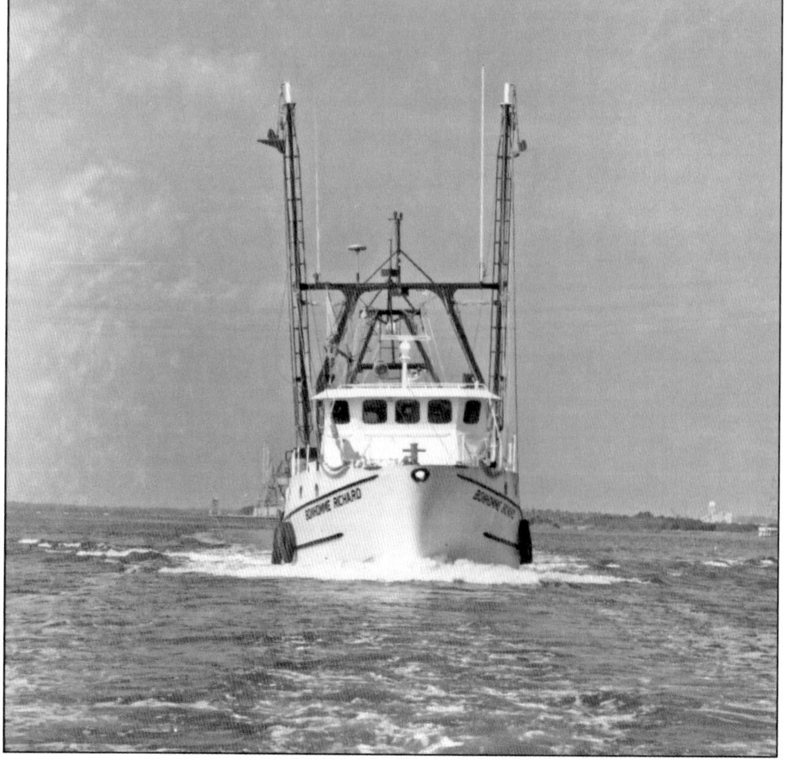

The highly respected seafood industry veteran Capt. Walter D. Toler owned the 65-foot, steel-hulled *Bonhomme Richard.* Captain Toler has been in the commercial shrimping industry for 32 years, and he owned and operated Mount Pleasant Seafood on Shem Creek. He served as president of the South Carolina Shrimpers Association (SCSA) and has contributed countless hours of service to the industry. (Courtesy Toler family.)

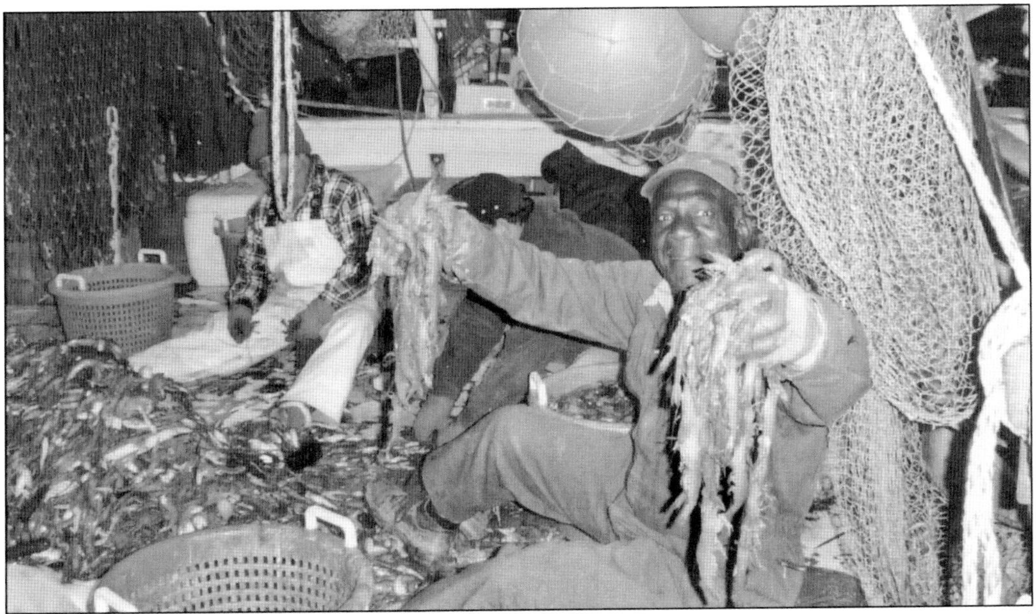

John Henry Middleton, pictured here, began shrimping in 1987. He owned, operated, and subleased his vessels, the *Stargazer* and the *Eva B*, while working full time for SCE&G. Losing his vessel to Hurricane Hugo, Middleton is currently retired from the industry, but he and his wife, Jessie, are still active within the shrimping community and are beloved by the creek family. (Courtesy Middleton family.)

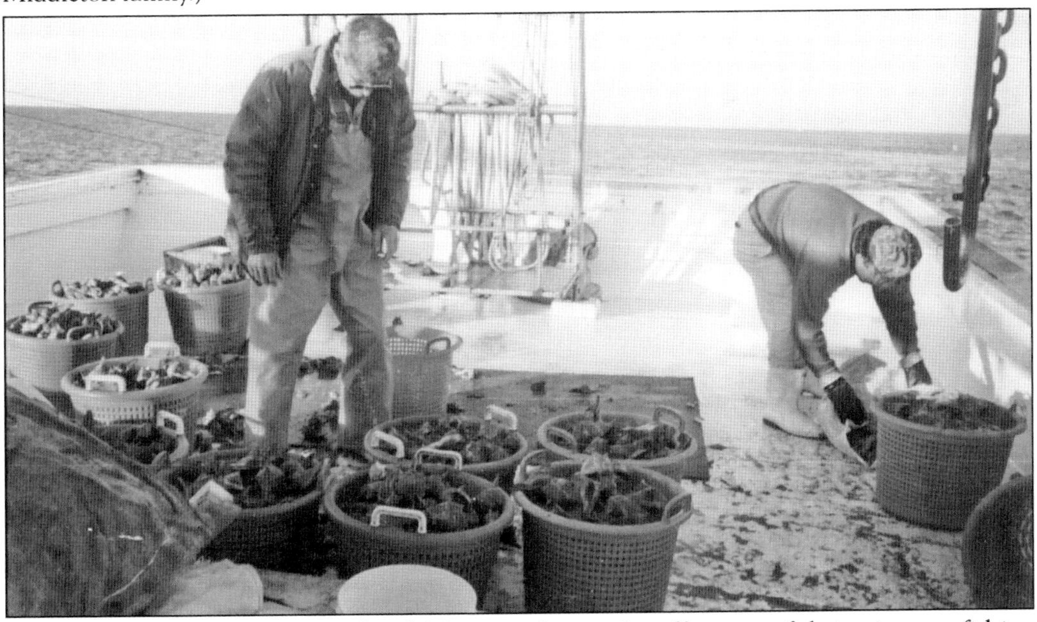

Another industry trawled for by local fishermen during the off-season of shrimping was fishing for conch in the early 1980s. Capt. Warren Rector recalls conch fishing aboard his vessel the *Miss Vivian* in March and April. Conchs were trawled for in waters 10 to 30 feet deep off beaches; this industry lasted around 15 years. Conch were placed into 85-pound sacks, unloaded via a conveyor belt onto trucks, and sold to markets in Virginia. Boats typically received $7.00 to $13.00 per bushel, and larger vessels could carry up to 500 bushels per day. (Courtesy Capt. Warren Rector.)

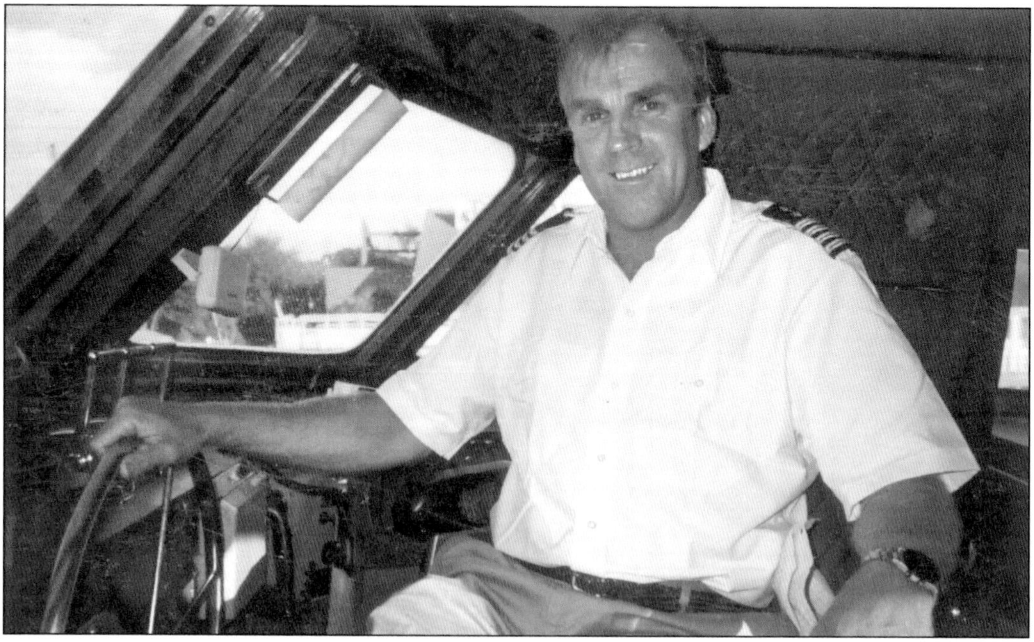

Capt. Harold Olsen began fishing coastal waters in 1978, and he currently owns and operates the *Bonsai* and the *Endangered I*. Captain Olsen is a rare shark fisherman on the creek, working offshore by setting a 10-mile line with up to 500 hooks bated with recycled fish parts. During his career, he has built a reputation of being a talented professional and has captained many vessels, including local boats the *Thunderstar* and the *Atlantic Star*. (Courtesy Capt. Harold Olsen.)

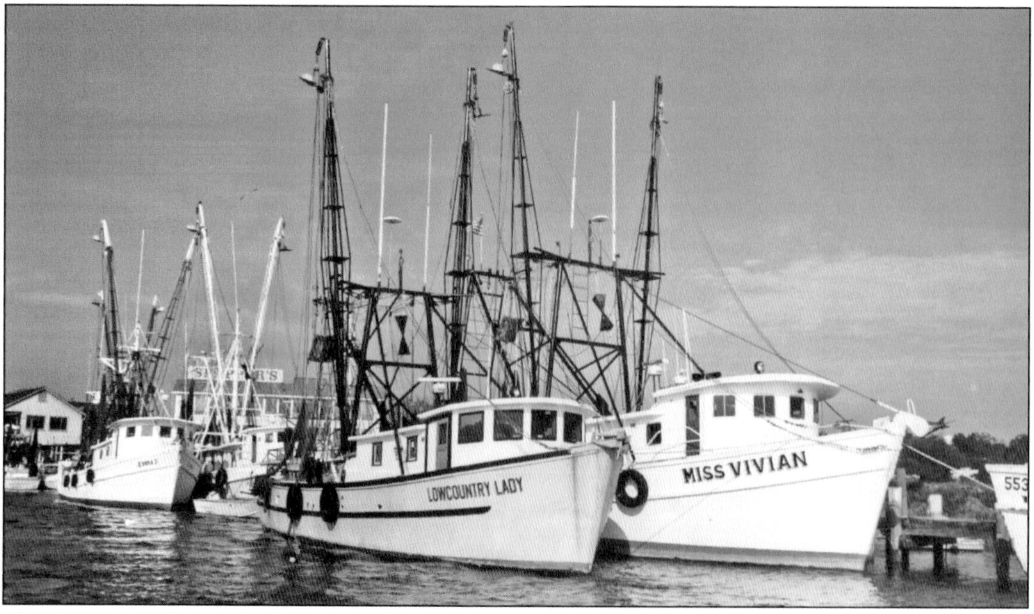

Shrimp season in South Carolina is regulated by the SCDNR and is generally six to eight months long. Two of the most common harvested species here are white and brown shrimp. These two vessels, the *Lowcountry Lady*, owned and operated by Capt. Randy Rhodes, and the *Miss Vivian*, owned and operated by Capt. Warren Rector, have "H" frame outriggers and step-up wheelhouses that allow captains to see behind them without stepping outside. (Courtesy Rector family.)

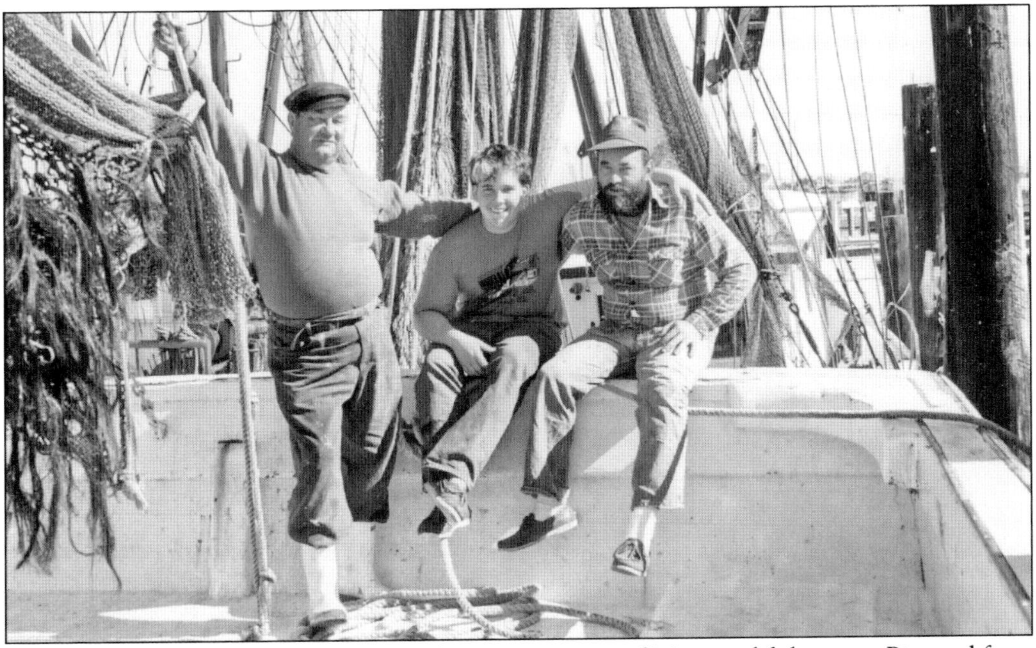

Seated on the rail of a shrimp boat are three generations of Magwood fishermen. Pictured from left to right are the late Clarence "Captain Junior" Magwood Jr., Clarence "Rocky" Magwood IV, and the late Clarence "Skipper" Magwood III. Rocky is the only fourth-generation fisherman on Shem Creek today and currently boasts the largest trawler on the creek. This local family has been working the East Cooper waters for nearly 100 years.

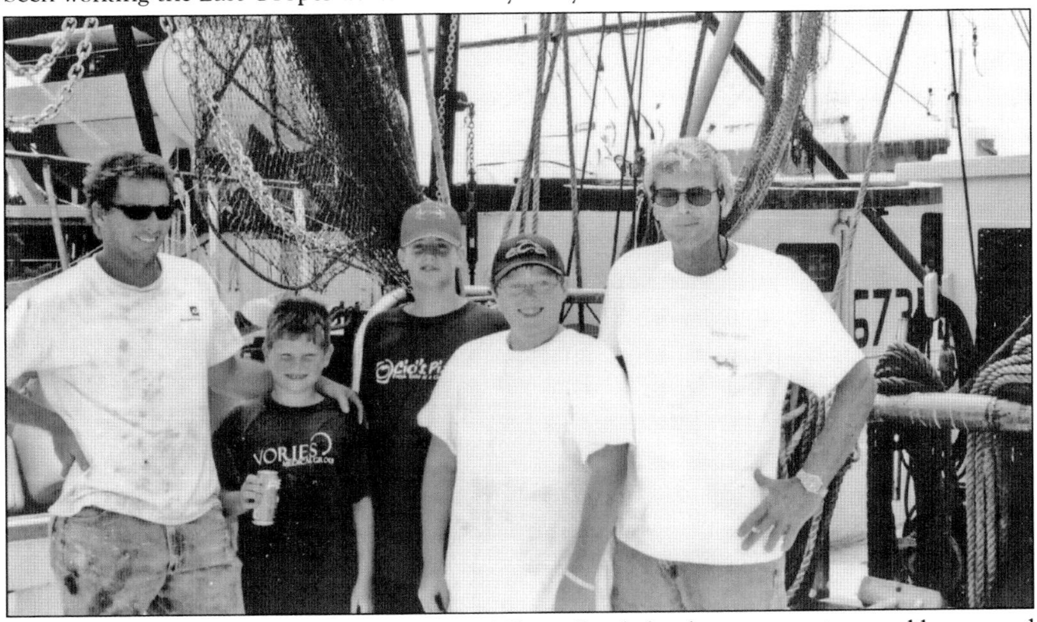

The Rector family has been shrimping out of Shem Creek for three generations and has owned and operated more than a dozen trawlers. Pictured from left to right are Lance Rector, his sons Christian and Joshua, his nephew Franklin, and his father, Capt. Warren "Bubba" Rector. Capt. Lance Rector remains hopeful that there will be a boat and an industry in the future for his children and others if they choose to make commercial shrimping a career. (Courtesy Rector family.)

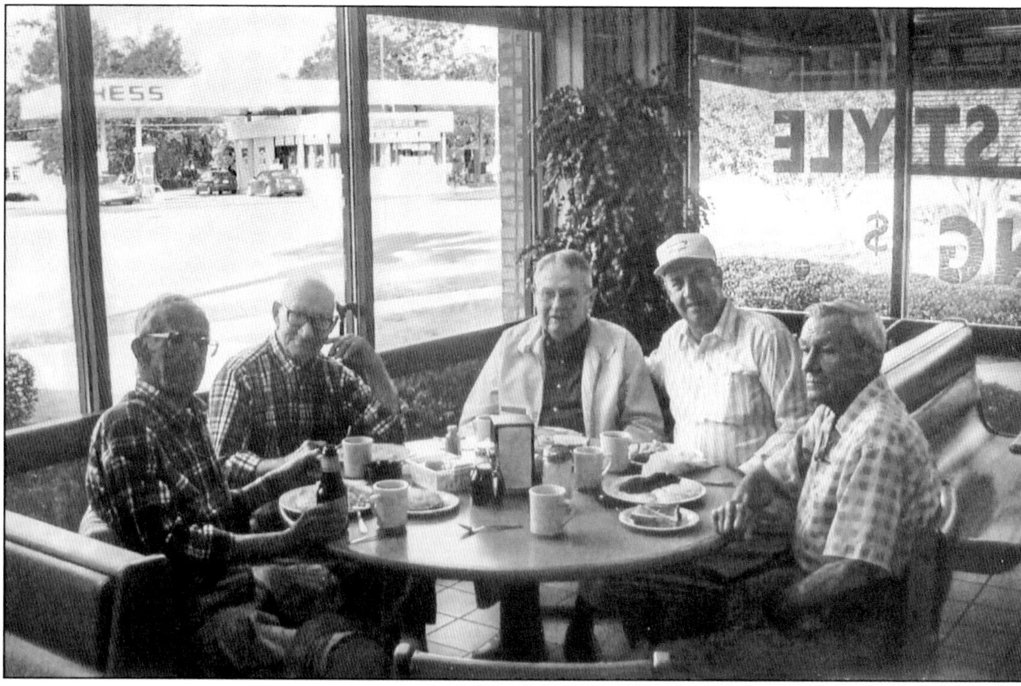

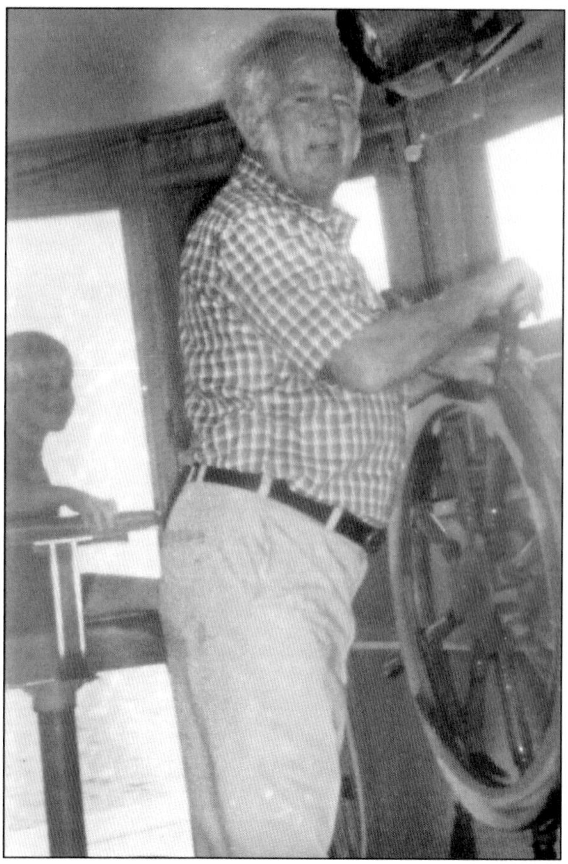

A cherished generation of fishermen from the creek share breakfast together at Alex's Restaurant. Pictured above from left to right are captains Robert Schirmer, Louis Williams, Walter O'Neil, Lawrence Van Essendelft, and Barry Wilson. Pictured at left, Capt. Jeffrey C. Thelning owned and operated the Wando Shrimp Company, which was established in 1949. One of the largest on the creek, the company unloaded commercial fishing and shrimping vessels in great numbers. Captain Thelning also ran the Thelning Diesel and Marine Shop and Wando Produce and Trucking, both located in downtown Charleston. After Captain Thelning passed away in 1995, his daughter Lisa T. Sigman took over the business, and with help from her husband, Chuck, and manager Alec W. Smalls, the business is still open, unloading shrimp daily. (Above photograph by Rob Royall, courtesy of Robert Schirmer Jr.; below courtesy Lisa Sigman.)

Capt. Wayne Magwood has taken over the family business, Magwood's Seafood, on Shem Creek and has added a dry stack facility. Captain Magwood is a respected member of the commercial industry, dedicating many hours of service to help promote local seafood. He is a third-generation fisherman with a close-to-40-year career as a shrimper, is a former president of the SCSA, and remains active in the industry today. (Courtesy Capt. Wayne Magwood.)

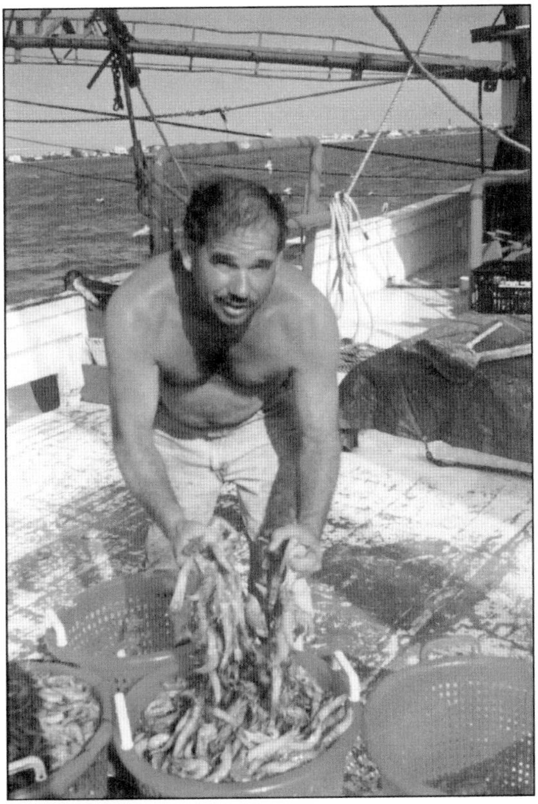

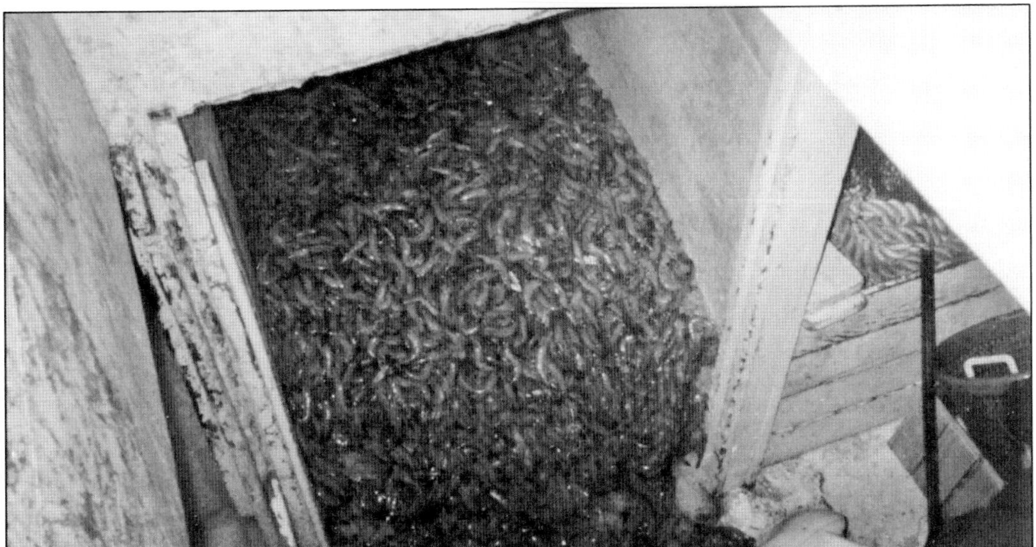

This image of shrimp being shoveled out of the fish hole was taken in 1999, the opening day of shrimp season. Capt. Wayne Magwood set the record of his career with an astounding 9,000 pounds of shrimp. The boat received a meager $2.77-per-pound price. In recent years, shrimpers have been battling the lower cost of imported shrimp, fuel costs, and maintenance expenses, forcing many to quit trawling.

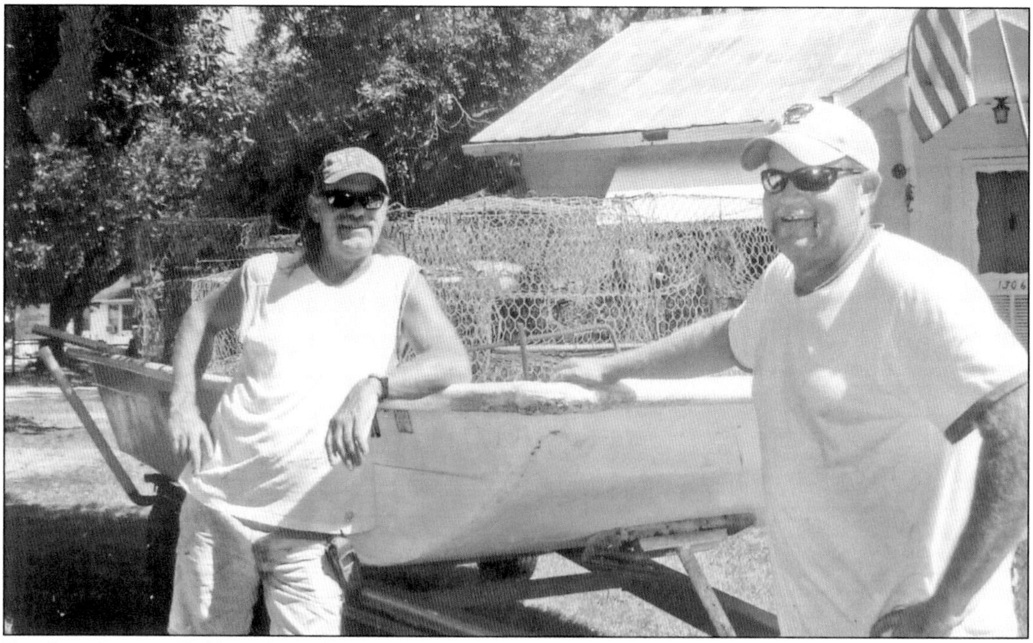

Brothers Jimmy (left) and Andy Crane, along with their best friend, Dee Magwood (right), have crabbed the local waters from Bull's Bay to Charleston Harbor since childhood. All three began shrimping part time while still in high school and crabbing in the off-season. All three retired from shrimping, and they now enjoy crabbing full time. Working together, they supply local and Northern Virginia wholesale markets.

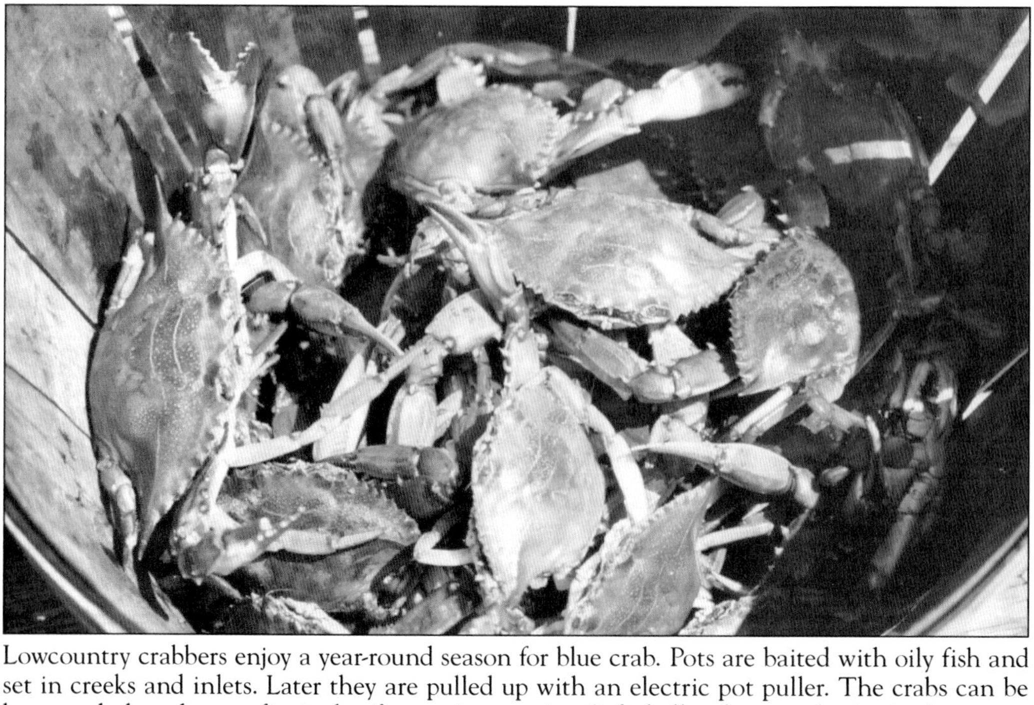

Lowcountry crabbers enjoy a year-round season for blue crab. Pots are baited with oily fish and set in creeks and inlets. Later they are pulled up with an electric pot puller. The crabs can be harvested when they are five inches from point to point. Soft-shell crab season begins in the spring, revolving around the full moons of March and April. Locals refer to female crabs as "sooks."

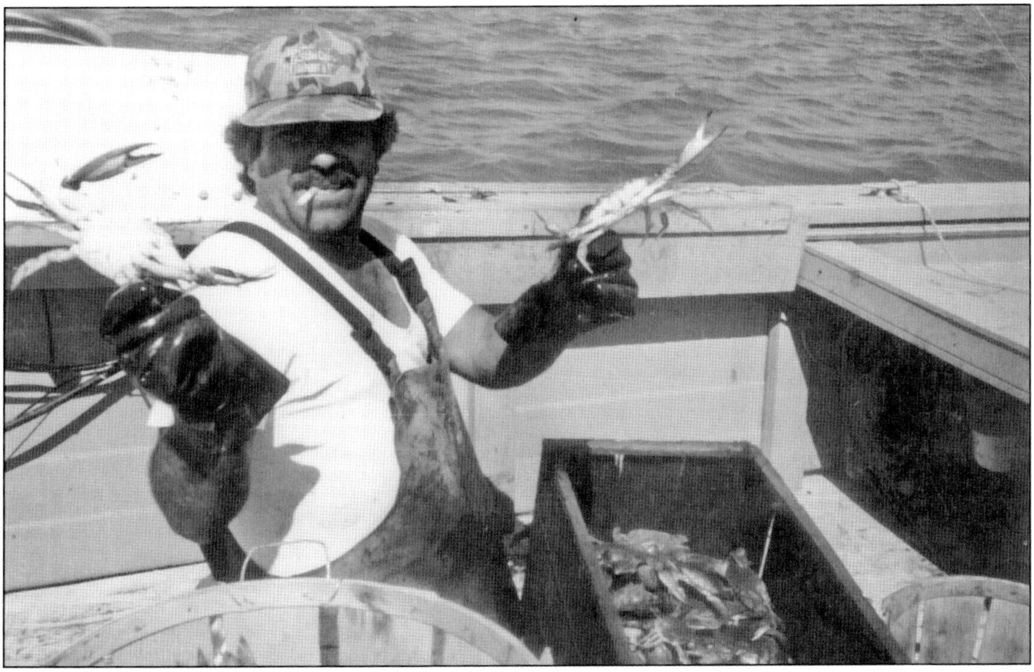

The late Raul Morales fled communist Cuba in 1967, arriving at Shem Creek in 1969. Finding work with local families shrimping and crabbing, he soon became a well-respected member of the creek. He acquired a small boat of his own, and fishing and crabbing for himself, eventually began his business, Raul's Seafood. Morales is celebrated as a skilled, hard-working businessman who cared deeply for wildlife. (Courtesy Kimberly Morales.)

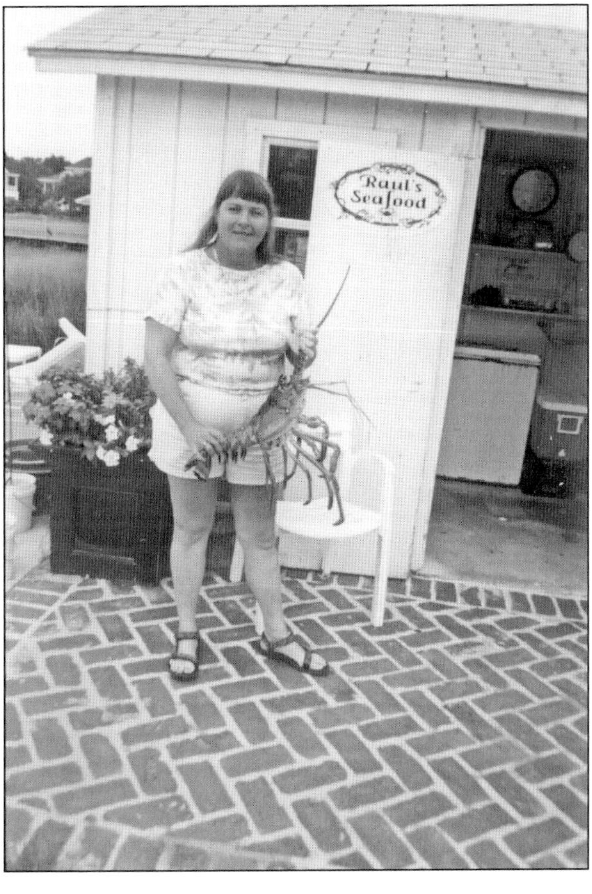

Kimberly Morales of Raul's Seafood continues to crab with the help of Capt. Bobby Carroll on the 24-foot *Miss Kimberly*, supplying fresh crab to local and Northern markets. Pictured outside Raul's Seafood, Morales holds a large spiny lobster. Open daily, the seafood market is located at the end of Magwood Lane and specializes in blue crab, fish, and shrimp. (Courtesy Kimberly Morales.)

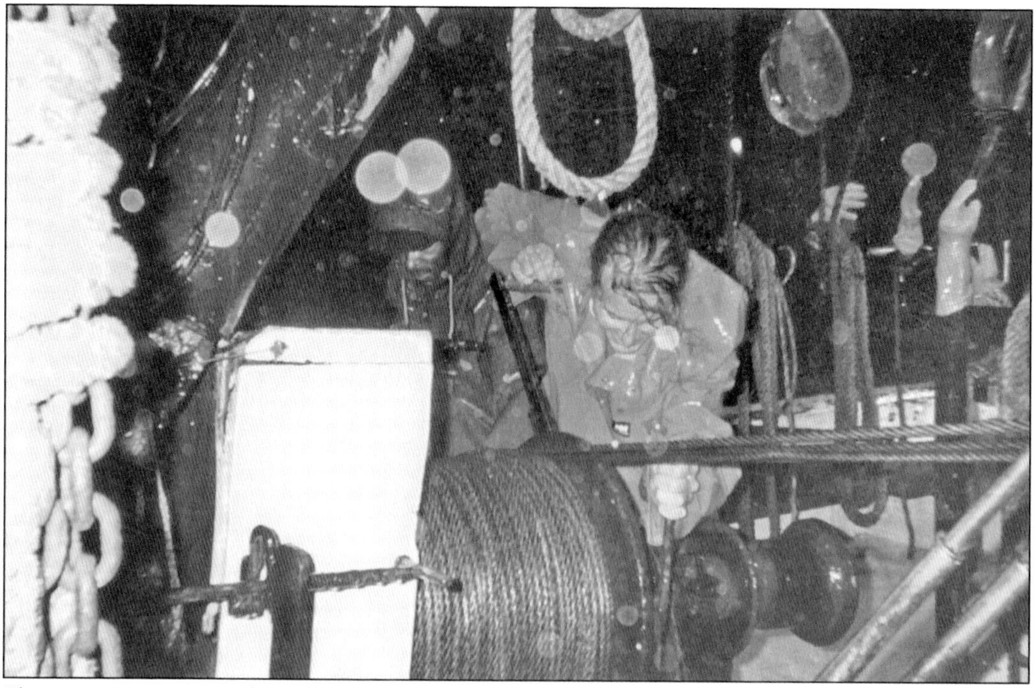

Shrimping is never without hazards. Capt. Lance Rector (pictured above) mans the winch on this stormy night. During rough seas or foul weather, a winch can be dangerous to handle, even for the most experienced crewmember. Dangling on the end of an outrigger 10 feet without a safety net, a striker (pictured below) has to retrieve the door line in order for a boat to bring up its nets. In this image, the skies are clear, and the water is relatively calm. On rough seas, crewmen are dipped into the ocean while holding onto the outriggers as boats rock. This necessary job is another hazard unique to the occupation of a commercial shrimper. (Courtesy Rector family.)

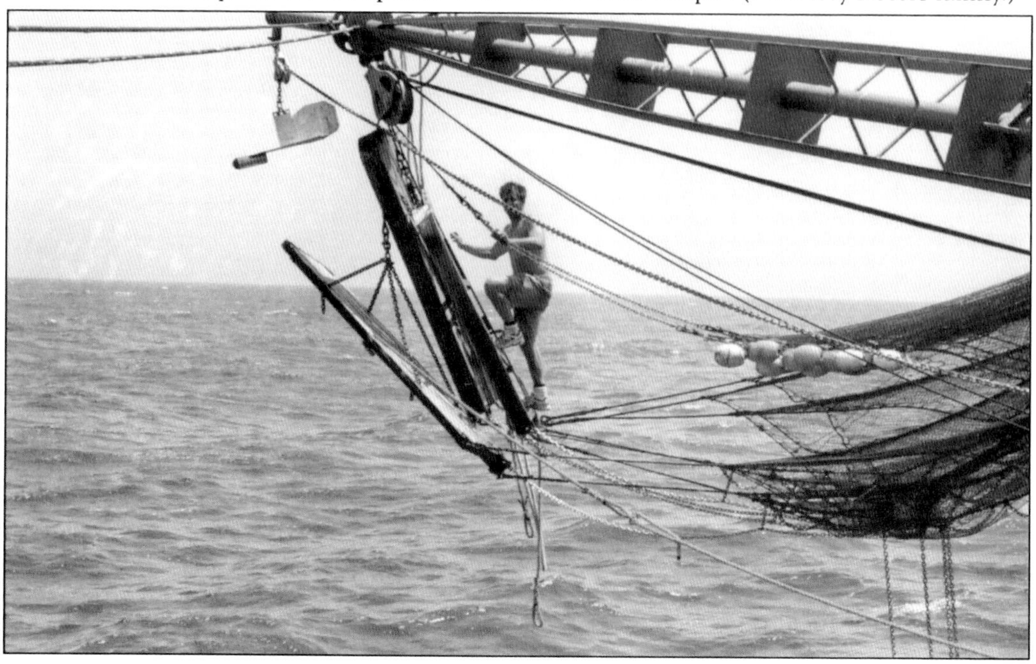

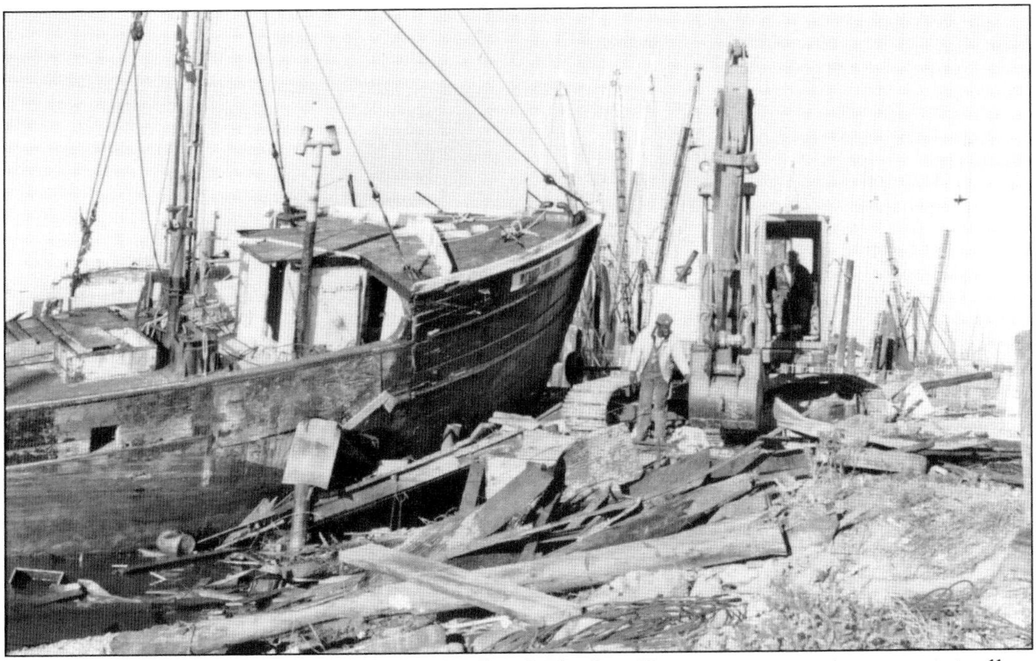

The building that The Wreck of the *Richard and Charlene* Restaurant occupies was originally a menhaden operation. It was home to many commercial seafood operations until being severely damaged during Hurricane Hugo ,when a shrimping vessel by that name was wrecked. The structure was restored, opened into a popular restaurant by Pat Scott, and named in honor of the wreck. The restaurant is so popular that it does not even have a sign. (Courtesy Fred Scott.)

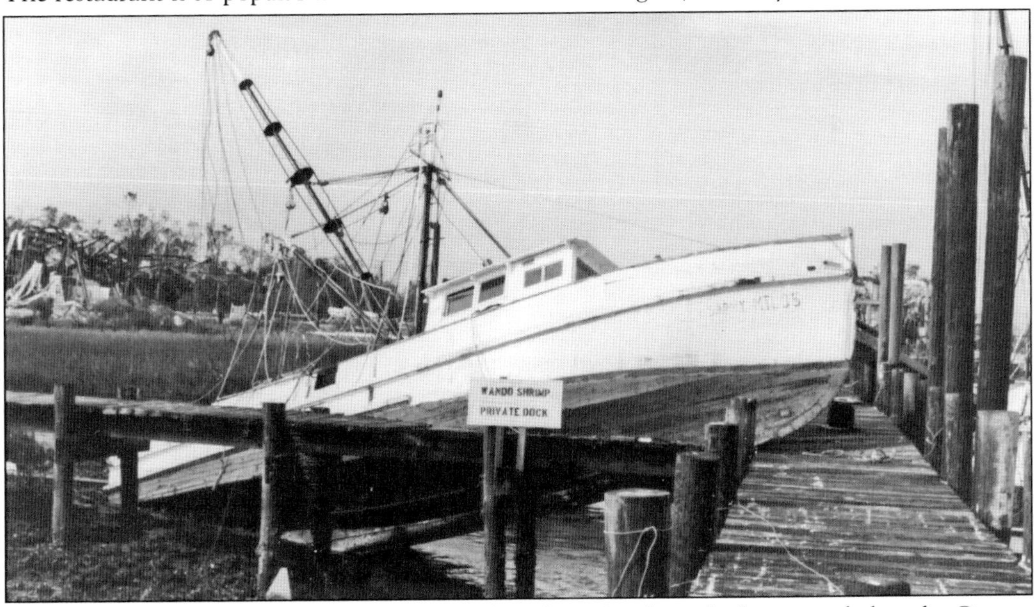

During Hurricane Hugo, a few boats remained at Shem Creek, and others traveled up the Cooper and Wando Rivers with their captains and crews aboard. The water and wind were so great that boats were floated above pilings, engines ran full-throttle into the wind, and people prayed not only for their boats to be spared, but also for their lives. The fleet lost eight vessels and two fishermen. Here the *MTL* lies across the Wando Shrimp Dock II. (Courtesy Rector family.)

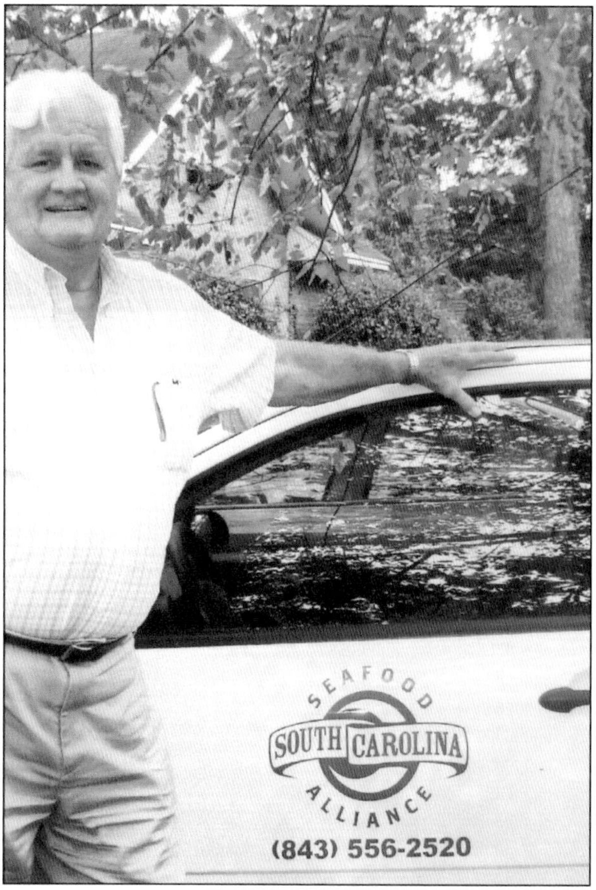

Capt. Frank Blum began fishing on the *Charleston Star* in the 1980s and has enjoyed a career long-lining and bottom fishing with electric bandit reels. He has fished the waters from Venice, Louisiana, to Wrightsville Beach, North Carolina, and owned and operated the Charleston Star Seafood Company on Shem Creek until the mid-1980s. Retired from the U.S. Air Force, Blum still owns and manages his vessel from the creek and is currently working with the South Carolina Seafood Alliance to help promote the industry and raise local awareness of the current issues the industry faces. Pictured below is the 55-foot *Charleston Star* and a visiting vessel, the *Can Do II*, dockside at Geechie Dock. A heavily regulated fishing industry is active in South Carolina, but fewer and fewer vessels exist as time progresses. (Courtesy Capt. Frank Blum.)

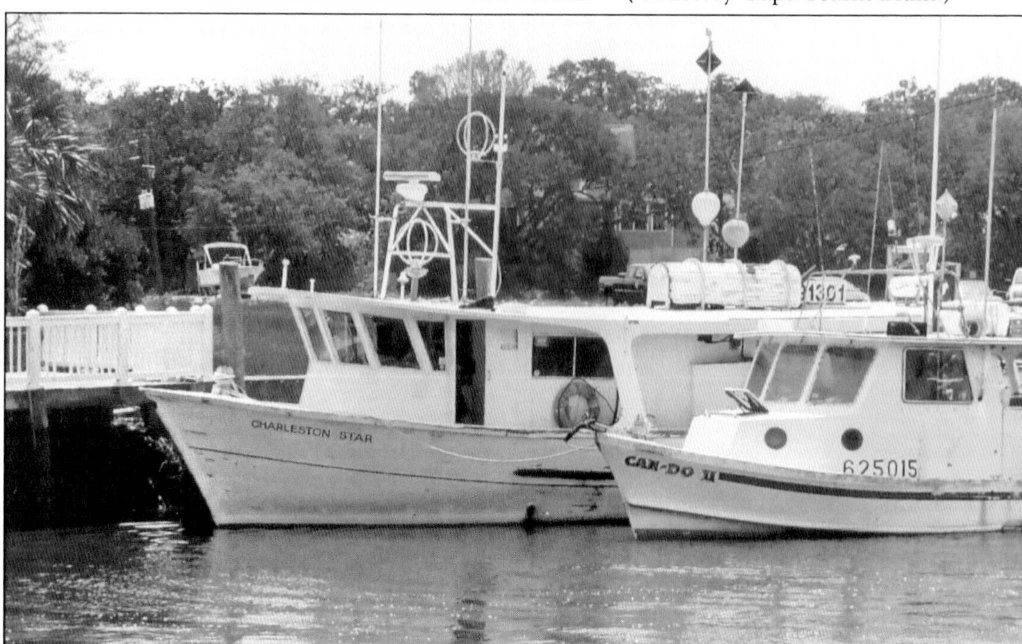

Six

EAST COOPER RECREATION

The East Cooper area remains the site of numerous water-based recreational activities, with hunting, fishing, sailing, swimming, boating, and diving all continuing to be attractions for both locals and visitors. On any given day, a variety of watercraft can be seen plying up and down the local waters, harkening back to the past and providing wholesome traditions for future generations. This coastal region also hosts many official recreational activities and events. Maritime traditions and relationships with the local waterways remain deeply rooted in East Cooper families. Whether it is a beloved, hand-made cast net passed down from an ancestor, a fishing pole given as a gift from parent to child, a seafood company still run by the family of the original founders, or even a favorite picnic spot on a local sea island, East Cooper residents cherish and appreciate their ability to maintain a connection to the water, if not in work, then definitely in play.

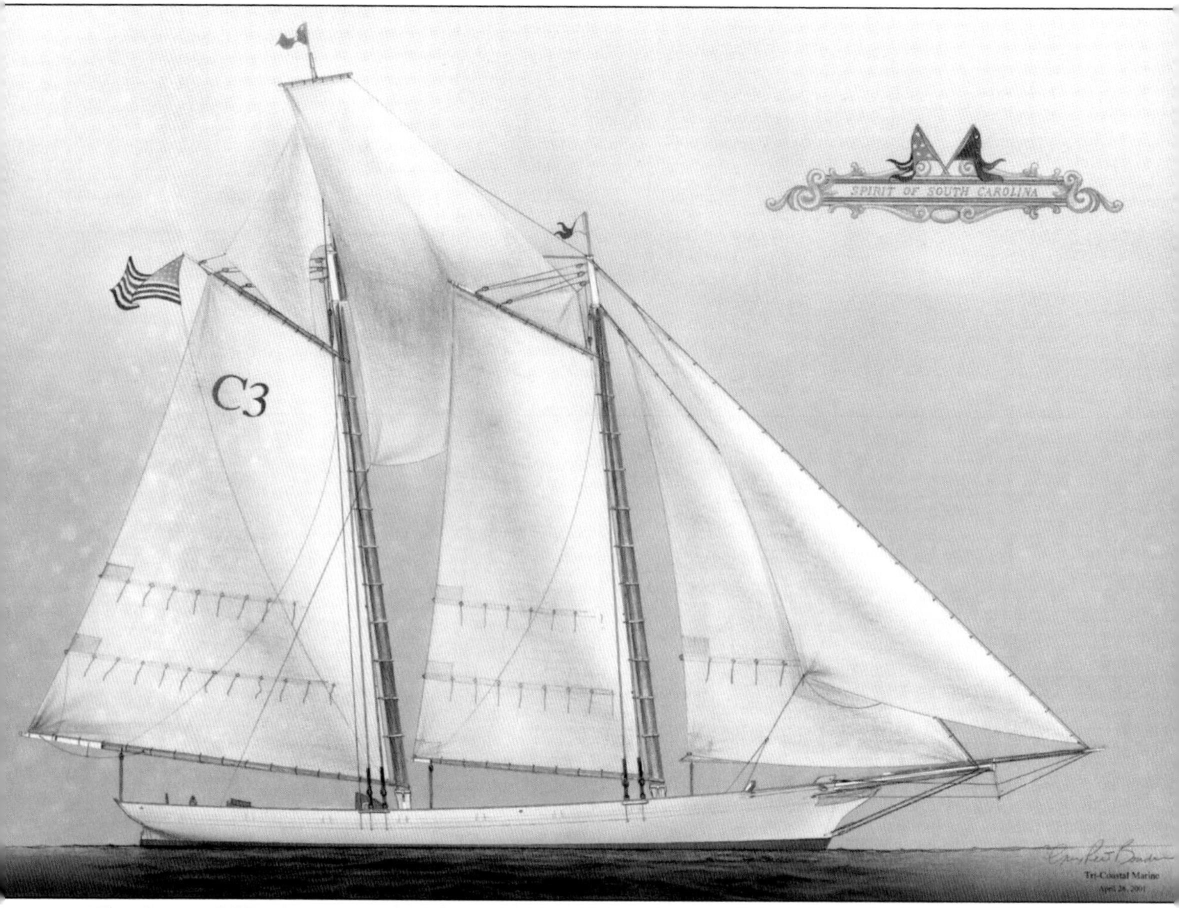

The *Spirit of Charleston* is a familiar sight to East Cooper residents. The incredible vessel, built on lines similar to those of a pilot schooner from the late 1800s, was constructed with the help of many volunteers and experts, including East Cooper native Mark Bayne. According to the South Carolina Maritime Heritage Foundation, there are three elements that the vessel is meant to represent and achieve: education, ambassador, and attraction. According to the organization, with regard to education, the tall ship provides sailing opportunities for young people to experience the sea. As an ambassador, she is a symbol that pays tribute to the resourcefulness and vibrancy of South Carolinians. As an attraction, she adds a nautical treasure to the state's already popular attractions while providing an enormous community resource to children and families of the state. (Courtesy South Carolina Maritime Heritage Foundation.)

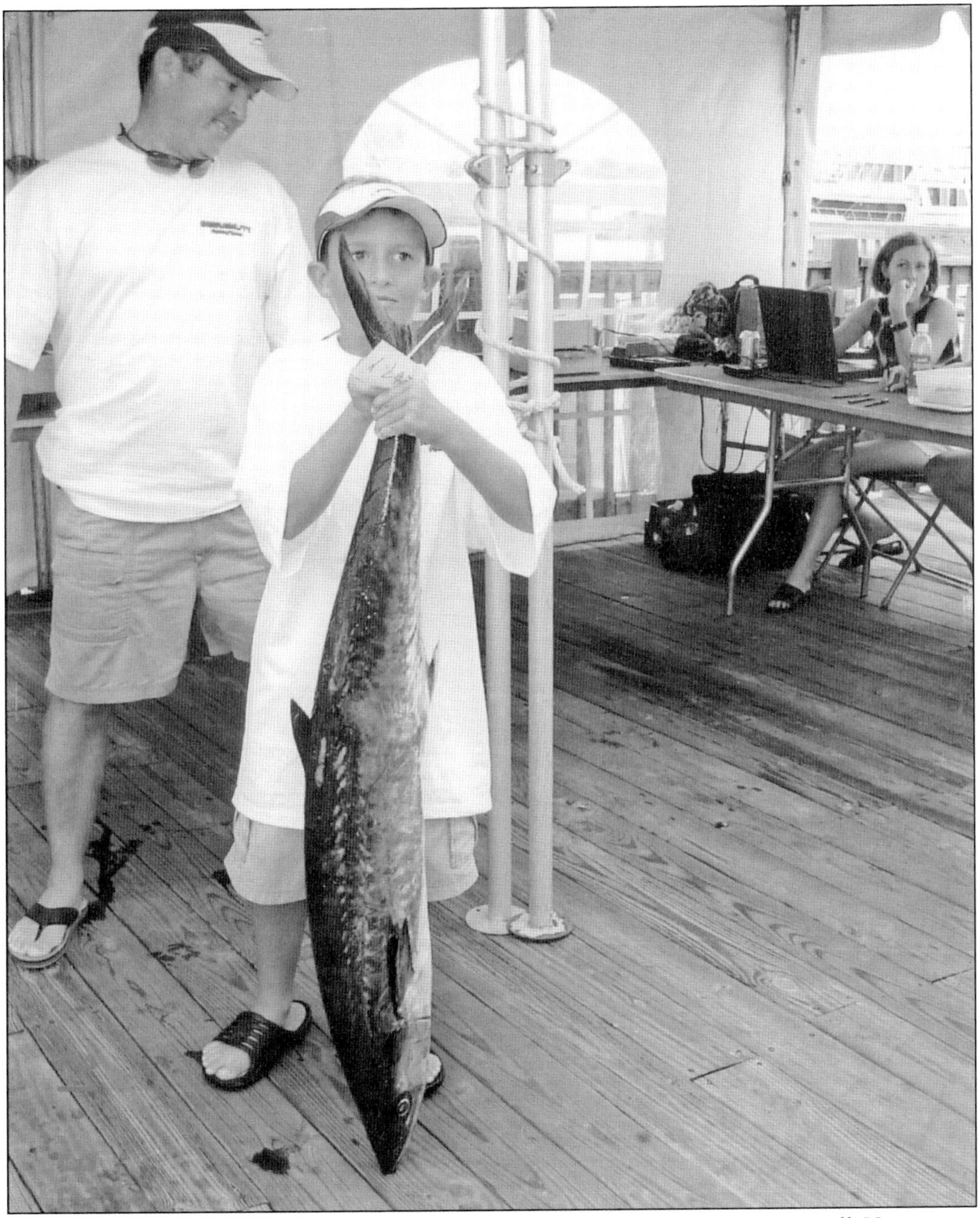

The East Cooper area plays host to many fishing tournaments, some large, some small. Here young Matthew Howard holds up his winning fish, a king mackerel almost as big as he is, that weighs in at more than 30 pounds. This catch was part of the Fishing for Miracles Tournament in 2004. Other area tournaments include the Patriots Point Kingfish Classic, the East Cooper Coastal Conservation Association (CCA) Fishing Tournament, the Working Man Bass Tournament, the East Cooper Anglers Classic, the Goldbug Island/East Cooper Outboard Motor Club Inshore Fishing Tournament, and the new East Cooper Fishing Club's Trout Tournament. The town of Mount Pleasant is actively encouraging more and larger fishing tournaments to consider the area as a venue. (Courtesy Matthew Howard.)

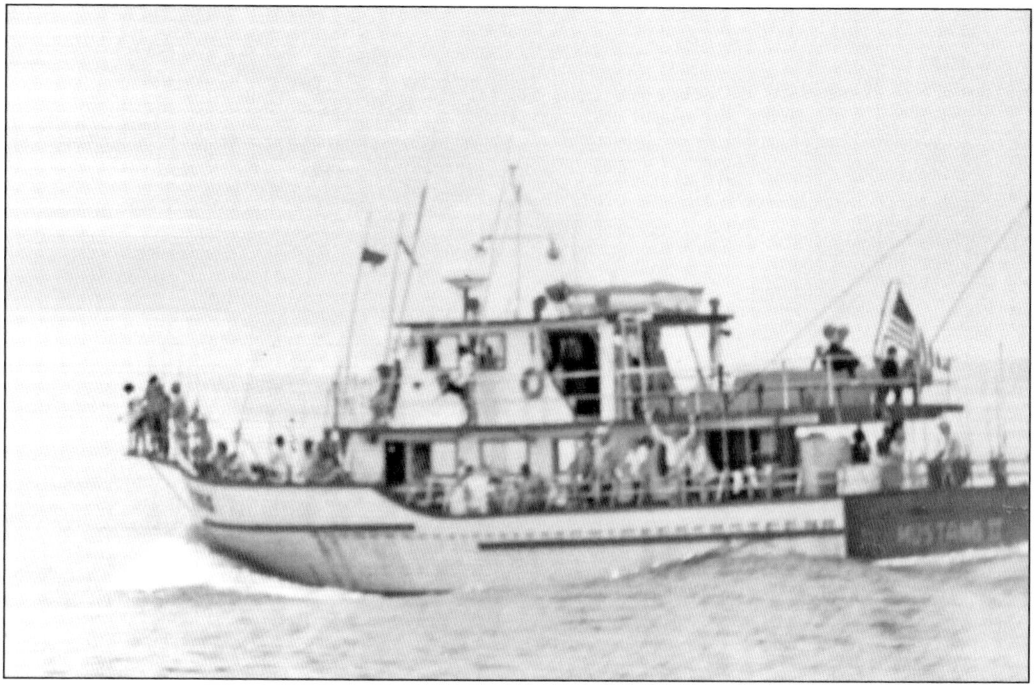

The *Mustang II* was a popular deep-sea fishing vessel. The boat left Shem Creek at what is now R.B.'s Restaurant and was boasted as being the only sonar scanner–equipped vessel in South Carolina. Day trips cost as much as $25 and included tackle, bait, and a fish bag during the 1970s. The brochure boasted that possible fish caught could include black sea bass, red and white snapper, and amberjack. (Above courtesy Capt. Barry Wilson; below courtesy Capt. Robert Santos.)

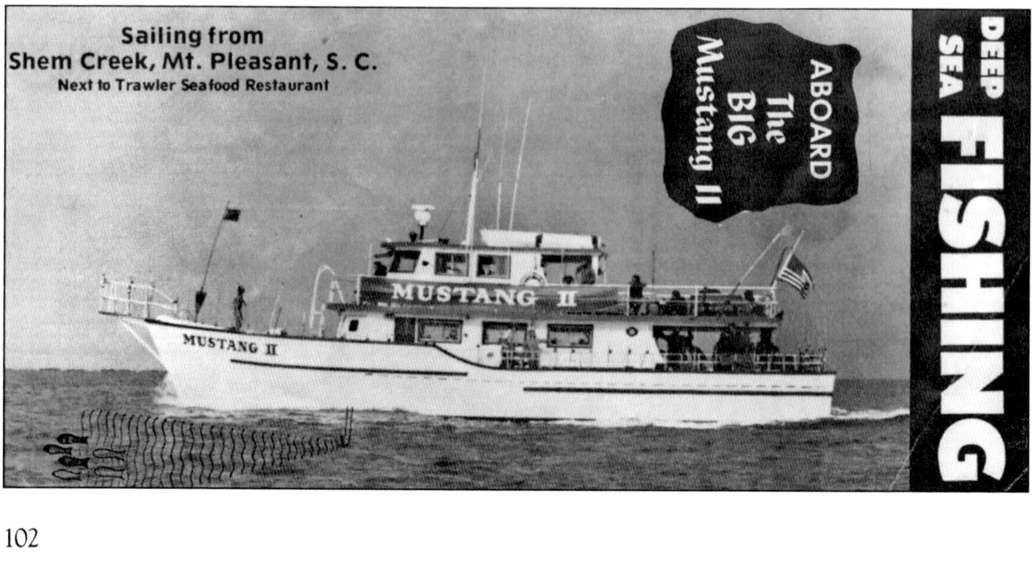

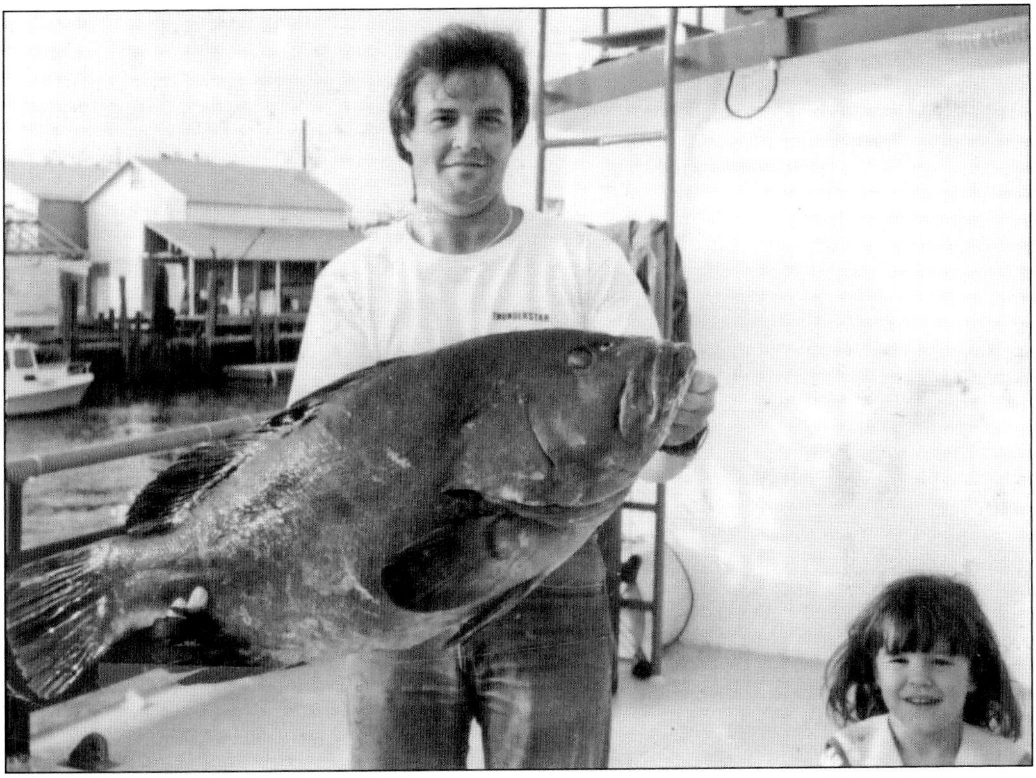

Capt. Stuart Reeves of Atlantic Offshore is a second-generation fisherman and a 25-year veteran of the charter fishing–boat business, providing countless fishing excursions to the Gulf Stream. His company offers full-day trips and has been operating for more than 25 years. In 1988, Reeves poses with his daughter Amber while holding a warsaw grouper caught aboard the *Thunderstar*. The *Thunderstar* is pictured below in 1989. (Courtesy Capt. Stuart Reeves.)

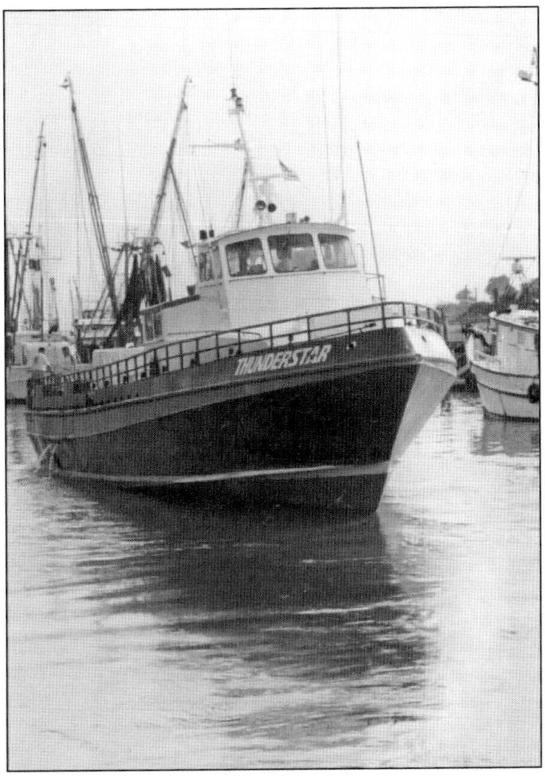

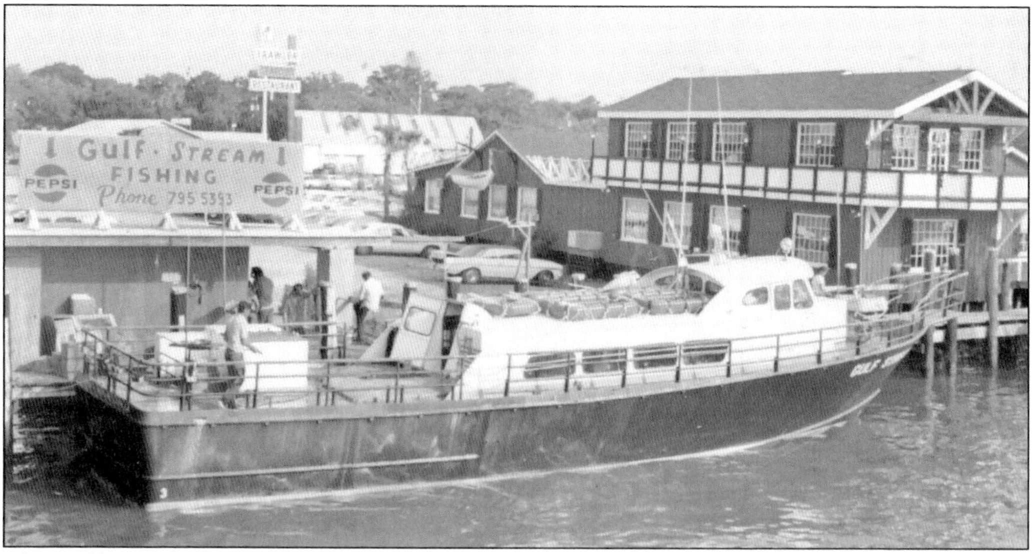

The *Gulf Stream II* is pictured above in front of the original Trawler Restaurant. Capt. Randolph Scott, pictured below, left the *Gulf Stream II* in 1984 and purchased his own vessel, the *Carolina Clipper*. As soon as possible, he moved the *Carolina Clipper* to Shem Creek, where he remained until his death in 1998. Captain Scott's widow, Alice, recalls the time a king mackerel jumped out of the water onto the deck of his vessel; the captain thereafter boasted that he was such a good fisherman that the fish decided to give up and now just jumped right into the ice boxes on board. (Both images courtesy Alice Scott.)

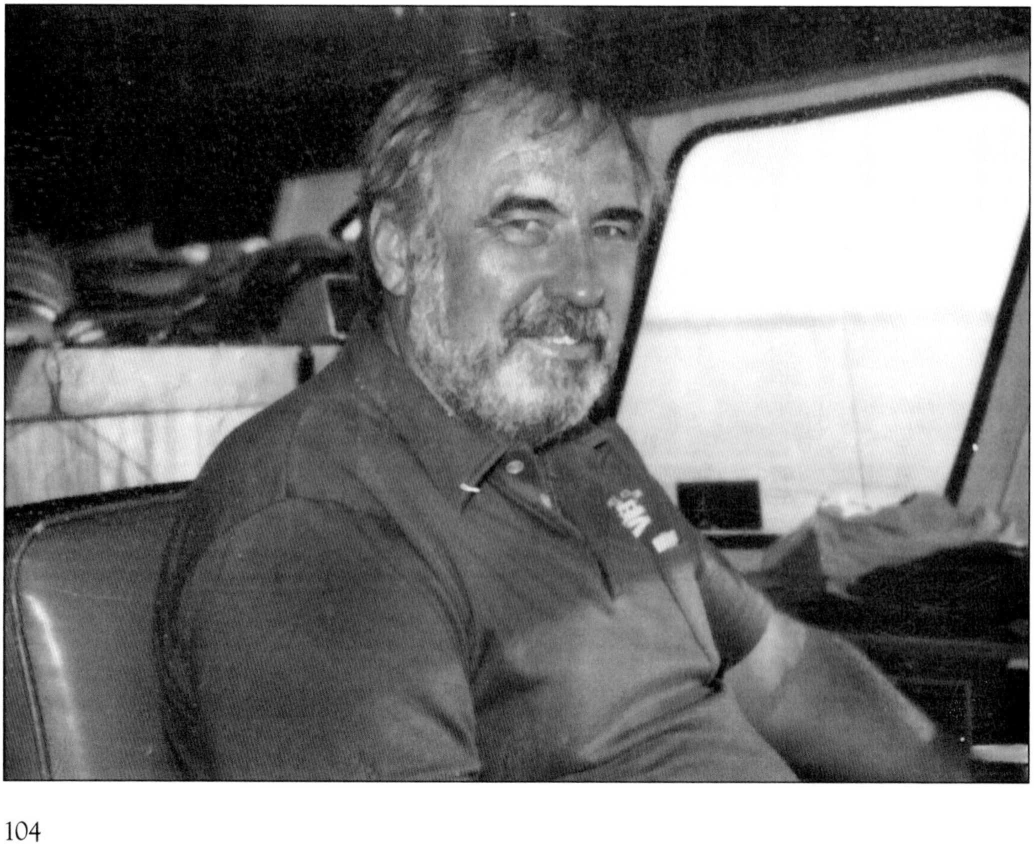

Seven

Modern Boatbuilding in East Cooper

The art of building boats has never left the East Cooper region. Local entrepreneurs are keeping the tradition alive and passing a valuable heritage onto future generations by commissioning local builders to craft needed vessels that continue to connect the community to the local waters. From small craft, to state-of-the-art research vessels, to ships sailing straight out of history into our modern waters, the East Cooper boatbuilding heritage continues. Like most seaboard communities, East Cooper has an unbroken tradition of boatbuilding and repair that has often been passed down through familial and community connections. While methods and materials often change, the passion and integrity of the art of crafting vessels remains the same. The eventual owners of these locally crafted vessels then became caretakers of yet another part of East Cooper's rich local tradition. The vessels themselves become the means of strengthening family and community ties, as friends and loved ones spend time together on maritime adventures.

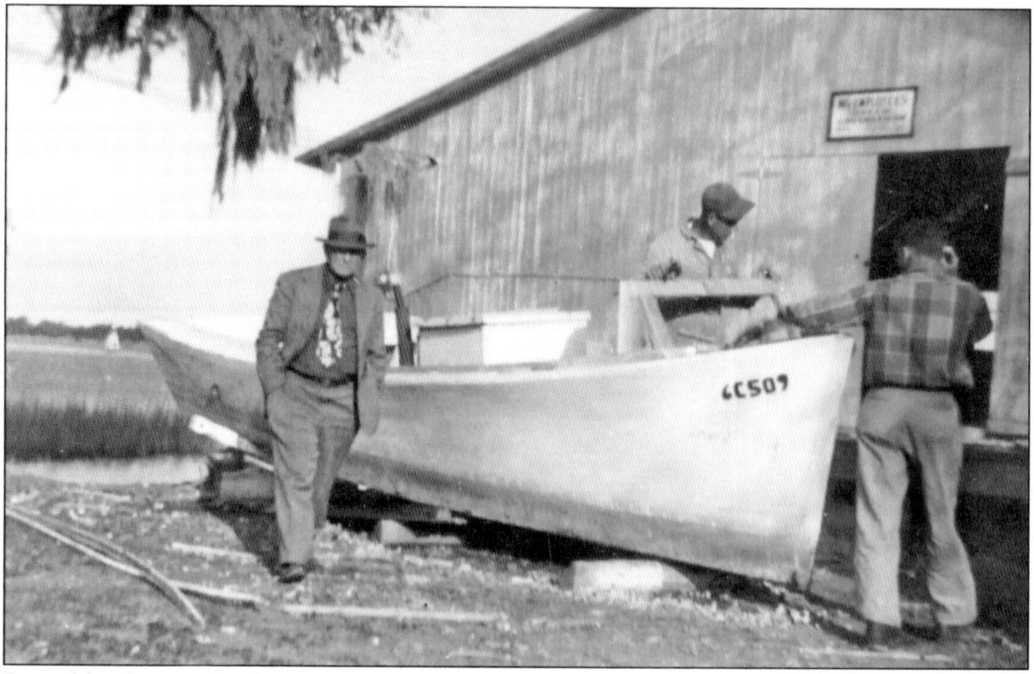

Boats like the *Speed Ball*, seen here in 1955 being outfitted at the Awendaw Shrimp Company, were used to drag in creeks and bays such as Bull's Bay, pulling nets approximately 35 feet in length. (Courtesy Capt. Barry Wilson.)

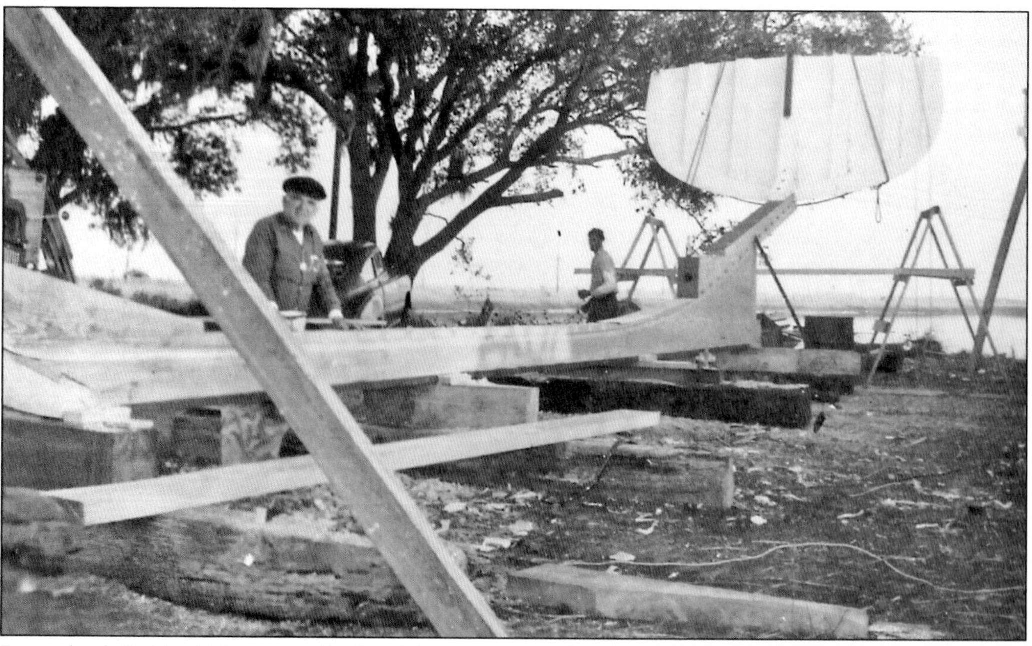

Boats built behind Simmons Seafood (near present-day Simmons Point) were built on a sandy beach and rolled into the creek on top of logs. On this site, master boatbuilder George H. Koutelas and his father oversaw and helped construct the *Little Lady*, the *Captain Fran*, and the *Norma K*. Here Koutelas's father poses beside the keel of the *Little Lady*, commissioned by Capt. Wally Shaffer. (Courtesy Phyllis Shaffer.)

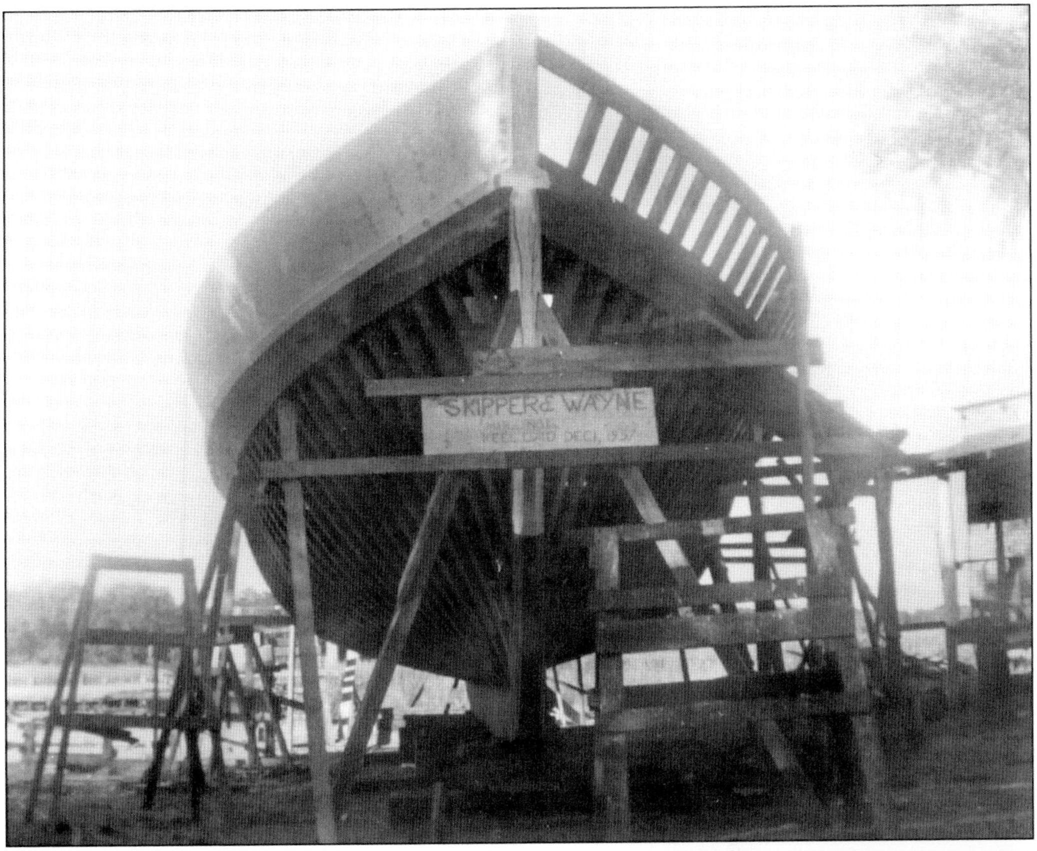

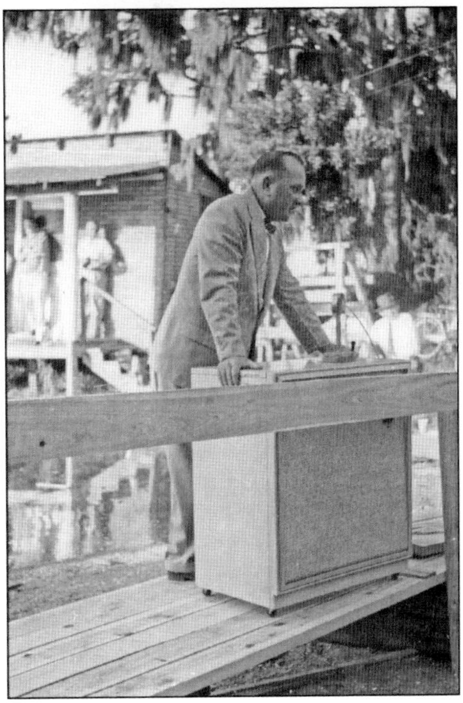

This image of the *Skipper and Wayne* shows the vessel being constructed on the banks of Shem Creek near present-day 5th Season. Andrew Magwood recalls helping his brother, Capt. C. A. Magwood Jr., build the vessel under the direction of boatbuilder George H. Koutelas. To shape the curved boards for the ribs of the vessel, the boards were placed in a tube, boiled, and then hammered into place, shaping the hull while still hot and steaming. A ceremony was held in June 1958 for the launching; the boat had difficulties sliding off the rail, and knowing the vessel had to clear the Shem Creek Bridge, Captain Magwood filled the bilge with seawater and partially sank her. The boat passed safely under the bridge, completing the ceremonial day. The engine, mast, and rigs were placed on the vessel later. (Both images courtesy Capt. Andrew Magwood.)

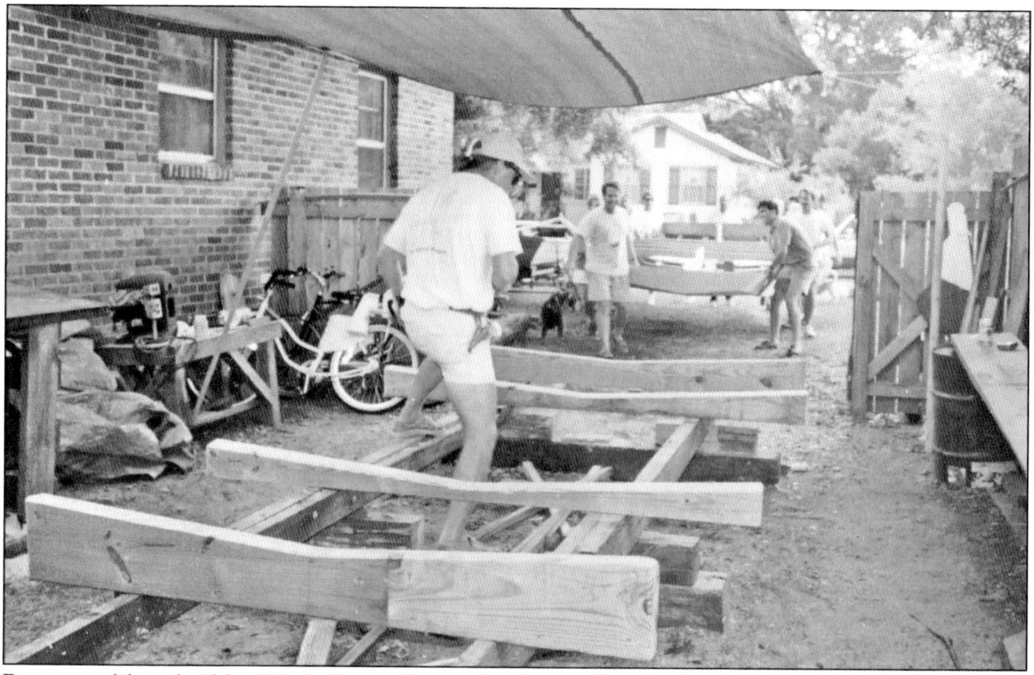

Renowned boatbuilder Mark Bayne began his love affair with custom-made wooden vessels more than 20 years ago after studying the craft in North Carolina. Coming back to the East Cooper area, Bayne decided to take a chance on making a living building custom wooden boats. Fortunately, he was in the perfect environment to undertake such an enterprise because old Mount Pleasant neighborhoods, such as the one he and his family lived in, were extremely accommodating toward those seeking to run businesses from home—even if it meant building boats in your own backyard. Here Bayne starts small, working under a tarp just off his house. Historically, East Cooper neighbors have always been helpful to those needing a hand or, in this case, a flip. Hence his favorite old-time tradition was born: a hull-turning party with friends and neighbors. (Both images courtesy Bayne family.)

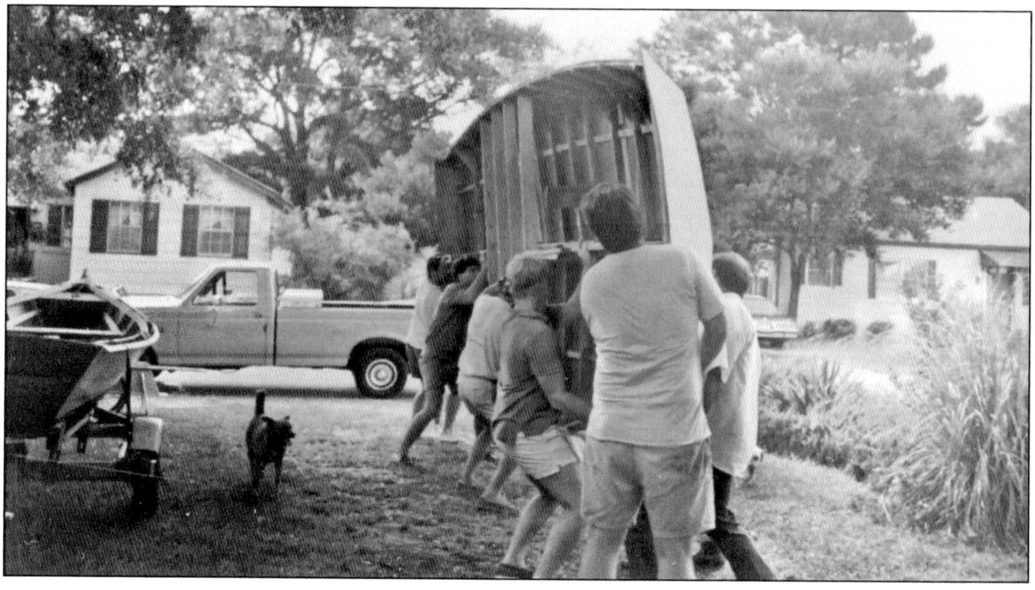

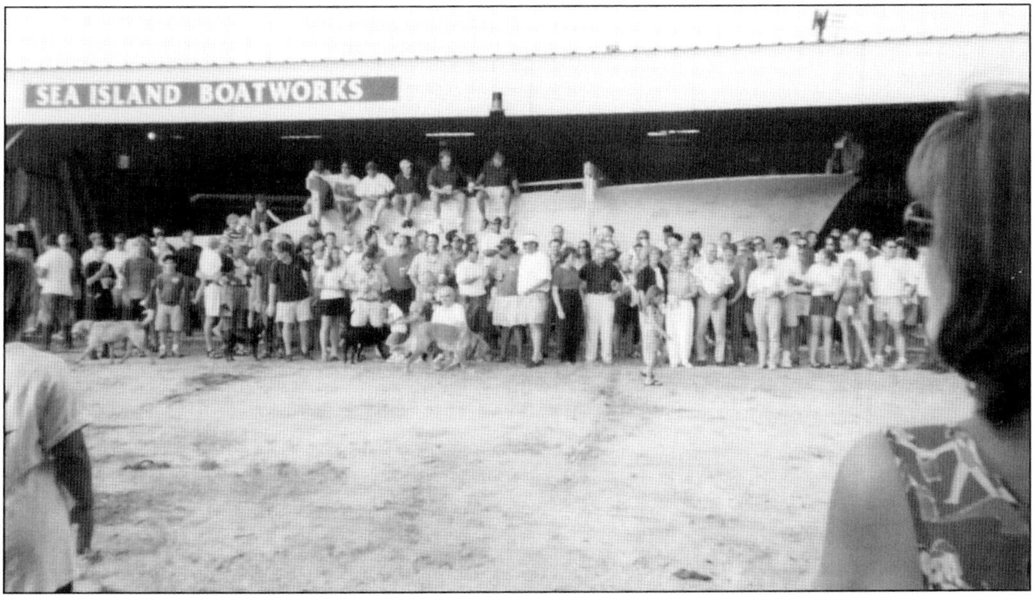

Mark Bayne's dream became a reality, and his company, Sea Island Boat Builders (formerly Boat Works) has been growing yearly, enabling him and his crews to craft hundreds of custom boats. Like many other boat builders in the East Cooper area, Bayne utilizes Shem Creek, having a facility there for putting boats in. Here is another hull-turning party, this one on a grander scale and on Shem Creek, reminding him of how far his little backyard company had come. He still loves the old neighborhood, though, and now builds boats on the corner of Pherigo and King Streets, often inviting neighbors in whenever a hull needs turning. Bayne has been involved with many intriguing projects, including the construction of the *Spirit of South Carolina*, a vessel reminiscent of a late-1800s-era pilot schooner. (Both images courtesy Bayne family.)

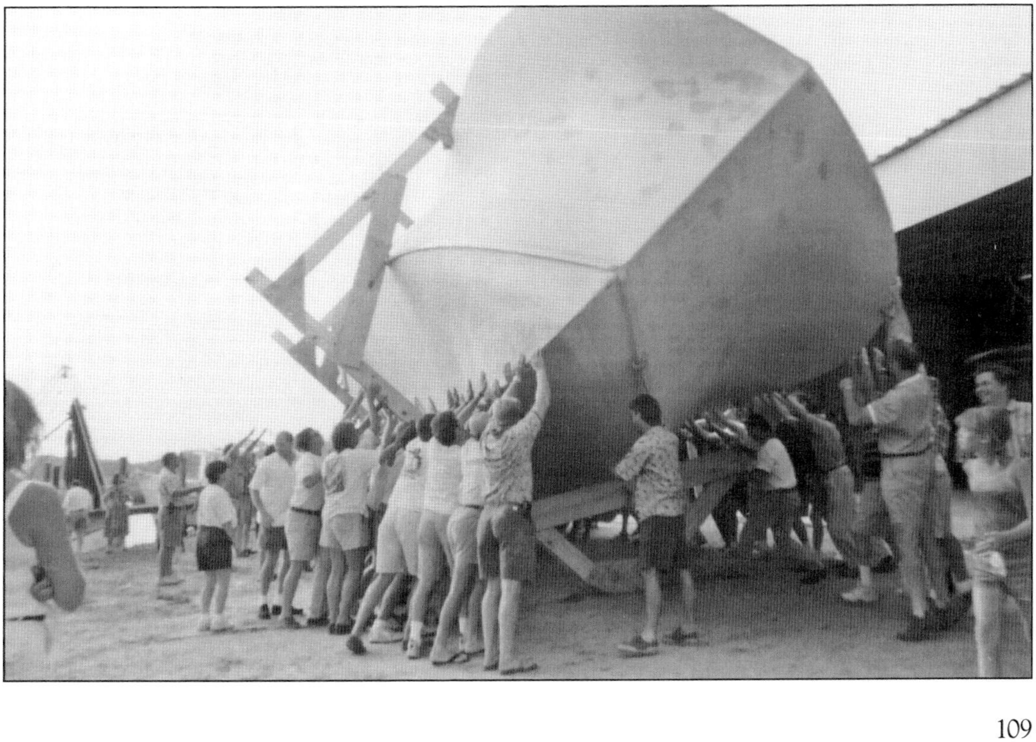

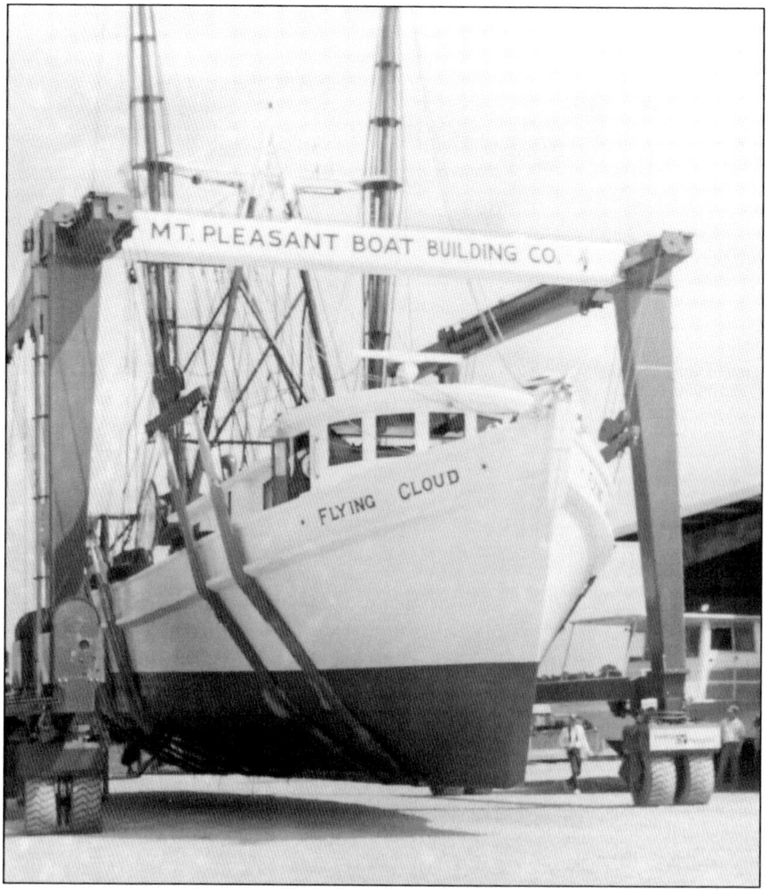

Another company associated with boatbuilding and repair was the Mount Pleasant Boat Building Company, pictured at left, with the *Flying Cloud* in her straps. Pictured below, former Mount Pleasant mayor Groggy Darby and his wife, Sara Jean, attend one of Mark's hull-turning parties. Darby owned Mount Pleasant Boat Building, which was located where the Boatyard Subdivision on Shem Creek is today. (Left image courtesy Capt. Barry Wilson.)

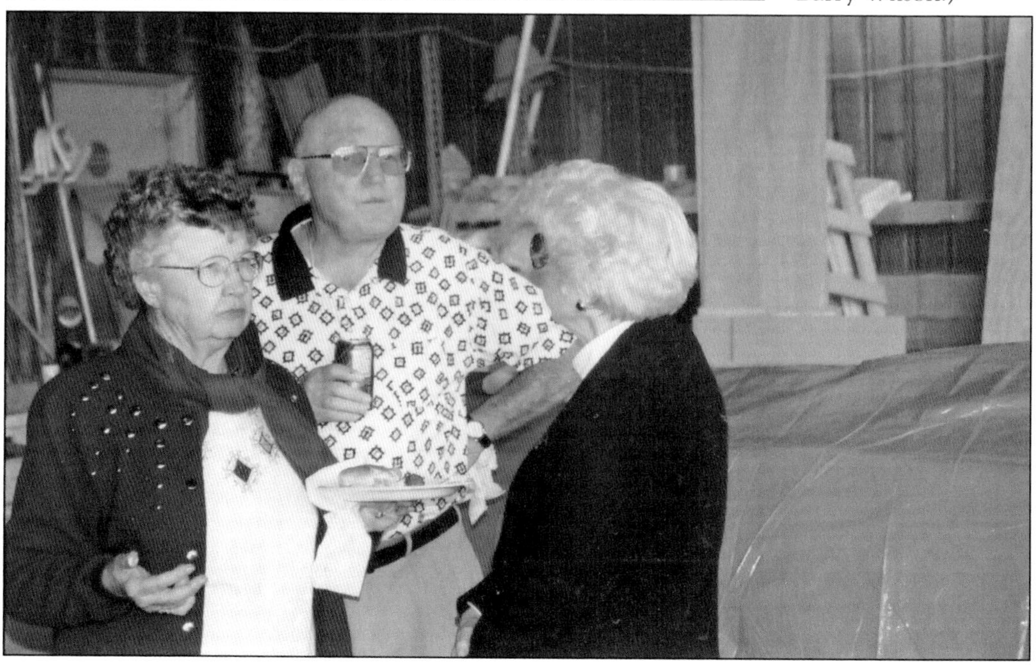

Eight

What Lies Beneath

What emerges from beneath East Cooper's murky waters can tell stories of the local history just as astutely as what lines the shores or skims the waterways. Salvagers, dredgers, divers, and even ordinary fishermen often uncover incredible clues to the past and provide valuable services to those wishing to traverse the waters now. From the earliest days, local residents have cleared sunken wrecks, salvaged valuable materials from submerged or sinking vessels, and explored nearby underwater sites for everything from artifacts to animals. As always, the water tells the tale of the local maritime heritage. With the continued commitment of SCDNR to creating an underwater habitat through their artificial reef program, the local waters enable sport fishers and divers to enjoy a live bottom environment, meaning areas filled with a myriad of living organisms that attract fish and other marine life, despite the fact that only about 5–10 percent of the local bottom has the appropriate geological conditions necessary for a reef community without the help of wrecks and other structures put carefully in place. Other companies, like Eternal Reefs, ensure that both the legacies of artificial reefs and those who loved the sea continue in this area, whereas local diving organizations and charter services always endeavor to promote and protect the regional underwater environment, enabling locals and visitors alike to visit the watery realm that lies beneath East Cooper rivers and the sea.

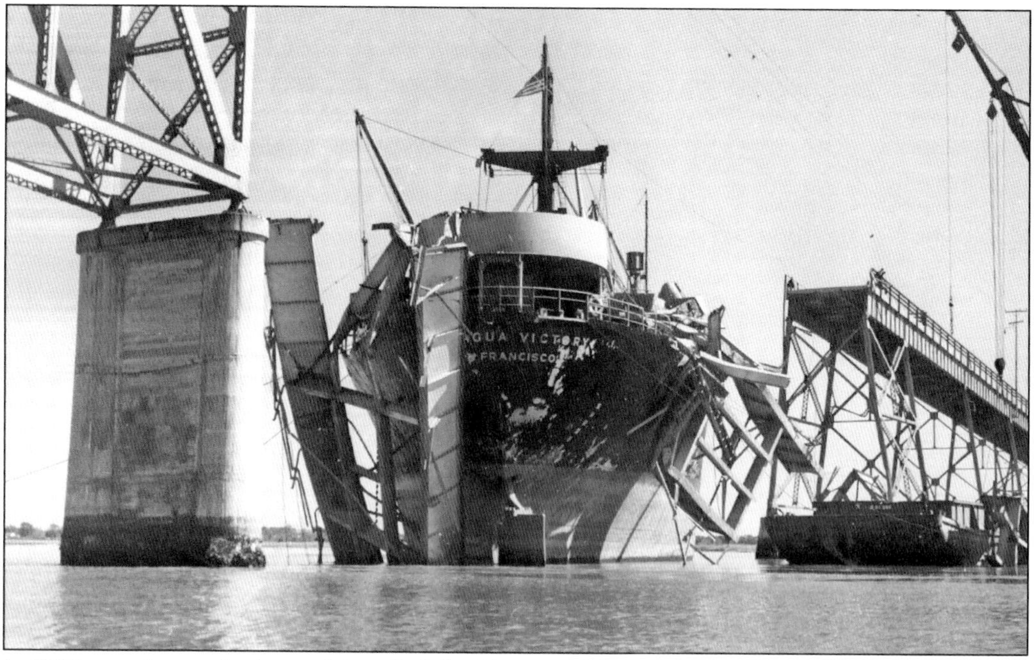

In 1947, tragedy struck when a ship called the *Nicaragua Victory* slammed into the Grace Memorial Bridge, causing the deaths of an entire family when their car plunged off the collapsing structure into the Cooper River. The ship was a 10,000-ton freighter and adrift. When the captain ordered the boatswain to take out the slack in the anchors' chains, he pulled up the anchors instead. The engines were not working, and the ship drifted right into the roadbed of the bridge. Marine contractor Salmons Dredging Corps was on the scene quickly and recovered the wreck of the car and its unfortunate passengers. Pictured above is a startling view of the ship and mangled pieces of the bridge. The always-dapper Salmon (below) supervises the removal of the car from the riverbed. (Both photographs by Ronald Allen Reilly; courtesy Richard Salmons, Salmons Dredging Corps.)

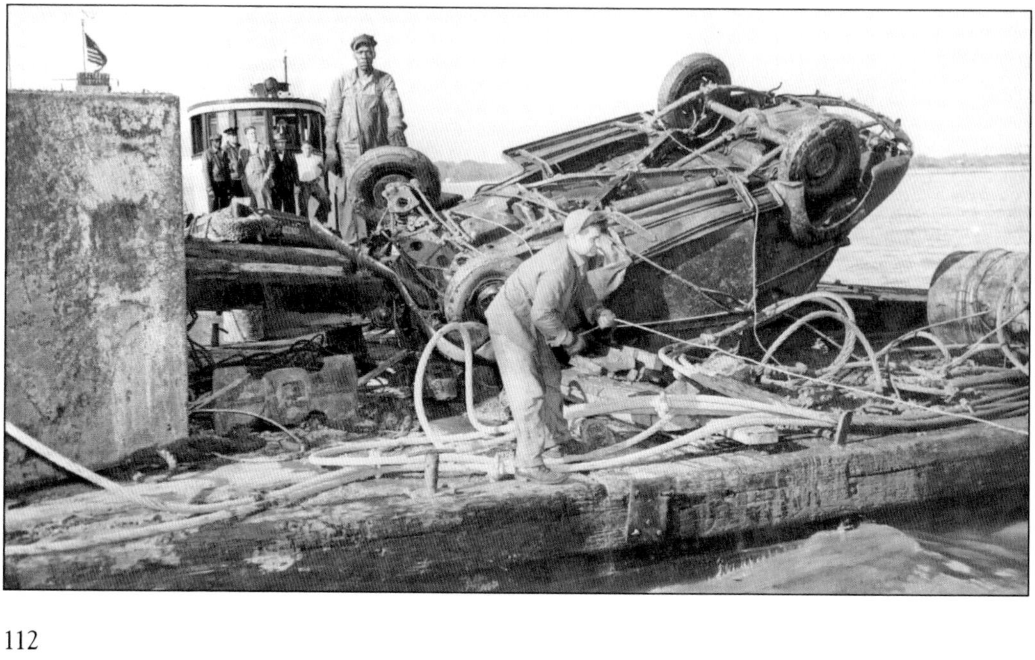

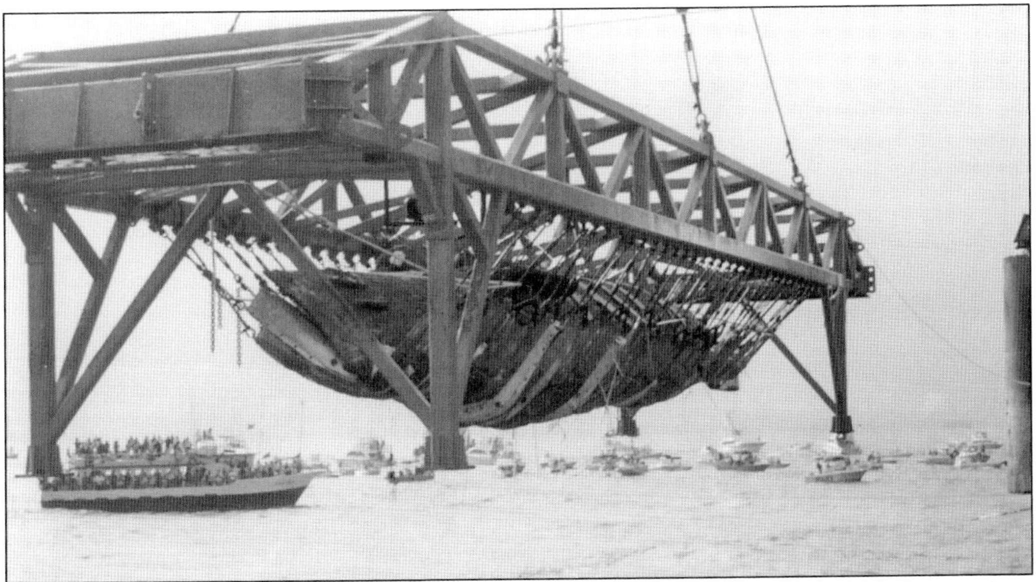

There are other underwater services provided by highly skilled divers and other maritime workers that are also invaluable. Seeking, finding, and recovering valuable pieces of local history is no easy task, and it is underwater experts like state archeologists, freelance researchers, underwater surveyors, and expert recovery teams who help learn more about the past. Pictured above is South Carolina's most famous underwater artifact, the Confederate submarine *H. L. Hunley*, which was launched, made history, sank, and was recovered all in local waters. The recovery effort was completed by a team of such experts, including Isle of Palms native and renowned diver and underwater surveyor Ralph Wilbanks, pictured below. Besides the experts, a wide variety of specialized maritime equipment and those who knew how to use it was necessary for the recovery. (Both images courtesy Ralph Wilbanks.)

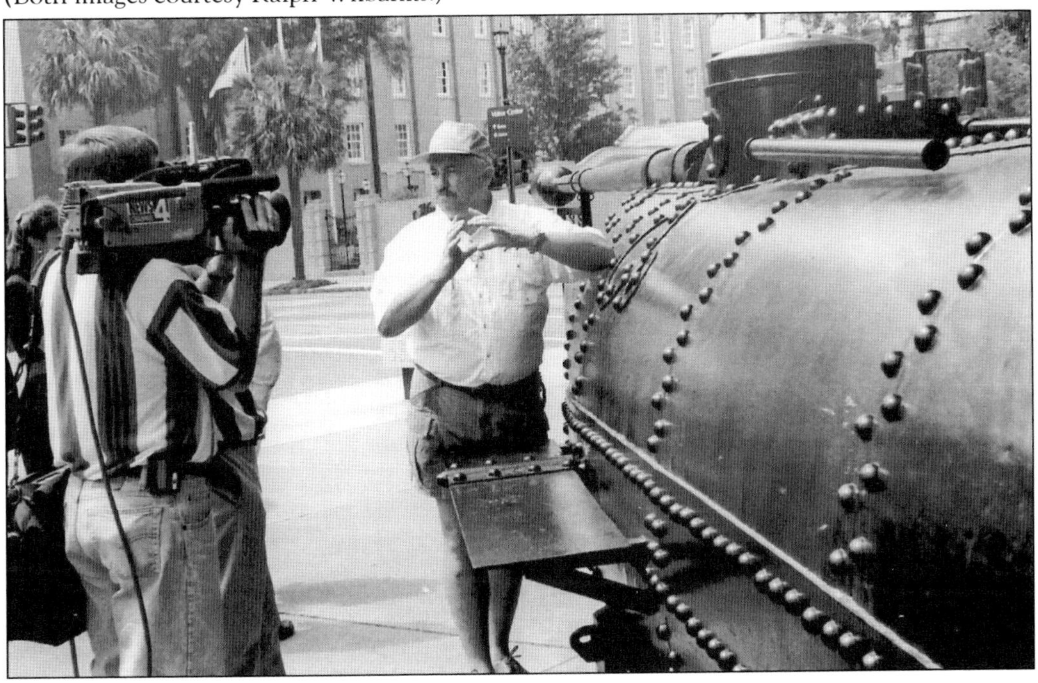

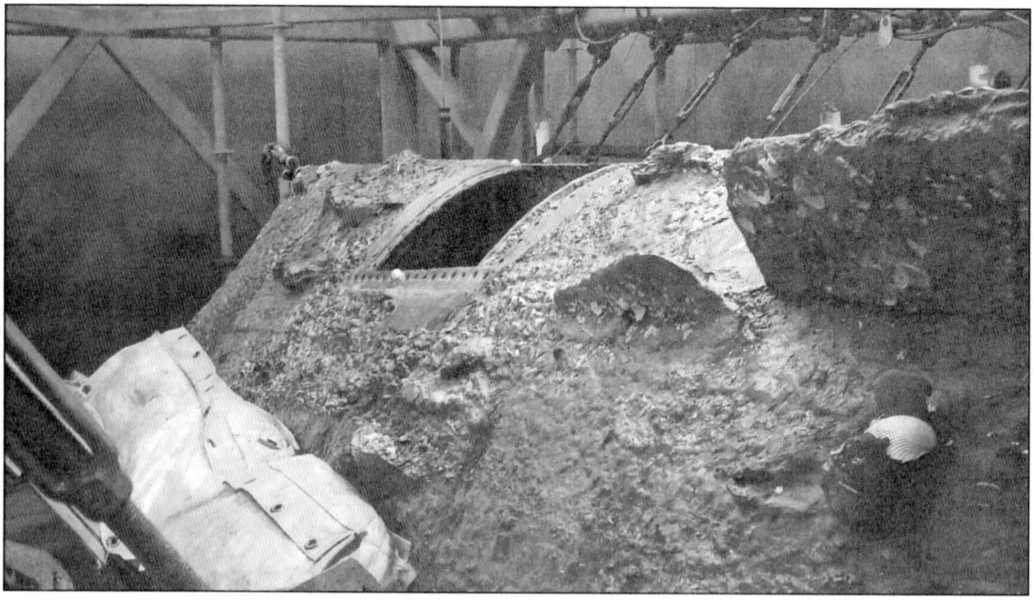

Suction piles were placed on the ocean floor and used as an extremely stable base for the large, elaborate truss that needed to be placed protectively over the wreck of the *H. L. Hunley*. Specialized straps, which could be pumped full of foam, had to be painstakingly placed beneath the entire vessel in order to lift and move it without jarring or damaging it in any way. A marine crane had to then lift the entire truss with the precious cargo strapped beneath onto a barge, which then transported the submarine to its new home on the old U.S. Navy base. It took teams of people to assist in the recovery and transport, and the combined maritime skill and knowledge associated with this project is astounding. Here the surface and interior of the *Hunley* are finally visible. (Both images courtesy Ralph Wilbanks.)

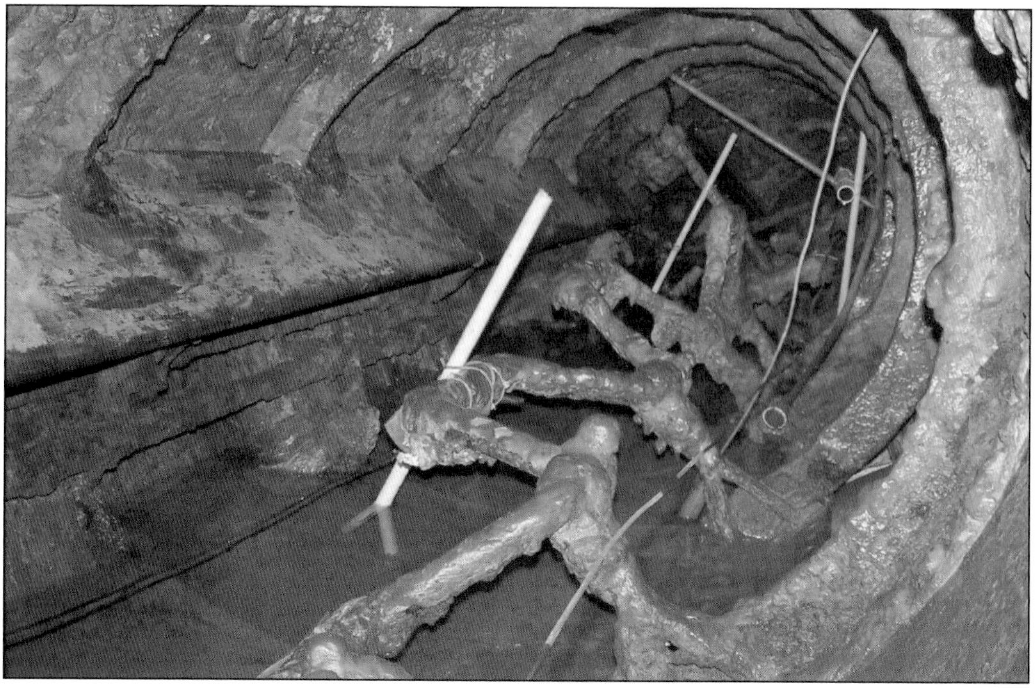

Not all artifacts are as important as the *H. L. Hunley*, but to the finders of historic maritime articles such as these anchors, the discovery can be just as thrilling—and pose some tricky recovery problems, as well. According to the caption on the back of the 1950 photograph at right, this enormous anchor was from a Revolutionary War–era British warship. It seems Walter G. Toler caught it in his shrimp net, and "it took three boats to pull it to the surface and get it to the dock." At right, his son, Walter D. Toler, poses next to the anchor. It is frequently shrimpers and other fishermen who discover sunken artifacts, which is hardly surprising considering their nets, the duration they spend in the water, and their thorough knowledge of the local waters. Pictured below is another anchor, this one from the early 1900s that, according to the caption, was found "south of channel" in 1985. (Right courtesy Toler family; below courtesy Magwood family.)

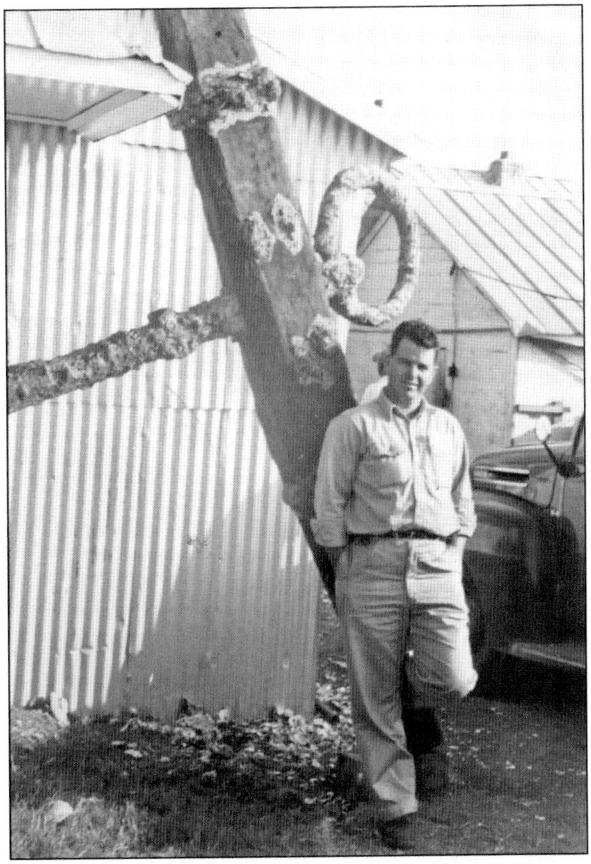

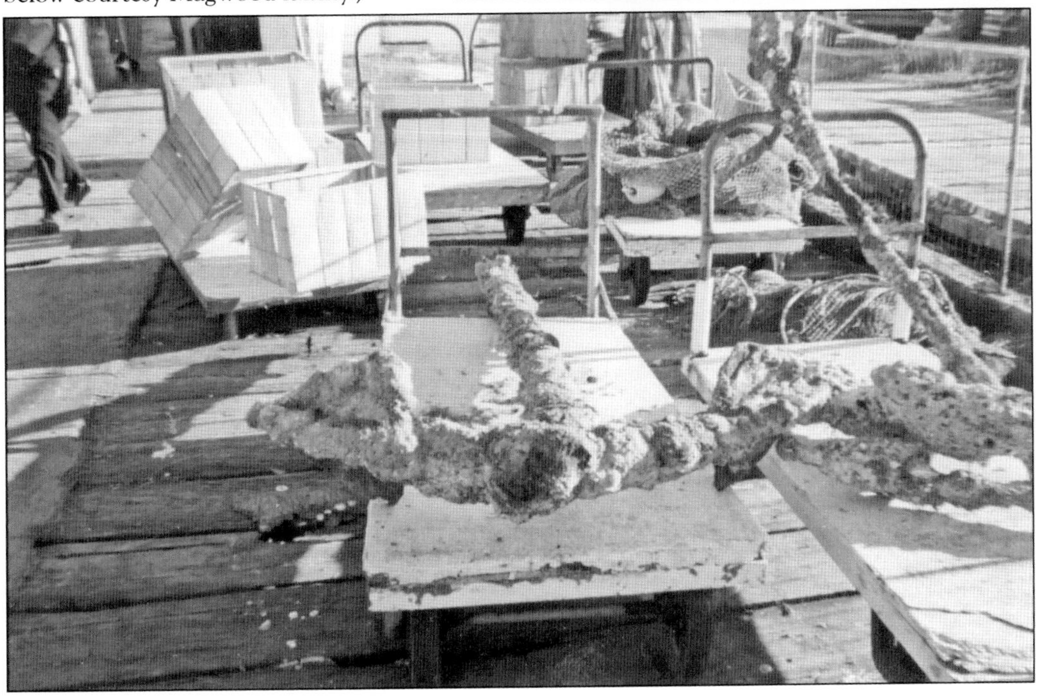

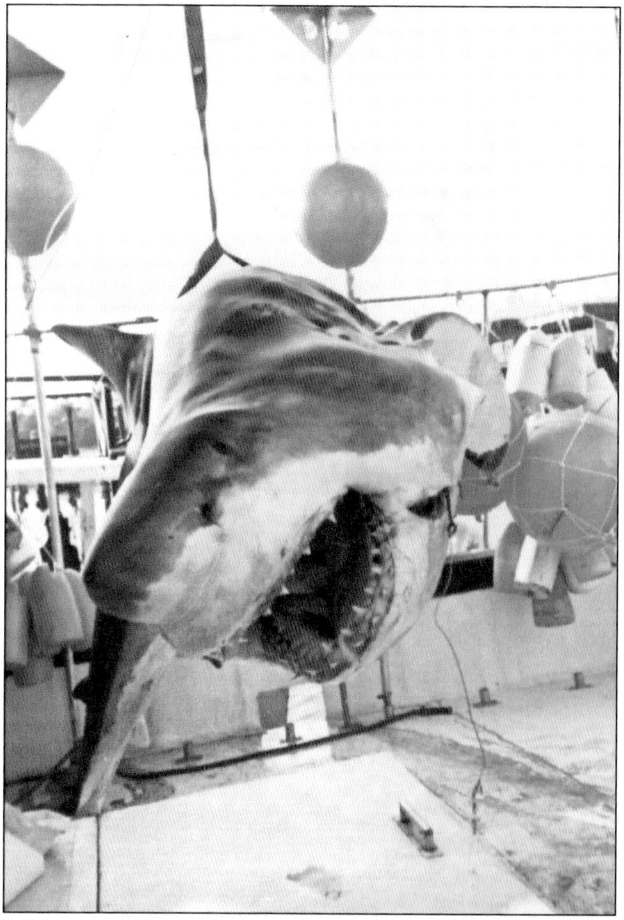

Some underwater finds are downright scary! Capt. Harold Olsen of the *Bonsai* caught this 1,236-pound great white shark while shark fishing off Bull's Bay. It was the biggest great white shark ever caught off the coast of South Carolina. (Courtesy Capt. Harold Olsen.)

Some beasts are more charming, as the Shem Creek shrimpers can attest, being well acquainted with the manatee that likes to swim up to a hose, seeking fresh water. There is less of an awareness of manatees in South Carolina, even though they do exist in good numbers. Some theorize that is because the water in South Carolina is so murky, meaning the manatees are seldom seen; out of sight, out of mind. (Courtesy Karen Brown.)

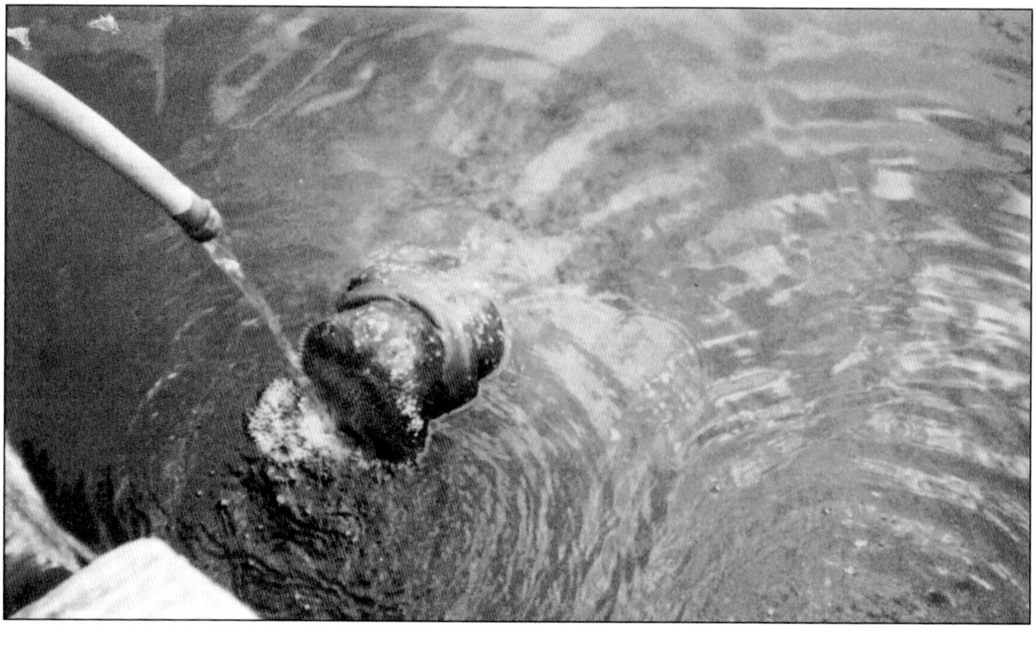

Nine

East Cooper Maritime Tradition

The annual Blessing of the Fleet is indicative of how East Cooper residents feel about their maritime heritage. Decorated boats are blessed, and the fishermen aboard them have the good wishes and prayers of the entire community as they continue their time-honored occupations. The wives and families of fishermen and other maritime folk are just as dedicated and active as their spouses in supporting their industry, as their activities clearly demonstrate.

Others appreciate that East Cooper celebrates maritime traditions in many ways, including Patriots Point, where locals and visitors can visit vessels and relics from World War II to honor their military heritage.

Still others think that the East Cooper area has the potential to more fully celebrate the past and are surprised that the area that is one of the few on the eastern seaboard without a general maritime museum.

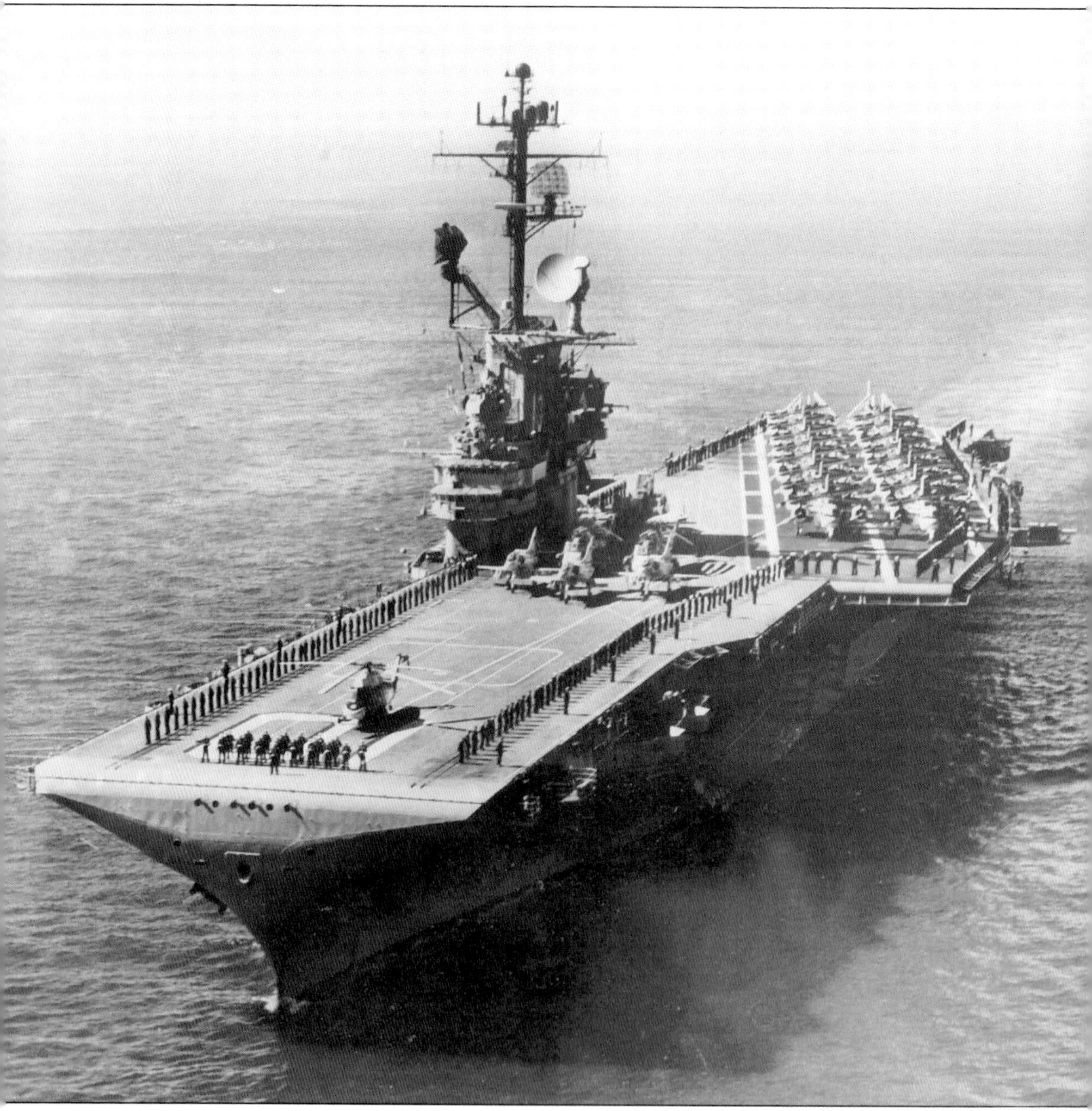

Patriots Point has become a landmark in Mount Pleasant. Exhibits including the USS *Yorktown* (pictured above), warships, a Medal of Honor Museum, a hangar and deck full of airplanes, a Vietnam support base, and a cold war memorial, all of which draw thousands of visitors per year and offer intriguing looks into the recent military past. (Courtesy Patriots Point Museum.)

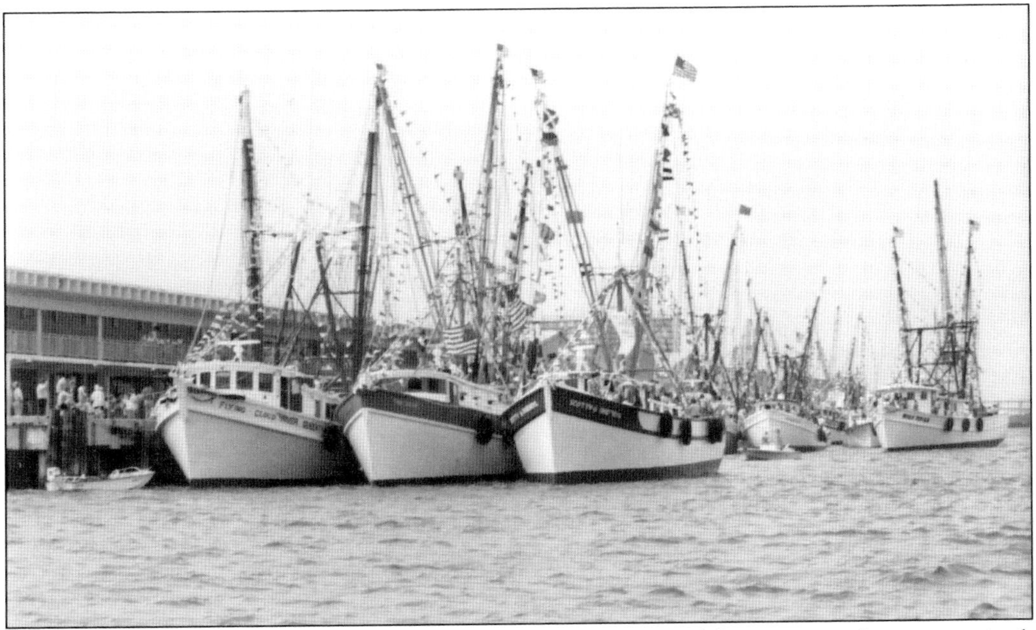

The Blessing of the Fleet, now in Mount Pleasant, used to be located downtown at the port terminal, as pictured here. Decorated boats parade in a procession as a clergyman gives a blessing to each vessel for a prosperous season of fishing and safe voyages at sea. At the end of the procession, a final prayer is offered and a wreath tossed to honor the fishermen lost at sea or who have passed away that year. (Courtesy Capt. Barry Wilson.)

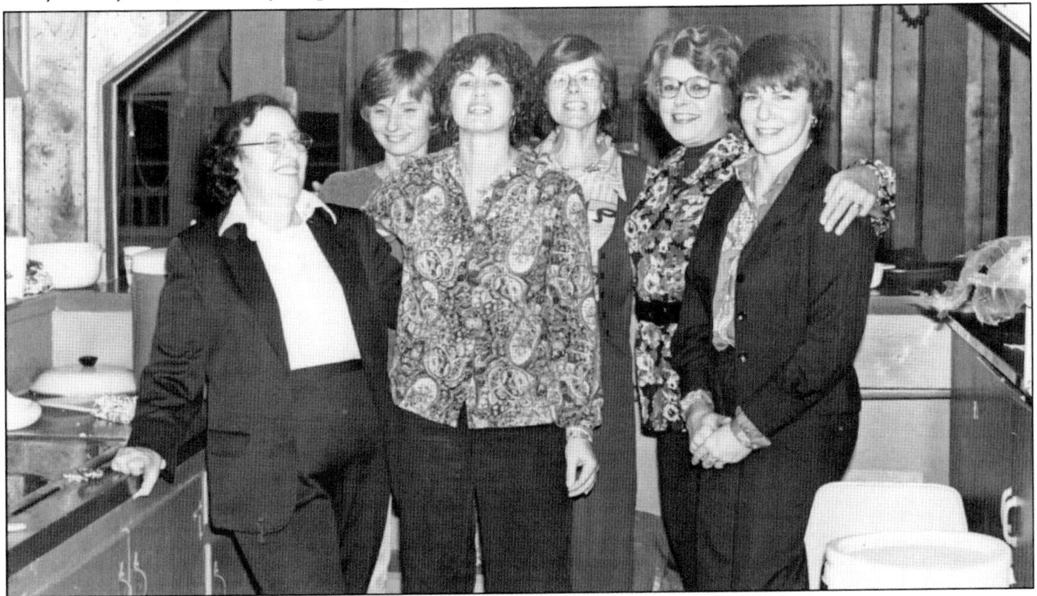

The wives of local fishermen formed the South Carolina Shrimpers Ladies Auxiliary in the early 1970s. They organized the Blessing of the Fleet, created the *South Carolina Shrimpers Association Cook Book*, which is still sold today, and organized the annual Christmas party for the South Carolina Shrimpers Association at Alhambra Hall, along with other charitable events. Pictured here from left to right are Alva Magwood, Pam Rector, Florence Magwood, Bunny Hills, Marian Puckhaber, and Ann Magwood. (Courtesy Ann Magwood.)

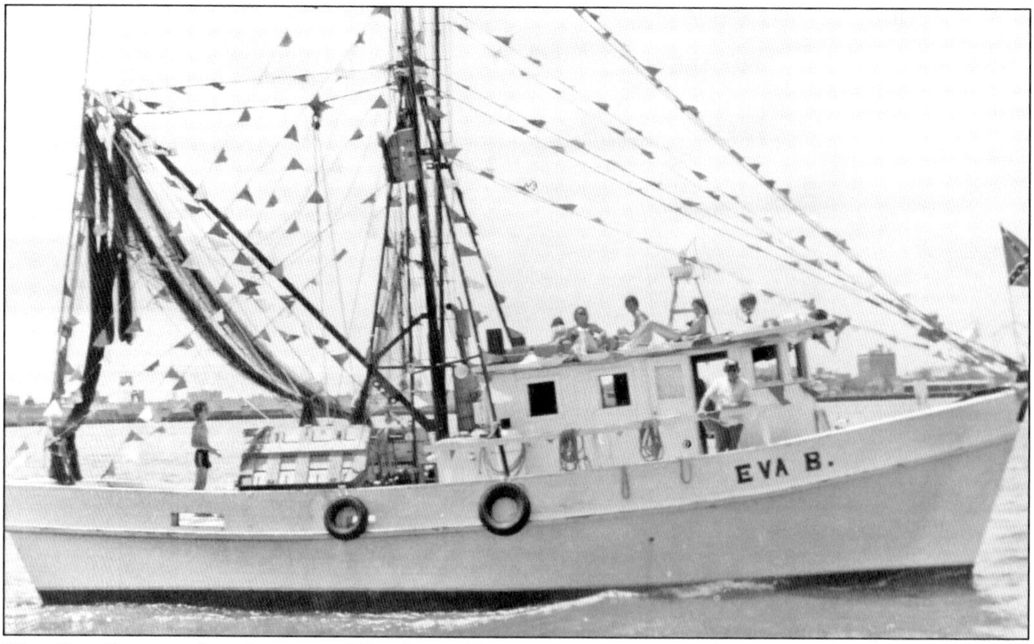

The *Eva B*, owned and operated by Capt. Tommy Cannon, parades at the port terminal for a blessing. The beautifully crafted wooden vessel had a 671 Detroit engine and was tragically taken by Hurricane Hugo in 1989. Captain Cannon operated two vessels from Shem Creek with a career spanning 15 years. His other vessel is the *Lady J.* (Courtesy Capt. Tommy Cannon.)

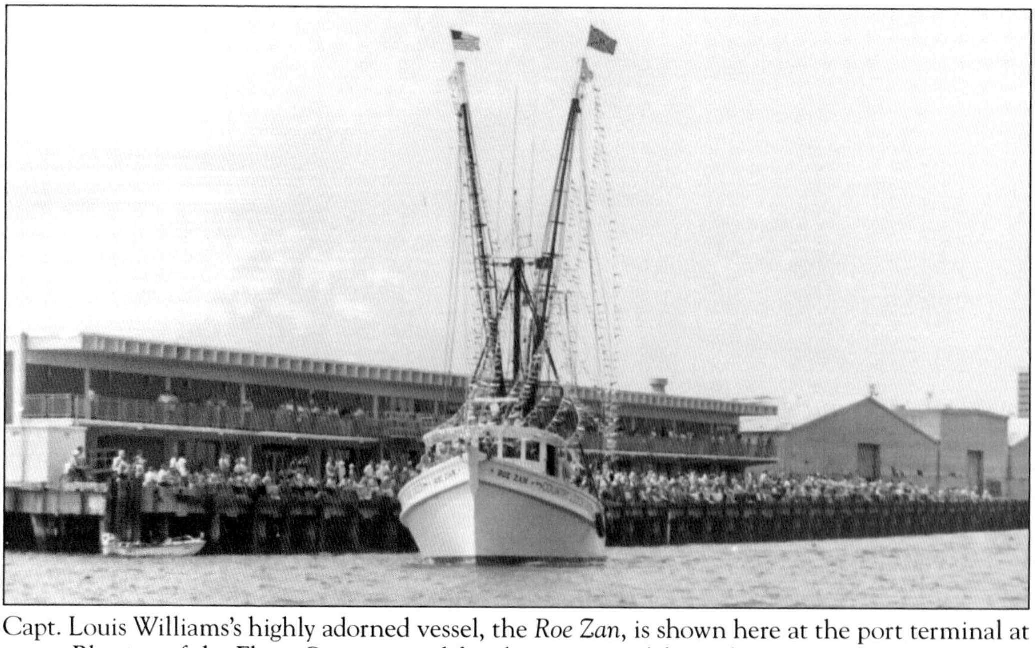

Capt. Louis Williams's highly adorned vessel, the *Roe Zan*, is shown here at the port terminal at a past Blessing of the Fleet. Captains and families competed for cash prizes in the early festival days, and friendly rival competitions between families provided for a spectacular parade of boats, reflecting the spirit of the day. Families spent hundreds of dollars and many hours making costumes and decorations for their vessels. Captain Williams's wife was one of the founding members of the South Carolina Shrimpers Ladies Auxiliary. (Courtesy Williams family.)

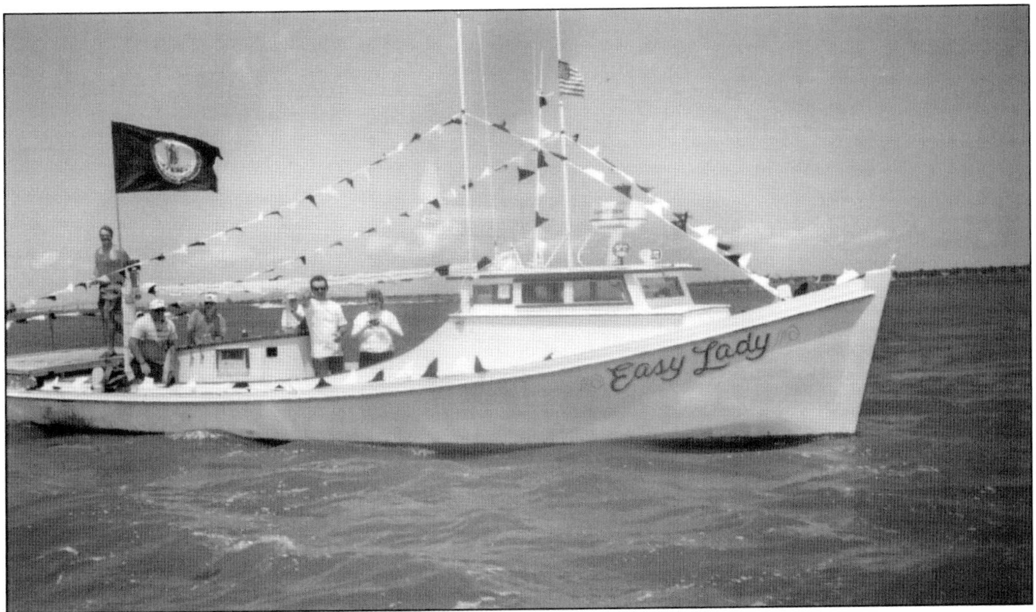

The late Capt. Dean Smith owned and operated the *Easy Lady*, a small Chesapeake crabbing vessel out of Shem Creek. With family and friends aboard, the decorated boat joins the parade for a blessing. Captain Smith was a beloved member of the creek who crabbed and trawled the Lowcountry waters for years.

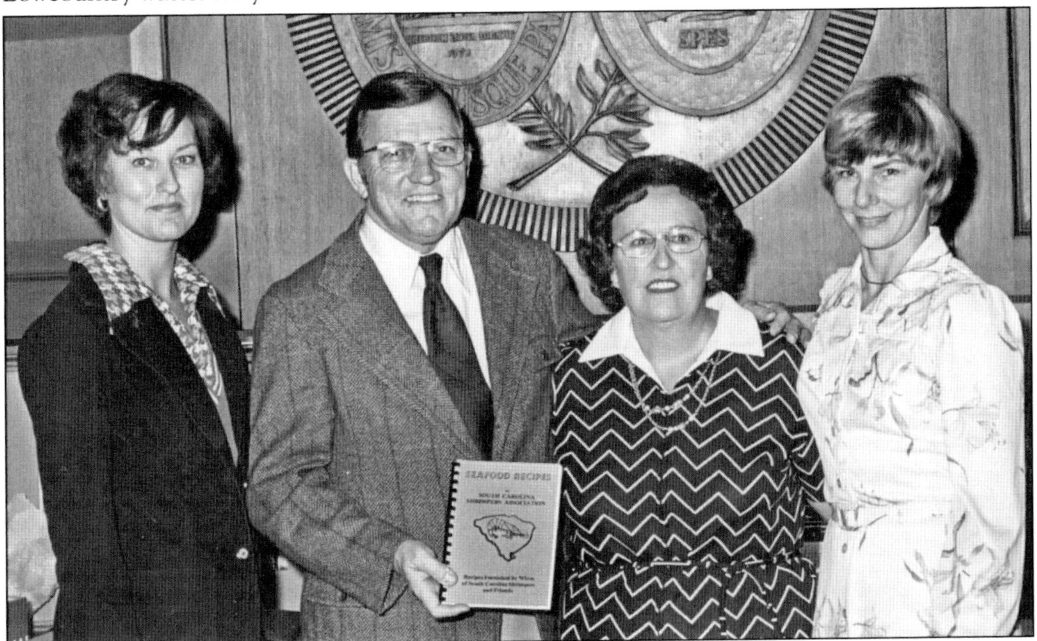

Former South Carolina governor Jim Edwards (above) stands with officers of the South Carolina Shrimpers Ladies Auxiliary, (pictured from left to right) Loy Marlowe, Alva Magwood, and Ann Magwood, who present him with a copy of the *South Carolina Shrimpers Association Cook Book*. In the past, seafood organizations have approached local and state governments to highlight the South Carolina seafood industry. In 1976, Governor Edwards declared a week to honor and call attention to this industry. (Courtesy Ann Magwood.)

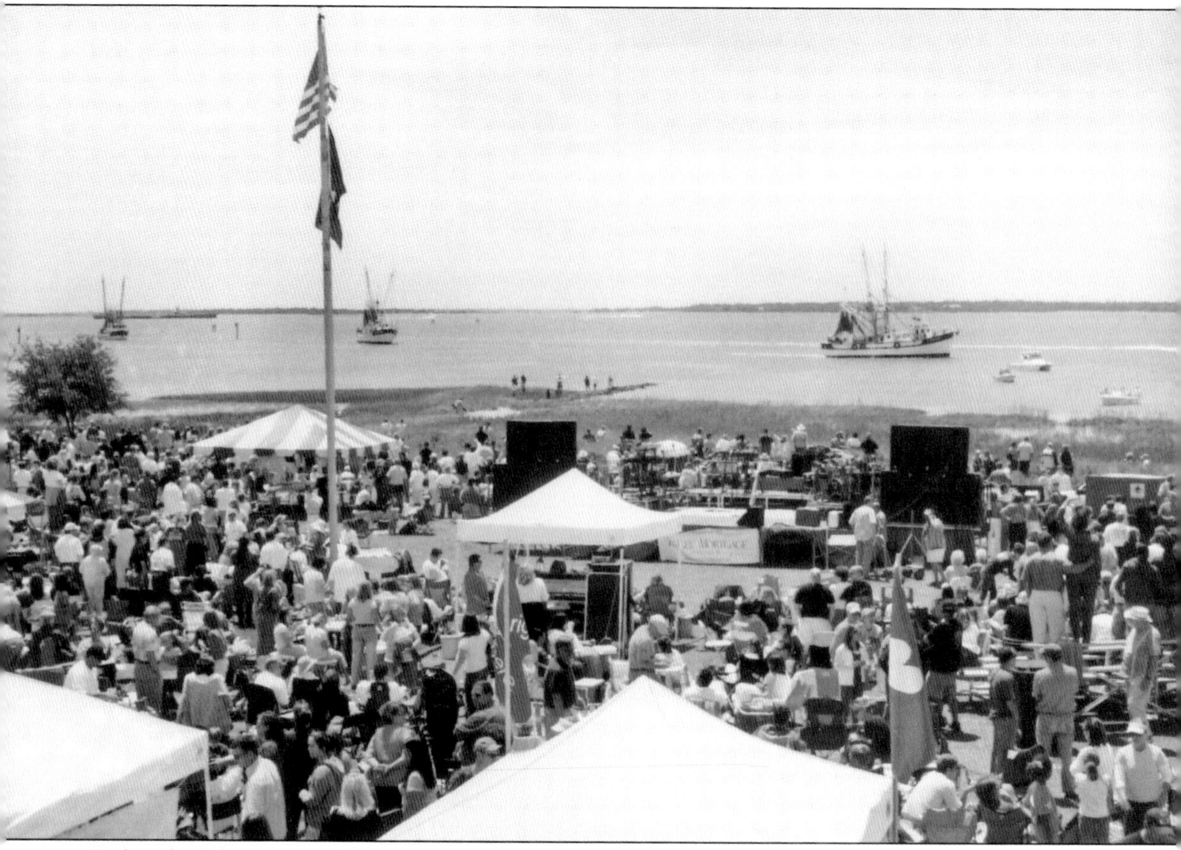

Today the Blessing of the Fleet and Seafood Festival is held in Mount Pleasant and is a highly celebrated event enjoyed by locals and tourists alike. The family festival, held at Alhambra Hall on the beautiful Charleston Harbor, hosts area restaurants, crafts and artisans, many children's activities, shag and shrimp-eating contests, local bands, and, of course, the ceremonial Blessing of the Fleet by local clergy. The free event, which benefits local charities as well as the South Carolina Shrimpers Association, attracted between 10,000 and 12,000 people in 2006 and recently celebrated its 20th season. (Courtesy Town of Mount Pleasant.)

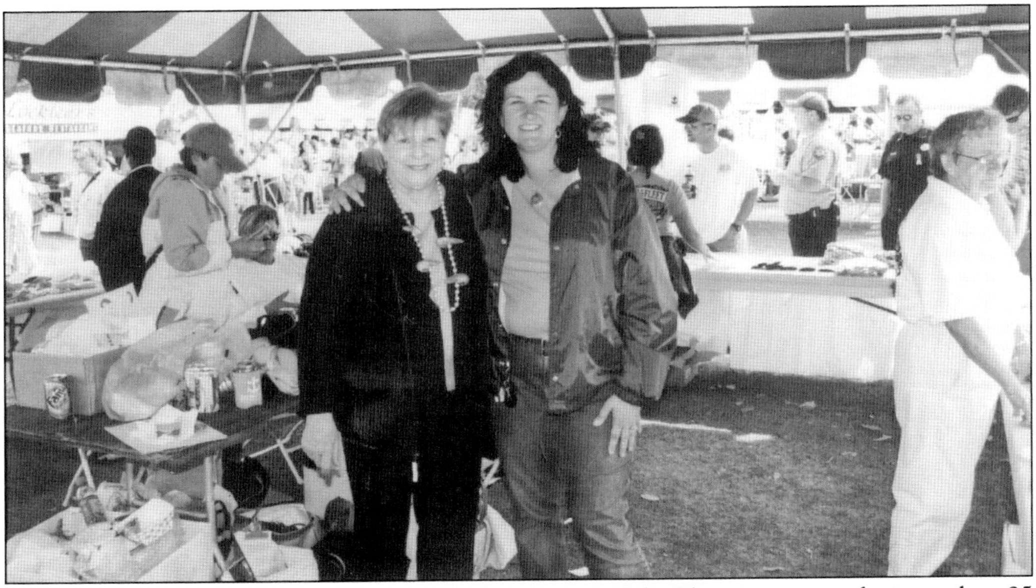

Ann Magwood (left), who has worked with the Blessing of the Fleet committee for more than 25 years, is credited with bringing the festival to Mount Pleasant. Su McManus-Frost, the Town of Mount Pleasant's special events coordinator, has served on the committee since 1997. Together they pose at the 2006 festival. (Courtesy Town of Mount Pleasant.)

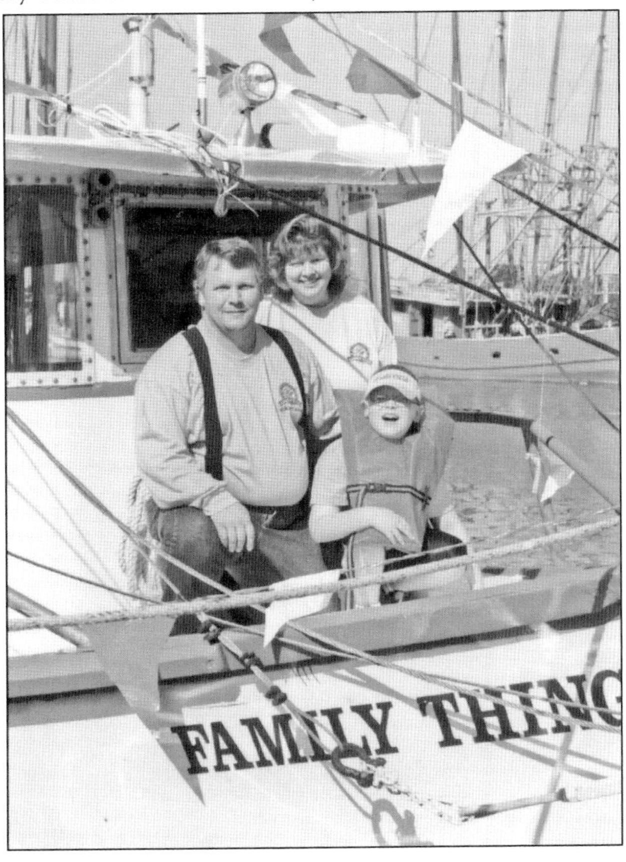

Michael Cobb and his family pose on the bow of their 42-foot vessel, the *Family Thing*, decorated for the 2007 Blessing of the Fleet. Captain Cobb is a second-generation fisherman, is currently working aboard local tugs, and is still trawling part time. The family remains active in the industry. (Courtesy Town of Mount Pleasant.)

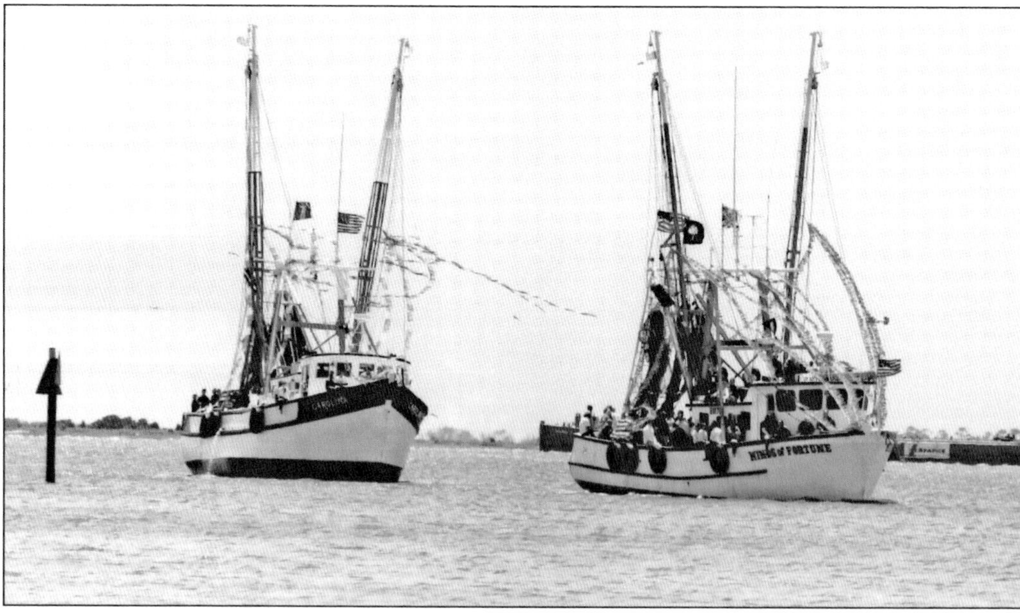

The highly adorned vessels the *Winds of Fortune*, owned and operated by Capt. Wayne Magwood, and the *Carolina*, owned and operated by his nephew Rocky Magwood, parade by Alhambra Hall, thankful for the blessings received from the community and the clergy. (Courtesy Town of Mount Pleasant.)

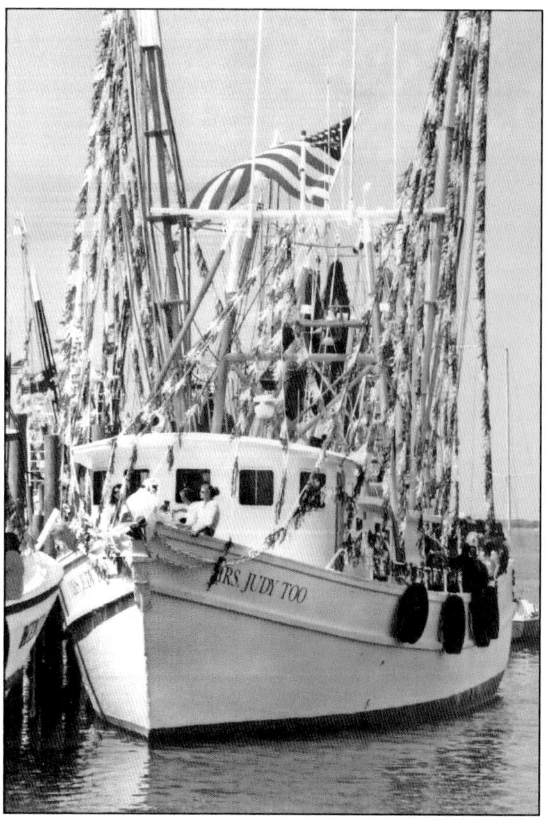

Capt. Tommy Edwards is a Mount Pleasant native who has been shrimping for 33 years. He began in the industry right after high school and is currently the proud owner of the 70-foot *Mrs. Judy Too*, named after his bride. She has a 365-horsepower engine capable of pulling four, 42-foot nets. (Courtesy Town of Mount Pleasant.)

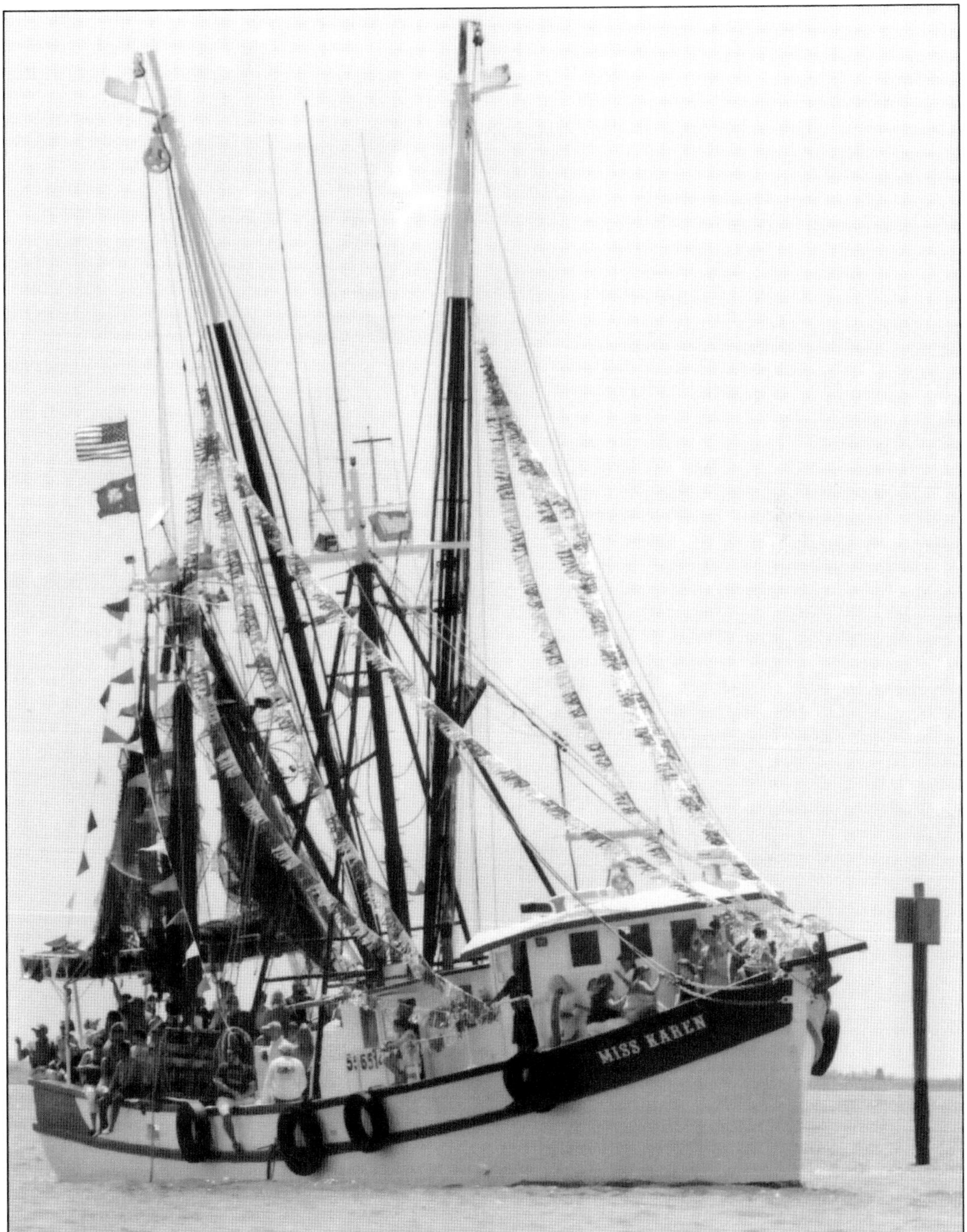

Capt. Donnie Brown, a Mount Pleasant native, began shrimping at age 17. He operated six boats, the *Silver Star*, the *Nora*, the *Miss Karen*, the *Pleasant Lady*, the *Miss Judy*, and the *Ethel and Clarence*, out of Shem Creek before acquiring his own vessels, starting with the *Crystal J*, then the *Lady Lynn*, and, currently, the *Miss Karen*, named after his wife. Captain Brown has fished the waters from Fort Myers, Florida, to Pamlico Sound, North Carolina. He can still be found trawling up and down the East Coast. This image is of the highly adorned *Miss Karen* at a Blessing of the Fleet ceremony. (Courtesy Town of Mount Pleasant.)

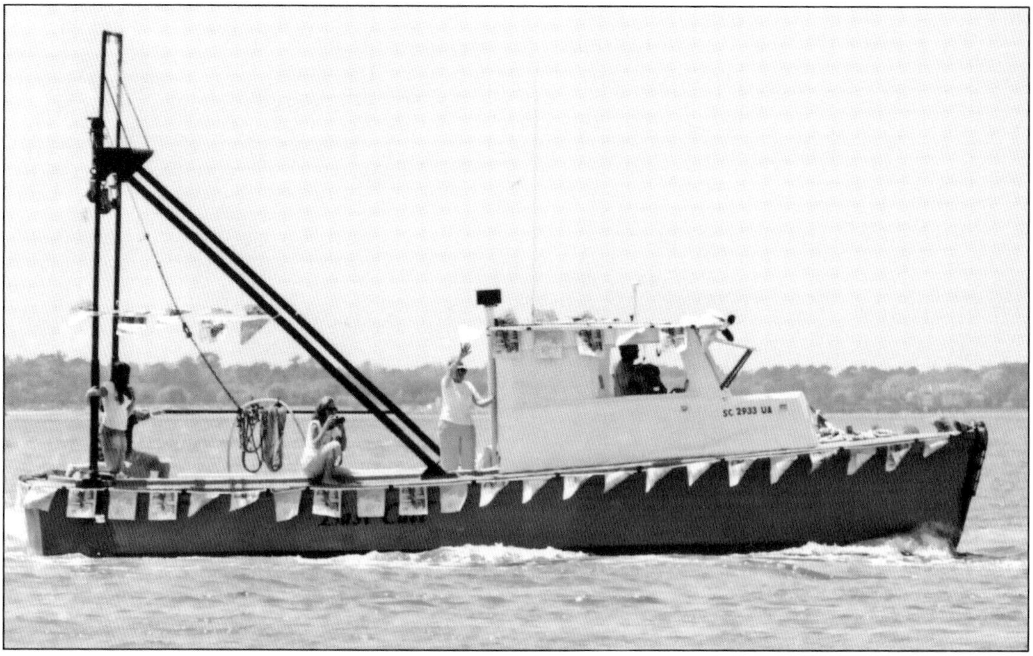

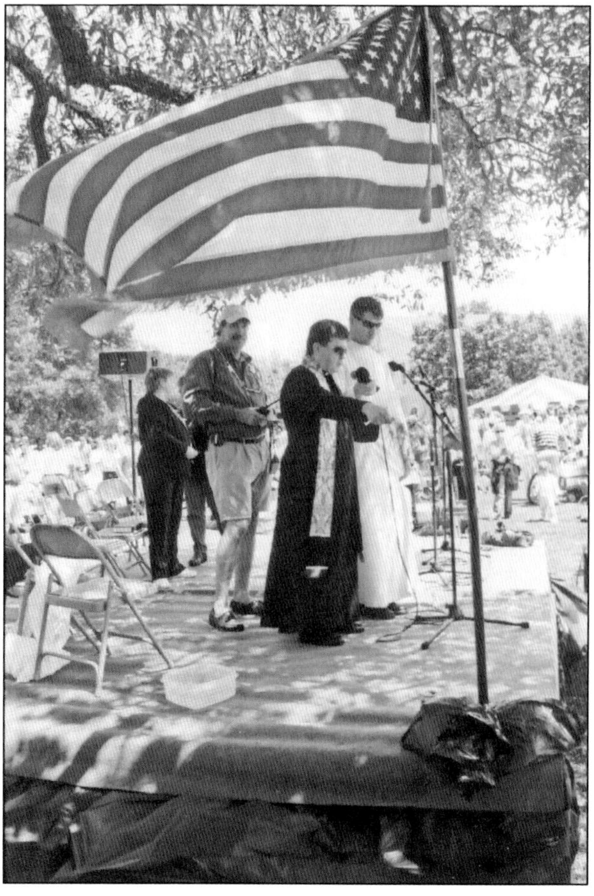

The vessel *Last Call* is a 33-foot converted U.S. Navy liberty boat that was once used to take sailors from ship to shore. Here she parades by Alhambra Hall at the Blessing of the Fleet in 2007. She was owned and operated by local brothers Jimmy and Jeff Isaac. (Courtesy Town of Mount Pleasant.)

Local clergy Rev. Len Williams (center) and Fr. John Parker (right), shown on stage at Alhambra Hall, offer prayers of protection and blessings to the shrimp fleet. Also pictured on stage is Wray Lemke (left) of Mount Pleasant Radio Company, a valued friend of the commercial fleet. (Courtesy Town of Mount Pleasant.)

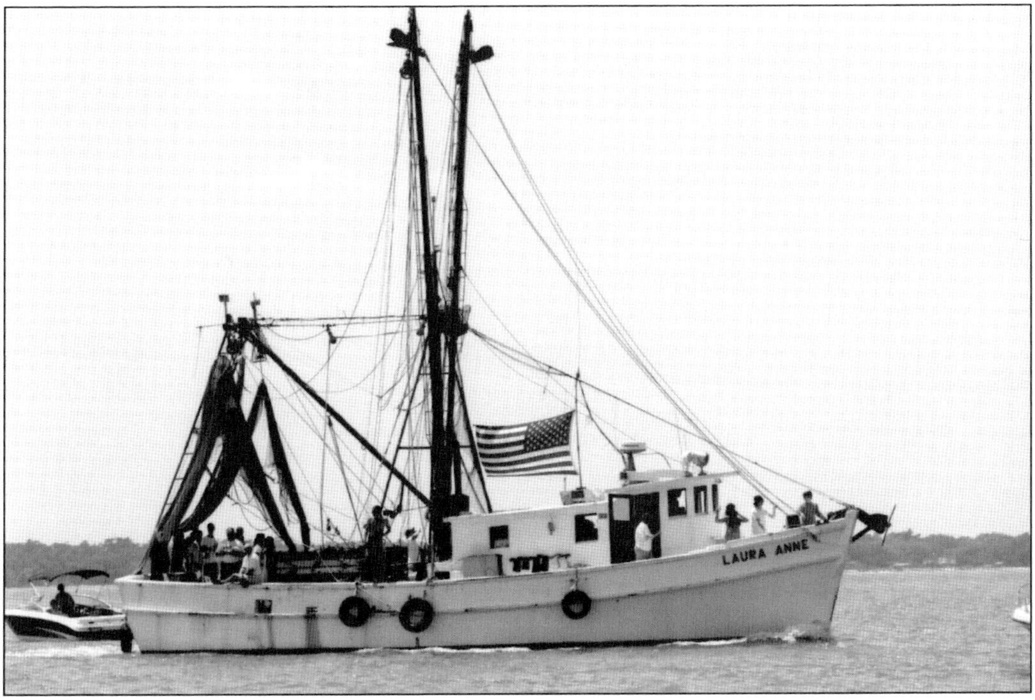

This is the beautiful *Laura Anne*, which is owned and operated by the Hills family. It was built in 1969 of cypress wood and heart pine and was named after Capt. Waring Hill's daughter. Pictured above, the vessel parades past the crowds at Alhambra Hall. Captain Hills, a near-40-year veteran of the commercial shrimping fleet, poses with his son Marion Hills (below). (Both images courtesy Town of Mount Pleasant.)

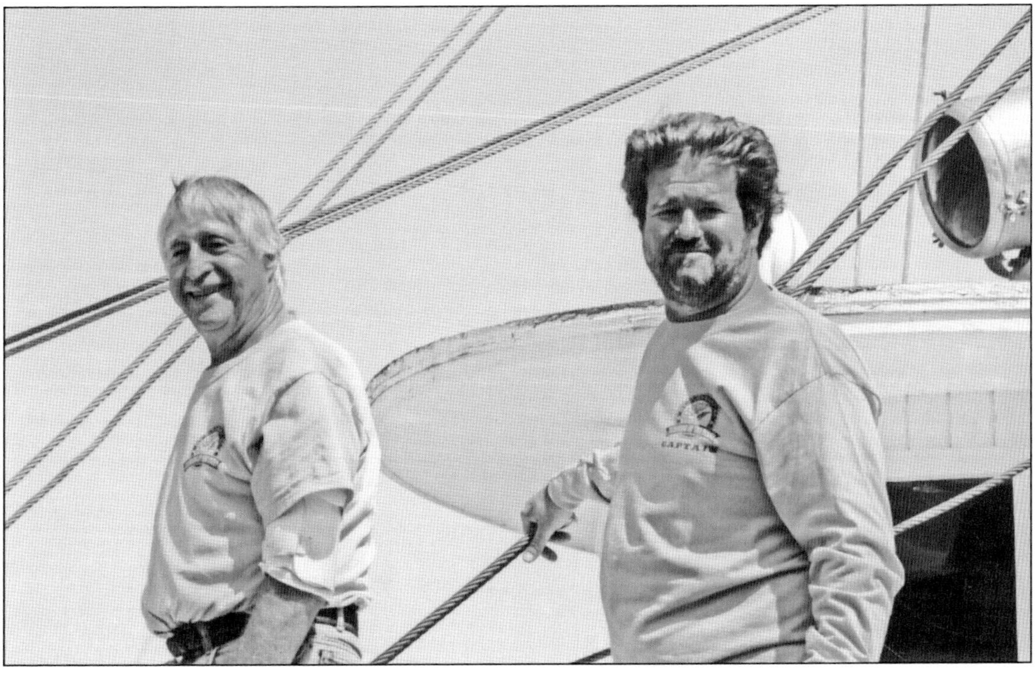

ACROSS AMERICA, PEOPLE ARE DISCOVERING SOMETHING WONDERFUL. *THEIR HERITAGE.*

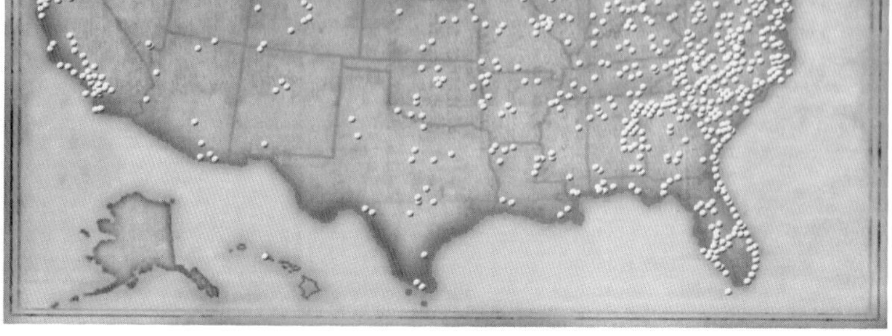